widening the circle

The Practice and Evaluation of Family Group Conferencing with Children, Youths, and Their Families

Joan Pennell and Gary Anderson, Editors

W9-DGC-692

NASW PRESS

National Association of Social Workers
Washington, DC

Elvira Craig de Silva, DSW, ACSW, President
Elizabeth J. Clark, PhD, ACSW, MPH, Executive Director

Cheryl Bradley, *Publisher*
Schandale Kornegay, *Manager, Publications*
Marcia D. Roman, *Managing Editor, Journals and Books*
Sarah Lowman, *Production Editor*
Gail Martin, Editorial Associates, *Copy Editor*
Cara Schumacher, Proofreader
Bernice Eisen, Indexer

Cover design by Poulos Design, Silver Spring, MD
Interior design by Cynthia Stock, Electronic Quill, Silver Spring, MD
Printed by Port City Press, Baltimore, MD

©2005 by NASW Press

Library of Congress Cataloging-in-Publication Data

Widening the circle : the practice and evaluation of family group conferencing with children, youths, and their families / Joan T. Pennell and Gary R. Anderson, editors.
    p. cm.
  Includes bibliographical references and index.
  ISBN 0-87101-367-3 (alk. paper)
  1. Family social work. 2. Social group work. 3. Child welfare. I. Pennell, Joan, 1949–
II. Anderson, Gary R., 1952–
  HV697.W53 2005
  361'.06—dc22

2005008407

Printed in the United States of America

To our families,

Charley, Ivan, Daniel, and Benjamin Pennell

and

Valerie Glesnes-Anderson and Lauren and Elizabeth Anderson

And our parents,

Kitty and Tom Stern

And

Richard and Carol Anderson

And our extended families

Who all helped us to appreciate the caring and strength in family.

Contents

Contents

Contents

Foreword

Child welfare systems across this country are committed to the safety, permanency, and well-being of children in care as a matter of public policy and organizational intent. Knowledge of family and its meaning in the lives of children as well as social work practice require that children are protected in the context of their family, culture, and community. Maltreatment by and separation from parents have potential short-term and long-term psychological and cognitive consequences, which can compromise a child's development. A major challenge for the child welfare system has been striking the right balance between a time-sensitive, child-protective approach and the efforts to engage families in problem solving and resolution of the issues that lead to placement. A second challenge confronting public child welfare agencies is to provide services in a manner that uses cultural and community strengths. This volume makes a major contribution to thinking and practice related to these two critical issues.

Child welfare systems have struggled with family engagement for the past three decades. Research has documented that most of the time and resources in the child welfare system are directed toward the children, with less investment in efforts to engage families in building their own capacity to protect their children. Among the social costs of these policies and practices are long stays in out-of-home care and no permanent attachments for the children. Public policy has attempted to address this issue through the reasonable efforts requirements, the funding of reunification services, and expedited adoptions. Despite these efforts, 126,000 U.S. foster children have no family of their own (AFCARS, 2001).

If the child welfare system is to be protective, fair, and just, it must serve children and families well and in the context of culture and community. This requires not only eliciting the voices of families and communities but also developing and delivering services in partnership with families and their communities. Family group conferencing (FGC) offers a powerful strategy for engaging families and holding them accountable for the changes that are essential to ensuring children's development in the context of safety and permanence.

This book is the most systematic examination of FGC to date. Looking through the lens of practice, research, and policy, the authors explore not only the state of the art but also the state of the science related to this approach. The volume describes what is and identifies future challenges. I hope the contribution made here will expand discussion of effective approaches to helping not only children but also families and their natural helping networks, resolve the problems that contribute to maltreatment.

CAROL WILSON SPIGNER, DSW
Kenneth L. Pray Professor
School of Social Work
University of Pennsylvania
and
Associate Commissioner for the
Children's Bureau, U.S. Department of
Health and Human Services 1994–1999

Preface

Joan Pennell and Gary R. Anderson

Widening the Circle describes and critically analyzes an intervention called family group conferencing (FGC). The guiding metaphor of "widening the circle" not only frames FGC practice, but also serves as the reference against which to assess the accomplishments and limitations of the model. Widening the circle refers to developing the family leadership, cultural safety, and community partnerships to safeguard children, young people, and other family members.

The volume is based on our experience with FGC in the United States and Canada as applied primarily in child welfare, but also extended into the fields of juvenile justice and domestic violence. Drawing upon our work as FGC developers, evaluators, and consultants, we have used a question-and-answer format to address commonly raised questions about the model's practice and evaluation. Typical questions are, Is it safe for children? Should domestic violence cases be ex-

cluded? Do we have enough resources to carry out FGC? How can we measure its outcomes? Does it change how we carry out child welfare and juvenile justice?

The responses to the questions highlight key points and use examples to illustrate FGC processes and outcomes. Summaries of research findings are used to substantiate patterns, and differences are explicated through an analysis of community contexts and family cultures. Joan Pennell's examples are from the North Carolina Family Group Conferencing Project, and Gary Anderson's examples are from New York City and the Michigan Family Group Decision Making Evaluation. All family material has been disguised to protect the participants' confidentiality.

Widening the Circle is devoted to examining how the principles of FGC orient the intervention and its evaluation and how they promote the three pathways to safeguarding children, youths, and their families—family leadership, cultural safety, and community partnerships. In chapter 1, "Widening the Circle," Joan Pennell introduces the concepts that form the basis of FGC; describes key features of FGC; defines family leadership, cultural safety, and community partnerships; and outlines the nine principles guiding FGC implementation (Pennell, 1999). Six of the nine FGC principles offer direction on how to work directly with the family groups and their service providers.

Section I: Conferencing

These principles are elaborated in the three chapters on conferencing in the first section of the book. Chapter 2, "Before the Conference—Promoting Family Leadership," addresses the referral process and conference preparations. In doing so, it relies on the following three principles:

- Have the conference belong to the family group.
- Foster understanding of the family and creativity in planning.
- Help the conference participants take part safely and effectively.

Referencing these principles, Joan Pennell emphasizes the importance of structuring the pre-conference work in a way that moves the family to the center of planning. Thus, it is necessary to define the conference's purpose in a way that is readily understood by the family group and encourages their best thinking, to weight invitations toward family members and away from service providers, to include a broad spectrum of family and "like family," to deprofessionalize the setting and process of the meeting, and to find ways for each participant to engage safely and competently in the deliberations. The aim is to advance the family's leadership from the outset.

Chapter 3, "At the Conference—Advancing Cultural Safety," reviews the five main phases of the conference: (1) opening in the family group's traditions, (2) sharing the information necessary for planning, (3) having a private time for the family group to deliberate, (4) finalizing the plan, and (5) closing the meeting. During these stages, Joan Pennell notes that two FGC principles offer guidance:

- Tap into the strengths of the family group in making a plan.
- Promote carrying out the plan.

The conference is geared toward creating a culturally safe forum in which family group members receive the necessary information and supports to make their own plan, privacy in which to express their views and draw on their traditions to find solutions, and authorization so that the plan can be carried out and revised as needed.

Chapter 4, "After the Conference—Maintaining Community Partnerships," examines the work carried out in the aftermath of the conference. The crucial tasks are carrying out the plan, monitoring and evaluating its implementation, and revising it as necessary. As Gary Anderson notes, the guiding principle here is the following:

- Fulfill the purpose of the plan.

The chapter highlights the importance of community partnerships to ensure the continued involvement of the family group and service providers.

Section II: Initiating and Sustaining Conferencing

Too often, conferencing falters because insufficient attention is given to developing a hospitable context for its implementation.

Three FGC principles are concerned with forming and maintaining an environment that will facilitate the success of conferencing:

○ Build broad-based support and cultural competence.
○ Enable the coordinators to work with family groups in organizing their conferences.
○ Change policies, procedures, and resources to sustain partnerships among family groups, community organizations, and public agencies.

These principles entail generating interorganizational linkages, policies, and evaluative approaches that support and correct model implementation. These are elaborated in the second and third sections of the book on, respectively, initiating and sustaining FGC and evaluating it.

Chapter 5, "Collaborative Planning and Ongoing Training," focuses on the development work necessary to begin the program and the continued effort necessary to sustain and enrich the program once it has been established. Joan Pennell stresses that before they begin the process, key participants must be oriented to the model and then engaged in planning the means for initiating, implementing, and evaluating the FGC program. Given the importance of community partnerships for successful conferencing, the author urges a collaborative approach to planning that brings together diverse partners from the outset of an FGC program. Once conferencing has started, the program must continue to offer training, consultation, support, and opportunities for exchanges—not only for the FGC coordinators, but also for other participants, particularly the referring social workers and their supervisors.

Chapter 6, "Family Group Conferencing and Supportive Legislation and Policy," addresses means of developing a hospitable national and state context for carrying out FGC. This is especially crucial for programs outside New Zealand, because most operate without legislation that mandates the model and none have legislation that explicitly incorporates Indigenous traditions and terms. Such legislation does not in itself guarantee cultural safety for FGC participants. Without legislation, however, FGC programs face an even greater challenge in resisting racist practices and respecting cultural diversity. The necessity of meeting this challenge is evident in child welfare systems that remove children of color from their families and communities in far greater proportions than white children (Roberts, 2002). As Gary Anderson discusses in chapter 6, U.S. child welfare legislation, while not mandating FGC, has values and practices that encourage its application, and federal reviews further support the implementation of FGC programs.

Section III: Evaluating Conferencing

Evaluation research on the implementation of FGC is relatively substantial; however, studies of its outcomes are more limited because of the recent introduction of the model in many locales. Cost analysis is the most limited of all, reflecting the nascent state of economic analysis in community-oriented services. Joan Pennell and Gary Anderson, joined by American Humane researcher Carol Harper, open the third section of the book by setting forth a program map or logic model encompassing FGC implementation, outcomes, and costs.

Chapter 7, "Checking for Model Fidelity," looks at ways to evaluate the implementation of the FGC intervention. Evaluation requires that researchers have a blueprint of the model against which to compare actual practice, and FGC processes are now sufficiently articulated for program evaluators to assess adherence to the model. At the same time, the model cannot be so rigidly specified that it prevents families from taking leadership in designing their own conference. To circumvent this danger, Joan Pennell discusses how key FGC guidelines can be used to assess faithfulness to the model in a way that respects FGC's flexibility and responsiveness to family cultures and local contexts.

Chapter 8, "Identifying Short-Term and Long-Term FGC Outcomes," describes ways to evaluate the results of conferencing. In general, assessing child welfare outcomes is difficult for many reasons, including the often conflictual nature of family–agency relationships. These conflicts are partly a function of the power of child welfare workers to remove children and partly the result of normative differences of opinion on child rearing. The latter, in particular, can lead to disagreements between child welfare workers and their clientele on the desired outcomes. Commonly, for example, the child welfare system defines the desired outcomes as removing immediate risks to children, whereas family groups tend to think in broader terms of safeguarding the children's long-term interests and keeping them connected to their community. As Gary Anderson notes, U.S. legislation encourages a broad look at outcomes, including child and family safety, permanency, and well-being, and he proposes that the evaluation assess immediate, intermediate, and long-term outcomes.

Chapter 9, "Calculating the Costs and Benefits of Family Group Conferencing," focuses on FGC expenditures and relates these to outcomes. In a climate of results-based accountability, fledgling social programs such as FGC too often are asked to demonstrate that they are a less expensive and more beneficial alternative to practice as usual. Economist Andy Rowe takes the stance that new programs can and should collect data on their costs and benefits, and he illustrates doable ways of gathering this information. He also takes the stance, however, that without external funding, new programs are not positioned to compare their costs and effectiveness with those of suitable alternatives. In a summary appended to this chapter, Joan Pennell reviews research on FGC costs.

Section IV: Reshaping Child Welfare

Family group conferencing is a method that is simple in terms of its concept, but complex in terms of its implementation. The complexity stems from its divergences in philosophy and practice from the conventional child welfare system in the United States. This system holds parents accountable for their failings without encouraging responsible interventions by the family group and community. The fourth and final section of this book examines the extent to which the FGC model is an effective alternative for safeguarding mothers and their children; its fit with other family involvement models now emerging in child welfare; its capacity to integrate planning efforts of multiple systems, including the juvenile justice system; and its overall contributions to reshaping child welfare and its challenges in doing so.

Chapter 10, "Safety for Mothers and Their Children," addresses the benefits and hazards of FGC in safeguarding family members. Family approaches in child welfare have been sharply criticized for endangering the safety and rights of children and increasingly scrutinized for their impact on abused mothers, especially when batterers take part in the decision making. In this chapter, Joan Pennell highlights the crucial role of the family group in stopping violence against both the adults and the children of the family, as well as the necessity of alliances between child welfare workers and domestic violence workers to prevent further family violence and promote healing in its aftermath. She summarizes findings on FGC processes and outcomes in situations of domestic violence and examines the consequences of including the maternal and paternal sides of the family. The participation of multiple sides of the family group points to a possible fourth pathway for safeguarding children and other family members: It is termed "inclusive planning" (Pennell, in press-b). In conclusion, she outlines a series of steps for carrying out FGC where there is a history of domestic violence.

Chapter 11, "Analyzing Family Involvement Approaches," reviews a range of models for engaging family members in child welfare planning. Family involvement models in child welfare are proliferating in the United States, and workers are often uncertain about which model to select for a particular family. Based in the American Humane's Family Group Decision Making Center, Lisa Merkel-Holguin and Leslie Wilmot compare three current U.S. models—FGC, family team conferencing, and team decision making. They also examine trends in family group decision making (FGDM) in the United States

and raise critical questions about whether these developments keep FGDM on track with its original aims.

Chapter 12, "Family Group Conferencing as a Strategy for Achieving Integration and Coordination in the Youth Justice and the Child Welfare Systems," addresses the conflicts that young people face in dealing with multiple public authorities, including the youth justice and child welfare systems. Drawing on his experience with child welfare, youth justice, and FGC, social work educator and researcher Gale Burford proposes a strategy to integrate planning from these two systems through FGC. He further stresses the importance of keeping distinct their different mandates: protecting young people versus holding them accountable for their behaviors and preventing further criminal activity.

In chapter 13, "Family Group Conferencing and Child Welfare: Contributions and Challenges," Gary Anderson presents FGC as a promising model for inclusion in child welfare interventions, but not a panacea. Drawing on legislation, professional codes of ethics, and trends in child welfare, he delineates the compatibilities between the aims of child welfare and the practices of FGC. At the same time, he sets forth challenges to mainstreaming FGC in the U.S. child welfare system—families' multiple problems, coordinator's capacity to reach out to alternative cultures, professional exertion of control, and the infrastructure of agencies. He concludes that although the idea may at first appear threatening to child welfare agencies, sharing power is the route to widening the circle and contributing to real change.

Acknowledgments

Any work is the work of many. Such holds true for family group conferencing (FGC) and for this volume. Accordingly, we need to acknowledge those who contributed in so many ways to our understanding of the model. We have learned so much from FGC participants and supporters in the United States, Canada, and other countries. Joan Pennell must first honor the teachings from Indigenous peoples in New Zealand, Canada, Australia, and the United States and those of her own cultural group the Society of Friends (Quakers). Gary Anderson has drawn upon his experience as a child protective services worker and lessons learned as a public child welfare worker in Michigan.

We each must note the support that made possible our ongoing study: for Joan, the State of North Carolina Department of Health and Human Services (particularly the Children's Services Section in the Division of Social Services) for the North Carolina Family Group Conferencing Project; and for Gary, the State of Michigan Department of Human Services (particularly the Office of Community Supportive Services and the Office of Evaluation and Policy Analysis) for the Michigan Family Group Decision Making Evaluation. None of this work would have taken place without the commitment of the participating North Carolina and Michigan counties and their families and staff. Our respective universities—North Carolina State University and Michigan State University—encouraged these endeavors, as did our colleagues in our home department or school.

Our contributing authors—Gale Burford, Carol Harper, Lisa Merkel-Holguin, Andy Rowe, Peg Whalen, and Leslie Wilmot—showed their commitment to participatory processes. Their contributions demonstrate the depth of their knowledge and their willingness to share what they have learned about the practice and evaluation of FGC.

For the North Carolina Family Group Conferencing Project, Joan wishes to acknowledge those involved in the training and evaluation work—training coordinator Teresa Turner, research coordinators Jennifer Hardison and Gretchen Koball, project assistant Amy Coppedge; faculty liaison at North Carolina State University Mark Macgowan, Lori Messinger, and Cheryl Waites; faculty liaison at the University of North Carolina at Chapel Hill Iris Carlton-LaNey and Marie Weil; the faculty liaison at the University of North Carolina at Wilmington, Karen Sandell; trainers Pat Dodson, Barbara Hollis, and Joyce Monney; research consultant Michael Calloway, statistical consultant Tom Gerig, publications associate Elizabeth Yerkes; and research assistants Shannon Bartle, Tanya Brice, Sarah Costantino, Matt Diehl, Linsay Everly, Stephanie Francis, Tonia Garrard, Marcella Hamilton, Jay Hemmingway, Jennifer Hendrickson, Erika Jones, Seong-Tae Kim, Julie Kimball, Alexsandra Manuel, Nancy Smyth, Alvin van Orden, and Charlotte Yongue. The Statewide Advisory Committee offered guidance throughout the project. Joan also appreciated the strong support of Rebecca Brigham with the Children's Services Staff Development of the North Carolina Division of Social Services and Dean Linda Brady at the College of Humanities and Social Sciences of North Carolina State University. Her prior work with the Newfoundland & Labrador Family Group Decision Making Project greatly influenced her work in North Carolina.

For the Michigan Family Group Decision Making Evaluation, Gary would like to acknowledge a number of colleagues who have contributed to the growth and development of FGC and his involvement in this work. These colleagues include (1) the managers and workers at the State of Michigan Department of Human Services who have supported FGC, including Deborah Hodge Morgan, Nancy Rygwelski, Diane Owens, Martha Tjhin, Carolyn Snyder, Charles Overbey, Steve Smucker, Christine Shedden, Blair Stieber, and others; (2) the managers, supervisors, coordinators, and advocates in the voluntary agencies that are piloting FGC in Michigan; (3) those involved in FGC evaluation projects, particularly evaluation coordinator Peg Whalen; evaluation associate Linda Lane; evaluation assistants Glenn Stutzky, Noriko Kubota, and Karen Wilson; and research assistants Sara Bacheller, Tamra Compton, Stephene Diepstra, Beverly Henrichsen, Bonnie Martinez, Kyle Savard, and Patricia Shropshire; (4) the faculty at the Michigan State University School of Social Work and the Dean of the College of Social Science, Dr. Marietta Baba; (5) the faculty at Hunter College School of Social Work and the staff at the National Resource Center for Permanency Planning, with special recognition of past director Sarah Greenblatt; (6) New York City child welfare agencies; (7) national leaders in FGC, particularly Lisa Merkel-Holguin, Joan Pennell, and Gale Burford; and (8) the child welfare professionals at the U.S. Children's Bureau, in particular former staff members Jake Terpstra, Carol (Williams) Spigner, and Ellen Carey.

Our hats are off to the two anonymous reviewers for their insightful feedback on the manuscript and to the NASW Press staff for their care in editing and moving forward this volume.

We have enjoyed our partnership in bringing this book to fruition and hope to continue the work of "widening the circle" with others.

JOAN PENNELL
Raleigh,
North Carolina

GARY R. ANDERSON
East Lansing,
Michigan

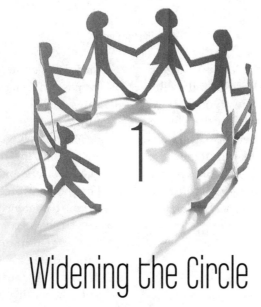

Widening the Circle

Joan Pennell

We know what children and young people need. They need supports, protections, clear limits, real opportunities, and pride in themselves and their heritage. These are the safeguards for their becoming full members of society. As social workers, we have repeatedly witnessed what happens to those who grow up without these safeguards. We can testify to the vicious cycles of neglect, abuse, poverty, and discrimination that stunt the potential of these children and youths. Everyone loses when young people cannot fulfill their aspirations of growing into responsible family members, workers, and citizens.

As social workers, we also know that we cannot help children and young people without attending to their key relationships and surroundings. They need us to take them seriously as individuals, and they need us to consider carefully where and with whom they live, study, work, and have fun. Our profession is founded on the principle of paying attention to both "person and environment." This principle appears simple and self-evident, but in practice is extremely difficult to follow. To assess and intervene in difficult situations, we are directed to take into account multiple, complex, and often volatile interactions. None of us can or should attempt this task on our own, especially when seeking to overcome the vicious cycles entrapping so many young lives.

This book proposes a means by which we can join with others to break down the vicious cycles and enlarge the lives of children and young people, as well as those with whom they have close ties. Called "family group conferencing" (FGC), this practice widens the circle of those committed to safeguarding children and other family members (Pennell & Burford, 1994). The use of this approach is becoming increasingly more common in child welfare, juvenile justice, and school systems, and it is gradually expanding into adult services (Bazemore & Schiff, 2004;

Burford & Hudson, 2000; Merkel-Holguin & Wilmot, 2000). To describe and evaluate FGC, the authors draw upon their experience with the model in the United States and Canada. Their primary focus is on its use in child welfare, but they also look at ways that its use in child welfare conferences can be extended to address juvenile offending and domestic violence.

What is FGC?

Family group conferencing is a means of involving family and close support people in making and carrying out plans to safeguard child and adult family members. The family group develops a plan to resolve the issues endangering young and adult family members. Before the plan can be carried out, the involved protective services must authorize the action steps and necessary public resources. Child welfare workers and family group members monitor the implementation of the plan and evaluate its impact. As needed, the family group may reconvene to make major revisions to the plan.

What is distinctive about FGC?

A conference belongs to the family group. Even so, the family group members are not left on their own. If they could have solved their relatives' problems without outside help, they would already have done so. Throughout the conferencing process, the family group receives supports and protections from involved public agencies and community organizations. The following features heighten family group ownership:

○ *Independent coordinators* organize and convene the conferences for the families referred for FGC. These co-ordinators do not carry the referred families on their caseload. This separates the FGC coordinators' role from that of the child welfare worker or other involved service providers. By minimizing role confusion, the FGC coordinators and family members can stay focused on preparing for the conference.

○ *Conference preparations* ensure that FGC participants can take part safely and effectively in making plans. The coordinator consults with the family group members on how to organize their conference and what supports they require. Preferably, there are more family group members than agency personnel invited to the conference. The service providers often need coaching on how to respect the family group's decision making while maintaining their own roles.

○ *Family private time* during the conference makes it possible for the family group to develop its own plan. During the private time, the FGC coordinator and other service providers leave the room, but are available as needed. (Before they leave the room, they make sure that the family group members have the information needed to develop a plan that will address the areas of concern.) Once the family group members have created a plan, they invite the coordinator and protective authorities back into the room so that the plan can be finalized and approved.

What is the origin of FGC?

The FGC model was first legislated in New Zealand. *The New Zealand Children, Young*

Persons and Their Families Act of 1989 entitled family groups to have a say over child welfare and youth justice matters related to their young relatives. The intent was to move away from expert-driven intervention and to promote family group responsibility, children's safety, cultural respect, and community–government partnerships (Hassall, 1996). The impetus for this radical redesign of the child welfare and juvenile justice systems came from economic reforms to reduce the role of the state in the lives of citizens, public demands for greater professional accountability to clients, and protests by Indigenous people against European-based models of intervention (Doolan & Phillips, 2000; Rangihau, 1986).

Is FGC a new approach?

Formally including FGC in the child welfare system and other human services is new, but its practice is not. The model is based specifically on the cultural institutions of the Maori, a New Zealand Indigenous people (Love, 2000), and generally on those of South Pacific islanders (Shook, 1985). In actuality, FGC is part of the traditions of people from many continents. Focus groups with African Americans, Latino/Hispanics, and Cherokee communities in North Carolina perceived FGC as congruent with their cultural practices (Waites, Macgowan, Pennell, Carlton-LaNey, & Weil, 2004). Furthermore, it is not an innovation for relatives to make plans to care for children when their parents die or fall seriously ill. It is, however, an innovation for the child welfare system to establish a program that invites the family group members to develop a plan and provide them with the supports, protections, and privacy for doing so. Taking these steps, though, is congruent with

"good" social work practice that emphasizes the safety of children and other family members, family empowerment, and a collaboration of informal and formal networks (Maluccio & Daly, 2000).

"We just get together, and we just do it."

—CHEROKEE WOMAN SPEAKING ON FGC

Similarly to New Zealand, *FGC in the United States and other countries builds on and complements child welfare initiatives toward family-centered practice and community–state partnerships* (Briar-Lawson, Lawson, & Hennon, 2001; Parton, 1997; Pecora, Reed-Ashcraft, & Kirk, 2001). The intent is to move from adversarial to collaborative relationships between child welfare agencies and families; encourage family involvement in decision making; draw upon community supports; respect the cultural heritage of families; and, thus, to advance children's safety, permanency, and well-being.

Gaining parental input into child welfare decision making is supported by the Child and Family Services Reviews conducted by the U.S. Children's Bureau. The reviews found that state systems that involved parents in case planning were more likely to have stabilized children's living arrangements, heightened families' ability to care for their children, and met the children's educational, physical, and mental health needs (U.S. Department of Health and Human Services, 2003).

How do child welfare systems encourage planning with families?

To encourage family involvement in child welfare planning, a number of models, including FGC, have been applied in the United States. Among these other models are Family Unity, Family Team Conferencing, and

Team Decision Making; hybrids of various models have developed over time. These models all share beliefs in family strengths and team approaches while retaining the mandate of child welfare to protect children at risk, and each has its "unique features" or guidelines on how to encourage family input (Center for the Study of Social Policy, 2002, p. 2; and see chapter 11). As previously discussed, FGC emphasizes that the conference belongs to the family and their close supports and advances this ownership by using independent coordinators, preparing participants, and ensuring family private time to deliberate. Data comparing the results of the various models are limited. Fairly extensive research is available on how FGC is carried out, and some studies examine its outcomes in child welfare.

What does FGC accomplish?

For family members, FGC is an opportunity to have a say over their lives. Repeatedly, studies have shown that family groups accept the invitation to take part, are willing to make a plan, and feel respected by the process (Lupton & Stevens, 1997; Paterson & Harvey, 1991). This is the case for families from diverse cultures and nationalities (Burford & Hudson, 2000).

"It was great. It was something to help me stay out of trouble and get on the right path."

—Teenager for whom a
conference was held

Research on FGC shows promising outcomes for children, young people, and their families. Multiple studies (Merkel-Holguin, 2003) have reported that FGC keeps children connected with their siblings, parents, and family group; stabilizes their placements;

and enhances family and worker relationships. Some studies report gains in the safety of children (Gunderson, Cahn, & Wirth, 2003) and their mothers (Pennell & Burford, 2000a) and reduced costs (Marsh & Crow, 1998). At a minimum, studies report that FGC is implemented without substantially endangering children's safety (Berzin, 2004; Sundell & Vinnerljung, 2004) and without a significant difference in total costs even when conferencing expenditures are taken into account (Andy Rowe Consultants, 1997; Berzin, 2004; McDonald, 2000; and see chapter 9).

How does FGC enhance child welfare services?

At the conference, social workers benefit from hearing the best thinking of the family group members on how to improve the lives of their relatives. Social workers make contact only with the mothers and children in much of child welfare work; with FGC, however, they make contact as well with fathers, grandparents, aunts, uncles, godparents, close friends, and many others with ties to the family of concern (Gunderson, Cahn, & Wirth, 2003). Family group members not only contribute their strategies, but also their resources. They may offer their homes to children, serve as a big brother to a teenager, or make regular telephone calls to a lonely single mother.

"The family worked as a team."

—Child protection worker
after a conference

"The social worker outlined everything well. . . . Brought up all of my concerns during the conference."

—Guardian *ad litem* after a conference

Family group conferencing can be used along with other approaches. In the United States, for example, FGC does not replace court proceedings that are mandated by law; nevertheless, the judge may choose to use an FGC plan in determining the disposition of a child welfare case. Judges often welcome such input, because they know that the plan has the consent of the family group and the approval of social services.

At other times, FGC may be the preferred means for planning. For instance, when the relationship between the family and the social services agency has become hostile, the social worker may decide against calling a case conference or family meeting. Rather than negotiating case decisions in a hostile environment, the social worker can make a referral to an FGC coordinator. Then the coordinator, who does not carry the case, can organize the conference with the family. By taking part in the conference, the family members and their caseworker often improve their relationship and are better positioned to implement the plan together (Marsh & Crow, 1998).

How does FGC widen the circle?

Family group conferencing widens the circle by combining the strengths of the family group, community organizations, and public agencies to resolve the issues threatening family members. Issues that bring families to the attention of public authorities are usually extensive and complicated. These kinds of issues require a cooperative effort to identify and assess what is happening, develop a plan of action, carry out the plan, and review and modify the plan as needed. This team effort is based upon five central values:

1. *Goal of Safeguarding*: The team effort should have as its goal the safeguarding of children, young people, and other family members. Against this goal, all of the key participants—family group, public authorities, and community organizations—need to evaluate their efforts.

2. *Family Voice*: To be part of a team effort to aid their young relatives, the family group members should have a voice. To exert a constructive voice, they need preparation to take part safely and effectively, an opportunity to communicate among themselves, and confidence that the involved authorities will listen to them.

3. *Worker Accountability*: In this team effort, child welfare workers should uphold their primary role of protecting their young charges. As part of carrying out this role, child welfare workers must be accountable for their actions to other key players, including the family group, the legal system, and other service providers and community groups.

4. *Community Involvement*: To strengthen this team effort, the role of other public agencies, community services, and cultural groups should be recognized. Their participation makes it possible to go beyond meeting minimal standards of protection and to establish longer term means of safeguarding young community members.

5. *Consensus Building*: To carry out a team effort over time, all of the key participants should build together a consensus on how to proceed. Consensus building requires opportunities to share ideas, build trust, form a plan, act on the plan, and regroup as needed.

These five values orient the team effort. In working together, the participants create pathways to safeguarding children, young people, and other family members. Three crucial and mutually supportive pathways for widening the circle are (1) family leadership, (2) cultural safety, and (3) community partnerships. The nature of these pathways is based on an analysis of participants' views on their conference (Pennell, 2004; see chapter 7). *Family leadership* means that extended family members and those who feel "like family" are central to planning with social institutions, such as public agencies and community organizations, supporting their efforts. Rather than a family therapist, the FGC coordinator can be characterized as a network assembler who connects people by cutting across generations and enabling them to share past experiences and future involvements (see Speck, 1998; Speck & Attneave, 1973). To exert leadership at an FGC, families require culturally safe forums.

Cultural safety refers to a context in which family members can speak in their own language, express their own values, and use their own experiences and traditions to resolve issues (Fulcher, 1998). Structures and practices that recognize the cultural background of the family, particularly if the family belongs to a group marginalized by the dominant society, create such a context (Polascheck, 1998; Ramsden, 1993). These structures and practices develop through *community partnerships* in which families work in collaboration with local organizations to achieve common goals. The partners each bring their own way of looking at the issue at hand and generate from their differences a direction in which to head together (Gray, 1989). In working as a team, the partners retain their distinctive roles while increasing their overall effectiveness in finding solutions that work.

The aim of widening the circle is to change for the better the lives of children, young people, and their families. As a theory of change, widening the circle is grounded on social work values, practice experience, and research on the FGC process and results. Widening the circle is conceptually specified by turning to theory on empowerment. Empowerment theory has been used by numerous FGC proponents to define the model's goals and principles (for example, Connolly & McKenzie, 1999; Hudson, Morris, Maxwell, & Galaway, 1996) and assess its results (for example, Lupton & Nixon, 1999; Marsh & Crow, 1998).

What is the theoretical framework for widening the circle?

Theory on empowerment frames widening the circle, and in the context of FGC, empowerment can be articulated through ideas on cultural inclusiveness, participatory democracy, and civil society. The profession of social work has a long and fruitful tradition of empowerment dating back to the late 19th century (Simon, 1994). This tradition is evident in social workers' efforts to form alliances with diverse groups to address human ills and right social inequities (Simon). The term "empowerment" gained prominence among social workers in the United States through Barbara Solomon's (1976) work in African American communities and then spread to other Western countries in the late 1980s and the 1990s (Parsloe, 1996). Empowerment does not mean to give power to an agent or subordinant. Instead it refers to the process and product of joining with others to responsibly share power and advance individual and collective well-being (Guetiérrez, Parsons, & Cox, 1998). Empowerment entails critiquing social relations, affirming people's strengths, and realigning power to achieve shared goals (Pennell, Noponen, & Weil, 2004). As discussed earlier, the team effort demanded by FGC is guided by five central values. The first and chief of these is the goal of safeguarding children, young people, and other family members. This goal is one of the intended outcomes of empowerment and recognizes that the well-being of individual family members is linked with that other members.

Cultural Inclusiveness. The second value concerns the family exerting a voice in case plans regarding their young relatives. This means more than family members having the opportunity to speak. It also refers to speaking in their own voice about matters of a deeply personal and emotional nature and knowing that they are heard by the involved protective authorities and community groups. This means that the service providers seek to be aware of their own preconceptions about those with whom they work and adopt a stance of learning from people of other cultures (Green, 1999). In such a culturally inclusive atmosphere, families can communicate the extent of their connections, push their own agendas beyond those specified by professionals, and affirm their sense of identity. For these expressions of caring to be received with respect, the deliberations cannot be restricted to reasoned and calm argument alone. This means opening the conference to encompass various forms of discourse:

○ Greeting or public acknowledgment—the explicit recognition that others are not objects of discussion but full participants;

○ Affirmative use of rhetoric—emotional and colorful expression that highlights injustices, appeals to varied audiences, and urges action; and

○ Narrative and situated knowledge—storytelling to break the silence, form a common identity, challenge preconceptions, and foster mutual understanding. (Young, 2000)

All of these approaches to discourse help to generate a context of cultural safety in which family groups can take part as full members.

Participatory Democracy. Encouraging multiple forms of expression deprofessionalizes the conference and makes it possible for families to join in the deliberations. With adequate preparation and acknowledgment of their competence, family group members can contribute productively to the planning process. The private time permits the family group to confront each other, express their mutual caring, and develop a sense of pride as they develop a plan for the benefit of their young relatives (Pennell & Burford, 1995). Contrary to fears that the private time will be dominated by abusive parents (for example, Bartholet, 1999), decisions are primarily made through democratic or inclusive processes—consensus, bargaining, and following an inspiring leader (Pennell, in press-a; and see chapter 3). The conference adheres to the value of building a consensus as it engages in collaborative planning, and through adopting strong democratic practices (Barber, 1984), the family's leadership is advanced.

Civil Society. A setting of cultural inclusiveness and participatory decision making fosters the trust necessary for promoting a civil society in which every man and woman has the right and responsibility to participate as a full member (Wollstonecraft, 1792/1975), to serve as a check on authoritarian government (Baker, 2002; Cohen, 2001), and to engage in non-coercive decision making (Fullinwider, 1999). With attention to their needs and level of maturity, children and young people can play an important role in the deliberations concerning their lives (Gal, 2004; and see chapter 3). A civil society differentiates and upholds boundaries among family, community, and government (Kelly, 2003) and, thus, allows space for family privacy while upholding the values of community involvement and worker accountability to the public. People with supports, protections, clear limits, real opportunities, and pride in themselves and their heritage are prepared to contribute to their society. These contributions, as occur often in smaller communities, may include taking part in conferences for their relatives and friends (Pennell & Burford, 1995). The family group members can develop "democratic competence" through conferencing about themselves or those close to them (Braithwaite, 2000). FGC educates young and adult family members about exercising the freedom and caring necessary for acting as responsible members of society. Social workers, given their enduring tradition of empowerment, have the commitments and competencies to encourage family members to take charge of their lives individually and collectively and to form community partnerships.

What are the key principles for implementing FGC?

To advance these three pathways, FGC must be responsive to the family group's leadership, culture, and partnerships. One way to conceptualize such a model is to depict it as a series of principles (Pennell, 2002c, 2003). This approach helps to prevent rigid prescriptions while still offering guidance on widening the circle. *Nine key principles give direction to FGC implementation* (Pennell, 1999):

1. Have the conference belong to the family group.
2. Foster understanding of the family and creativity in planning.
3. Help the conference participants take part safely and effectively.
4. Tap into the strengths of the family group in making a plan.
5. Promote carrying out the plan.
6. Fulfill the purpose of the plan.
7. Build broad-based support and cultural competence.
8. Enable the coordinators to work with family groups in organizing their conferences.
9. Change policies, procedures, and resources to sustain partnerships among family groups, community organizations, and public agencies.

These principles have been derived from empowerment theory, based on a study of the intervention in diverse cultural contexts, and tested in training and consultation in different countries. The following chapters explicate how these nine principles can be translated into empowering practices with families, communities, and agencies.

SECTION

Conferencing

Joan Pennell and Gary R. Anderson

Family group conferencing (FGC) is designed to widen the circle of those committed to safeguarding children, young people, and other family members. Section I describes the three main stages of conferencing to assist others in carrying out the model. Although the New Zealand model influences the description of FGC in this volume, the description is geared to child welfare settings in the United States or Canada. Unlike those in New Zealand, jurisdictions in the United States and Canada typically operate under no or only limited legislation on conferencing in child welfare.

Is there one way of doing FGC?

The model must be flexible in order to respond to the diversity among family groups, communities, and agencies, and to deal with the unexpected events that almost inevitably happen at conferences. At the same time, the process can be distinguished by its key principles as described in chapter 1. These same principles make it possible to monitor faithfulness to the model, to adapt it as necessary, and to prevent drifting into practices that take away from the family group's role in decision making. The intent is not to promote one "pure" model but, rather, to show how FGC principles are translated into action within different contexts. To emphasize responsiveness to local conditions and cultures, the following three chapters illustrate the conferencing process with diverse families. As discussed later in the fourth section of this book, significant variations on the process can be found in child welfare (chapter 11) and juvenile justice (chapter 12), and particular caution needs to be taken in situations of family violence (chapter 10).

Who coordinates FGC?

Conferences are organized and convened by FGC coordinators. These coordinators may work from a child welfare agency or in another agency to which referrals are made for a conference. Preferably, the FGC coordinators do not carry the family on their caseloads. In other words, they are "independent" of other functions in regard to a family for which they are arranging a conference. Such independence helps to reduce role confusion, keeps the family and coordinator from entering into case negotiations, and enables the family group and the coordinator to focus on organizing the conference together. Clarity about the FGC coordinator's function also helps to reinforce the role of the child welfare workers. The referral for FGC does not mean that the workers are delegating their responsibilities to the FGC coordinator. On the contrary, the child welfare workers retain their functions as both child protectors and family helpers. In this section, all examples illustrate the process with an independent coordinator.

What are the main stages of FGC?

An FGC approach involves work before the conference, at the conference, and after the conference. If the family has subsequent conferences, the stages are repeated, often in an accelerated manner, because the participants are familiar with the process. Figure I-1 depicts the process. In chapter 2, Joan Pennell describes the FGC referral and preparations for the conference; in chapter 3, she provides an overview of the phases during the conference; and in chapter 4, Gary Anderson reviews the follow-through on the plan after the conference. These stages are similar to those used for analyzing group development (Macgowan & Pennell, 2002), and all are designed to broaden the family's supportive network and keep the focus on

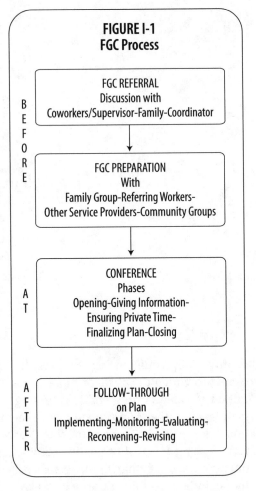

FIGURE I-1
FGC Process

BEFORE

FGC REFERRAL
Discussion with
Coworkers/Supervisor-Family-Coordinator

FGC PREPARATION
With
Family Group-Referring Workers-
Other Service Providers-Community Groups

AT

CONFERENCE
Phases
Opening-Giving Information-
Ensuring Private Time-
Finalizing Plan-Closing

AFTER

FOLLOW-THROUGH
on Plan
Implementing-Monitoring-Evaluating-
Reconvening-Revising

building solutions (Berg & Kelly, 2000; De Jong & Berg, 1998).

Before the conference, the FGC referral and the FGC preparation take place. As with the formation of social work groups in general (Garvin, 1997; Shulman, 1999; Toseland & Rivas, 2001), the coordinator works before the conference to ensure that the purpose of the group is clearly specified; the FGC participants are identified and prepared for participation; and the meeting's timing, location, and structure are determined to encourage attendance, alleviate anxiety, and increase safety. Chapter 2 shows how the family group is constructed as both a natural group based on kinship and friendship, and a formed group brought together for the purpose of creating a plan. As illustrated in chapters 2 through 4, this dual structure helps family members to draw on their existing network while broadening their social supports. As discussed in chapter 1, this approach is consistent with empowerment practice. The presence of familiar supports shifts the power relationships within the family and between the family and child welfare. These power shifts help family group members to exert constructive leadership in resolving major issues identified by child welfare and themselves. During this process, the child welfare workers retain their role as child protectors, while also joining with the family to help them.

During the conference, five phases take place: opening the conference, giving information, ensuring private time, finalizing the plan, and closing the meeting. Because of the time-limited nature of FGCs, one conference encompasses all phases from the beginning to the working phase through to the ending phase. The group is charged with an emotionally loaded task during the meeting—agreeing on a plan to resolve issues that are literally close to home or at home. Given this charge, the conference has both the affect of a natural group and the focus of a task group. During the course of the session (sometimes, sessions), the group must establish norms to reinforce collaboration, encourage participants to express their feelings and ideas, and build their commitment to effecting changes. Several strategies facilitate the development of such a context: opening in a way that deprofessionalizes the meeting; providing sufficient information so that the group can develop a sound plan; ensuring the family group's private time

in which to vent, confront each other, and develop a sense of ownership for the plan ultimately developed; validating the family group's good thinking without endorsing unsafe or infeasible plans; and closing with appreciation of the group's effort. As described in chapter 3, all of these strategies help to generate the cultural safety requisite for fostering participation and creating a plan based on the family group's values and strengths.

After the conference, the group follows through on the plan, not only implementing, monitoring, and evaluating the plan, but also reconvening the group and revising the plan as needed. It is the hope—and often the case—that by the end of the conference, family group members feel reconnected, hostilities between the family and service providers are lessened, and participants depart energized to carry out the plan. The transition into the follow-through stage is facilitated if the plan specifies a system of monitoring and evaluating progress, the workers incorporate the FGC plan directly into their service plans, and the family group members strengthen their positive bonds as they carry out work on behalf of their relatives. Many bumps, however, may arise along the way in implementing FGC plans, including lack of follow-through by family group and service providers. Because family members' lives do not hold still, plans often become outdated. Minor adjustments can be made with individual family members; however, the group should be brought back together to review and revise the plan in the event of major developments. One strategy applied in Michigan to keep the work on track is to designate an FGC advocate who is responsible for assessing safety, supporting the family group's efforts to carry out the plan, and linking the family with needed services. Chapter 4 reviews all of these steps to cement the family–community–agency partnerships and assesses their efficacy in facilitating the cooperation necessary for safeguarding young and adult family members.

Can the FGC partnership approach be applied in child welfare?

The short answer is "yes." The efforts made before, during, and after the conference are all designed to encourage family members to share their concerns and resolve problems together. The group participants may not start with the same concerns, but in hearing the same information together and working to-gether to reach solutions, participants come to common commitments.

For the longer answer to this question, it is necessary to take into account the authority position of child welfare workers. Because their legal mandate to protect children gives them authority to remove children from their families, child welfare workers often face clients who fear their involvement and resist the provided services. Social workers have learned what does not work with involuntary clients (Trotter, 1999, pp. 40–41). As shown in Table I-1, FGC is structured so as to avoid these ineffective behaviors and to emphasize the family's strengths in generating solutions and carrying out their plan.

TABLE I-1
Ineffective Behaviors and Family Group Conferencing (FGC) Approach for Involuntary Clients

Ineffective Behaviors	*FGC Approach*
Being unclear about the worker's dual role as authority and helper	Upholding the referring worker's dual role of protecting children and helping families Distinguishing the referring worker's role from that of the FGC coordinator as conference organizer and facilitator
Revealing pessimism about the possibility of positive change	Referring a family to gain their input on how to resolve issues
Blaming and punishing clients	Organizing the conference in a way that respects families and their traditions
Focusing on insights or relationships rather than the task at hand	Promoting safe participation in finding solutions
Ignoring the clients' goals and emphasizing only the worker's goals	Generating shared concerns and solutions
Viewing the client as a problem rather than as an individual in a family and social context	Working with family members, both individually and as a group, to carry out the plan

2

Before the Conference–
Promoting Family Leadership

Joan Pennell

If family group conferencing (FGC) is to be successful, it is essential to affirm the family members' leadership from the start. In making the referral, the social worker acknowledges that the family group is crucial to planning for the well-being of its young relatives. In organizing the conference, the FGC coordinator reaffirms the family group's role and coaches the service providers on how to support the family group's participation. In preparing to take part, the family group members remind each other of their ties and the contributions that they can make to resolve family issues. Thus, this initial stage of forming the group sets the groundwork for a partnership in which the family group members are central and the participating community organizations and public agencies support their leadership.

Social workers know that in advance of holding any group, the groups' purpose, composition, and structure must be determined and its members prepared to take part in a safe and effective manner. This holds true even if the group meets for only one session, as in the case of many family group conferences. For a family group conference, the planning work is both simple and complex. In part, the membership is predetermined by kinship and friendship; in part, the membership is constructed by seeking out a broad range of perspectives and resources. Thus, the FGC coordinator may push for representation from different sides of the family or creative thinking on who is "like family" for an isolated mother or a long-term foster teenager. The family group includes more men than most child welfare interventions (Veneski & Kemp, 2000) and cuts across generations. As discussed further in chapter 3, this inclusiveness enriches planning, but it also requires attention to the dynamics of age, generation, and gender in organizing the group. In addition to the family group, the conference includes service providers. Careful thought is necessary to determine how service providers can lend their support without dominating the session in numbers or influence.

Creating this hybrid of a natural and formed group involves two main stages: referrals and preparations. In the referral process for FGC, as is true of group work in general, the social worker needs to provide a clear reason for holding the group so that the participants do not spend their time trying to guess their worker's intention (Northen & Kurland, 2001). If participants are clear about the worker's reason, they are better positioned to determine their own goals for taking part, and the worker and participants can agree on the purpose for the group. With this understanding, they can prepare for the conference.

What types of families are referred?

Programs vary in their referral policies, depending on local needs and contexts. In new FGC programs, workers are often hesitant to make referrals at first, particularly if they view the family as highly dysfunctional or inarticulate, or if there is child sexual abuse or domestic violence present (Marsh & Crow, 1998; Merkel-Holguin, 2000a; Pennell & Burford, 1995; Sundel, Vinnerljung, & Ryburn, 2002; Trotter, Sheehan, Liddell, Strong, & Laragy, 1999; Walter R. McDonald & Associates, 1999). The reason for the referral is usually constructed around the children such as where they will live, how they and their parents can get along better, or what supports are needed for young people to live independently (for example, Pennell & Burford, 1995; Trotter et al., 1999; Walter R. MacDonald &

Associates, 1999). Referral rates increase if policies require workers to consider referring cases, but with the later possibility of opting out by the family or social worker (Marsh & Crow, 2003).

In terms of outcomes, family groups with a range of issues, including child sexual abuse and domestic violence, benefit from conferencing (Morris, 2002; Pennell & Burford, 2000a). It is not necessary to exclude families from conferencing because of specific conditions, such as parental mental disabilities or substance addictions. In fact, social workers are more likely to refer parents who are abusing substances (Crampton, 2001). For their part, families are more likely to agree to take part in FGC if their issues involve parental substance abuse, domestic violence, parental mental illness, homelessness, previous experience with child protective services, special needs children, improper supervision of children, or child sexual abuse (Crampton, 2001). Incarceration of a mother or father may appear to prohibit participation, but can be handled by escorting parents to the conference. In keeping with research findings and practice experience, referrals should reflect the case situation rather than the characteristics of individual family members.

Who refers the family to FGC?

Commonly, the referral to FGC is made by child welfare workers, ideally in consultation with their supervisor, the FGC coordinator, and the family. If they are aware of the FGC program, the family may request a conference (Lupton & Nixon, 1999; Pennell & Burford, 1995), and family groups often write into their plans a date on which to reconvene. In some jurisdictions, other service providers such as juvenile justice or child mental health workers may make the referral or request such a referral. For cases before the court, judges may offer the option of a conference to the family and may consider the FGC plan in making their disposition or sentence. To encourage participation in FGC, it is advisable to use a number of referral routes—child welfare workers, family group members, and community members. Self-referrals are in keeping with advancing the family's leadership.

When does the social worker make the FGC referral?

The referral to FGC is made once the child welfare worker has determined a clear reason for seeking the input of the family group. The conference should not be viewed as a fact-finding expedition, but rather as a planning forum. It should be convened only after some baseline of facts about the situation has been established, but the delay should not be unduly prolonged.

Although it is preferable to hold the conference as early as is feasible, FGC is also useful for long-term situations, such as when a foster teenager is leaving state custody. For new or reopened cases, the referral should occur after the assessment or investigation is completed and a specific protection concern is identified. Court proceedings do not have to be concluded—provided that information from the conference is not used to allocate guilt or responsibility. If the family group members feel under scrutiny during the conference, they are less likely to volunteer their views.

If workers are not sure what is happening in the family, then they and the FGC coordinator cannot convey to the family the reason for the conference. A compel-

ling reason serves as a strong motivator for family groups to attend, and justifies holding a conference. When relatives understand that the children have been placed or are about to be placed in care, for example, they may feel that they can step forward and offer their homes to the children without appearing to betray the parents (Horwitz, 2003). A conference is an intrusive intervention in that it involves sharing confidential material related to the family. There should be a legitimate reason for sharing such information.

What does the social worker tell the FGC coordinator about the referral?

The referring social worker needs to provide sufficient information so that the FGC coordinator can approach the family in an understanding manner. In particular, the coordinator needs to be informed of any potential risks to the safety of family members taking part in the conference. At the same time, the worker should avoid biasing the coordinator toward the worker's perspective on the family.

Agencies differ on whether the FGC coordinator should read the family's case file; some want the coordinator to be fully versed in the history, and others see this as unnecessary and, possibly, prejudicing the coordinator. This choice is often an administrative one. The FGC coordinator who works inside the social services organization has ready access to files, but those who work in an independent agency may find that reading files is contrary to social services' policies on confidentiality. Whatever procedure is adopted, referring workers need to retain their role as child protectors, while FGC coordinators carry out their role as conference organizers and facilitators.

How are referrals screened?

The FGC coordinator assumes responsibility for screening referrals in consultation with the worker and the family. In determining whether to go forward with a referral, the coordinator faces a series of decision points (see Figure 2-1).

Is there a clear reason for referral?

In discussing the referral with the worker, the FGC coordinator gains information about the family's situation and ascertains if the worker has a clear and sound reason for making the referral. Often, workers know that they want family input on a difficult situation, but are uncertain about a specific reason for holding a conference. In these cases, the FGC coordinators can help the workers and their supervisors articulate a clear reason that can be conveyed to the family, their relatives, and their friends. The reason must be presented in a straightforward and positive way that encourages the family group to seek solutions together. The group's purpose is not the intended activities (for example, "to inform," "to discuss," "to plan"), but instead, the ends to which all can work collaboratively (Northen & Kurland, 2001). Some examples of FGC reasons are

- to support and keep all four children in the parents' home
- to ensure a peaceful home where all family members can live safely
- to plan a permanent residence for all six children
- to help the teenager and his father live together
- to help the mother stay sober and take care of her baby.

Can worker use family input?

The coordinator needs to ensure that the reason for the referral fits with the aim of FGC. The intent is to give the family group a voice in planning. For the family members to feel that they have a say, their social worker must be interested in receiving their input. If the worker is making a referral only to meet an agency policy or a federal guideline, the family will quickly ascertain this. If the worker cannot or will not listen to the family's input, there should be no conference. Sometimes workers already have a plan from which they are reluctant to deviate, or they are obliged to follow a court order. A conference should not be convened to secure the family group's compliance with a predetermined plan. If the family is already out of compliance with a service plan or court order, however, a conference can be called to develop a workable plan for approval by the agency or the judge.

Child welfare workers may worry that giving the family a say is not in the best interest of the children. In these instances, the supervisor and the FGC coordinator need to remind the worker that the child welfare agency or the court will have final approval over the plan. Although workers are usually pleased with the plans that come out of conferences, they may need to establish that family members' "having a say" is not necessarily the same as "having their way."

Is the family interested in learning more about FGC?

Workers discuss with their supervisor and the FGC coordinator the suitability of a referral and the best ways of describing a conference to the family. If a referral seems

16

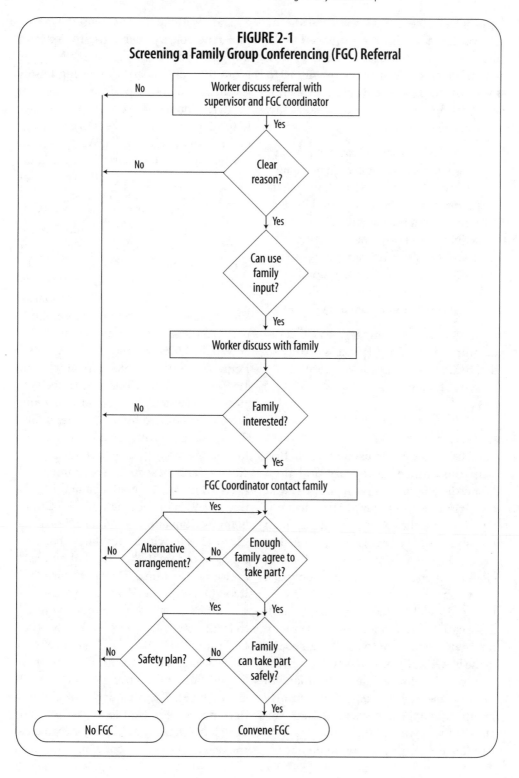

FIGURE 2-1
Screening a Family Group Conferencing (FGC) Referral

appropriate, the worker raises the idea of the conference with the primary family member or members, such as the parent(s), and asks if they are willing to meet with the FGC coordinator. In describing a conference, it helps if workers say, for example:

○ "A conference is a way for you and your family to have a say in planning."
○ "Social Services doesn't have all the answers; we need the family's help in making the best plan."
○ "No one has to come to a conference, and each person can choose to accept or decline the invitation."
○ "Whether a conference is held or not, we will continue to work with you."

In subsequent meetings, the FGC coordinator can explain the process further so that the family can make an informed decision on taking part.

Does enough family group agree to take part?

The FGC coordinator usually meets first with the immediate family and then branches out to relatives, friends, and other close supports. Gradually, the family group and the coordinator develop an invitation list. The intent is to pull together those who have a stake in the well-being of the children and their family. If only one or two family members agree to attend, the group will be too small for FGC. In these cases, the child welfare worker may meet with the one or two willing people, or the FGC coordinator may work with the family to develop an alternative that will involve more members of the family group. It may be necessary to think creatively about who is "like family," and to redefine the purpose of the conference.

The coordinator can extend the invitation in person, by telephone, in a letter, or through a mix of these approaches. Using more than one means of inviting family group members helps to increase their participation (Anderson, 2003). It is also helpful for family members to encourage other members to attend. As a rule, the invitees agree to take part (Crow & Marsh, 1997; Paterson & Harvey, 1991) or, if they do not attend, to send a message to the conference (Pennell & Burford, 1995). At some conferences, relatives may decline to attend if they anticipate being asked to serve as kinship care (Crampton, 2001).

On average, conferences have from five to 11 family group members in attendance. The numbers may grow far larger, however (Anderson, 2003; Gunderson, Cahn, & Wirth, 2003; Marsh & Crow, 1998; Pennell & Burford, 1995; Trotter et al., 1999; Walter R. McDonald & Associates, 1999). In New Zealand, children and young people are entitled by law to attend family conferences with consideration given to their wishes, age, developmental stage, culture, and best interests (Paterson & Harvey, 1991). The New Zealand legislation (1989) is in keeping with the United Nations Convention on the Rights of the Child (1989), which stipulates that children, according to their level of maturity, are to participate in decisions affecting their lives. Outside New Zealand, policies and practices on including children younger than 12 years vary considerably (Merkel-Holguin, 2003); their exclusion may be more a function of adults' concerns than the wishes of the youngsters (Marsh & Crow, 1998). The attendance of children does not have to lead to a "yes" or "no" decision. A flexible arrangement can meet the needs of both the child and the adult participants. For example, a playroom next to the conference room allows children to exit when the proceedings become too tiresome for them.

Can family take part safely?

On meeting with family members, the FGC coordinator tries to assess whether they want to take part and, if so, what do they need to take part safely. The coordinator may ask:

- "How do you feel about taking part in this conference?"
- "What are your hopes for the conference?"
- "What are your fears?"
- "Is there someone who scares you?"
- "Has this person been violent in the past?"
- "Is this person violent now?"
- "What would help you take part?"

In talking with family group members, the coordinator learns not only what they each need to participate in the conference, but also what they know about their relatives' needs. This group planning helps to build strategies and norms for safety that benefit all participants, both family and professional. With a safety plan in place, FGC can proceed.

Research studies report that violence seldom occurs at conferences (Marsh & Crow, 1998; Paterson & Harvey, 1991), and that violent retaliation does not appear to result from conferencing (Burford & Pennell, 1998). On occasion, FGC coordinators may exclude certain family group members to protect the physical and emotional safety of participants (Lupton & Nixon, 1999; Walter R. McDonald & Associates, 1999). This step requires much reflection and discussion, however, because the excluded person may be crucial to making and carrying out the plan. A restraining or protective order forbidding contact and communication should be respected, but legal, feasible, and safe alternatives may be found for participation, such as a telephone hook-up and letters. (See chapter 10 for further discussion of safety measures in family violence situations.)

How do FGC coordinators prepare themselves to work with a family?

As the FGC coordinator engages with the family, the focus is on helping family group members decide if they want to take part and, if so, in what way. In these discussions, *the FGC coordinator needs to listen closely to learn how differences among conference participants may affect the group's working together*. As with other types of groups, the coordinator tries to determine how prospective members are likely to experience the meeting (Shulman, 1999). The FGC coordinator may reflect on such topics as the following:

- How will an 11-year-old child feel in a room with adults?
- How will the down-country side of the family respond to their suburban in-laws?
- How will an abusive father and husband react when he must face his wife's grandmother, mother, and three sisters?
- How will a family whose multiple generations are the products of foster home placements relate to the child welfare worker?

Differences in age, culture, gender, or position may separate conference participants. In thinking through the resulting dynamics, *the FGC coordinator should seek out guidance from family group members and community groups sensitized to these issues.* It may mean consulting with advocates for children or women, or with elders in cultural or faith-based communities. In addition, FGC coordinators should consider how they themselves respond to various families:

○ How can I work with this family when I don't even speak their language?
○ This referral hits close to home. My mother has emphysema just like the mother in this family.
○ I went to school with the grandparents in this family. I know this family really well, but should I be their coordinator?

In addition, the FGC coordinator must be ready to engage with a family who may be facing crises or traumatic events. For instance, an aunt caring for the children may attempt suicide, or a teenager may run away from home. In these situations, the family requires immediate help, and the coordinator must respond. It may be necessary for the coordinator to contact the child welfare worker or another service provider, but the coordinator should not assume responsibility for providing service. FGC coordinators have to juggle meeting a family's needs with focusing on their role—that of FGC coordinator.

If more than one person is organizing the conference, these individuals need to define their roles. Sometimes, two coordinators share the tasks; in other instances, one person takes responsibility for the preparations, and another takes the lead on facilitating the conference (see chapter 11). In other locales, one person serves as coordinator, and the other serves as an advocate who supports the plan's imple-

mentation (see chapter 4). For a smooth operation, support staff assist with FGC arrangements. Conferencing involves a great deal of organization; having more than one person helps both with preparations and with monitoring developments during and after the FGC.

How do family group members prepare themselves to take part?

First, *the family group members require information before they can decide whether to take part.* They need answers to the following questions:

○ What is FGC?
○ Why is this conference being called?
○ Who will be at the conference?
○ What will I be expected to do?

Some of the answers come from the FGC coordinator, but many more may come from other family group members. As the family group members gear up for a conference, they talk among themselves and decide how to organize their conference:

○ Do we want to go?
○ Who else should be invited, and who should contact them?
○ When and where should we hold the conference?
○ How will we get there?
○ What food should be served?
○ Which interpreter do we trust?

They may also be aware of what individual family members need to participate and tailor solutions to specific needs:

○ a playroom for the children
○ a support person to stay by an abused wife during the meeting
○ a ramp for grandfather's wheelchair
○ security outside the door

○ a telephone hook-up for a teenager in detention

○ several smoke breaks.

All this networking in advance reaffirms their family connections and readies them for making good plans. In some families, this pre-conference networking yields plans for resolving the issues that prompted the referral and makes the actual conference unnecessary (Horwitz, 2003). These successes demonstrate the effectiveness of conference preparations in activating the family's informal supports.

How do service providers prepare themselves to take part?

Often, child welfare and other service providers are accustomed to working with clients one on one. *The FGC coordinator can coach them as they move from working with individuals to working with a group that consists largely of the client's family, not the professional's network.* They need to know how to carry out their parts at the conference and how to tune in to their own feelings. For the child welfare workers, a key task is getting ready to give their reports at the conference on the family's situation and the areas that need to be addressed in the plan. In preparation for the meeting, the child welfare worker is likely to wonder:

○ How can I be clear about the areas of concern while highlighting the family's strengths?

○ How should I word my presentation so that the family follows what I am saying?

○ How much confidential information can I share?

○ What questions am I likely to get from the family?

○ How am I likely to feel at the meeting? Will I be in the hot seat?

Commonly, other service providers are invited to the conference and may be asked to give information about a health condition, the impact on children of witnessing domestic violence, or the services available for addictions treatment. In preparing for their presentations, these information providers need to consider:

○ How can I avoid using jargon while still conveying the necessary information?

○ Can I give my presentation without telling the family what to do?

○ Will I want to take care of the family rather than support their planning?

As discussed further in chapter 5, workers generally welcome training on how to conduct themselves at meetings.

What steps do FGC coordinators carry out to organize a conference?

Preparing for FGC is akin to organizing a major event to which the participants bring a multiplicity of hopes, concerns, and commitments. *The wise coordinator knows that it is essential to work with others in the family, community, and agency in organizing the conference.* Sharing the workload makes it more manageable and, even more important, heightens the likelihood that the family group members can exert their leadership in a constructive manner.

In organizing a conference, FGC coordinators may find it helpful to develop a guide listing the steps that they must take. The North Carolina FGC Project developed an FGC preparation guide to remind coordinators of standard organizational tasks (Pennell, 2000b). It first outlines the steps involved in discussing the referral with the worker, then continues with those necessary in contacting and planning the conference with the family, and finally addresses specific tasks. The latter include developing an invitation list and extending the invitations; making arrangements for travel, facility, food, and child care; meeting participants' special needs, such as a support person, interpreter, telephone hook-up, or a temporary release from prison or detention; and compiling a package of likely resources for inclusion in the family group plan.

In the North Carolina FGC Project, the coordinators who filled out the preparation guide indicated that they had carried out most of the tasks (Pennell, 2002b). Their diligence yielded good returns, according to conference feedback. At the end of the conferences, the participants completed an evaluation form, of which three items related to preparations. Table 2-1 lists the 16 items rated on the extent of satisfaction; the first three items refer to preparations (for the complete questionnaire, see Pennell, 2002c). Overall, participants agreed that preparations for their conference had been good. They generally liked their conference location, usually a church or community center. The main shortcoming, if one was noted, was the absence of some key family group members or service providers. They often missed a father or simply wanted more family members at the conference. On occasion, they identified a particular service provider or community member who would have contributed to the planning.

How long does it take to prepare for a conference?

Organizing conferences takes time. *Usually, the time between the referral and the confer-ence, during which preparations take place, is two weeks to one month* (Marsh & Crow, 1998; Paterson & Harvey, 1991; Pennell & Burford, 1995; Walter R. McDonald & Associates, 2000). If the number of referrals is high, the time from referral to convening the conference increases (Thoennes, 2003).

In terms of coordinator hours, the averages run from 10 to 30 hours, but the overall range is wide (Marks, 2002; Marsh & Crow, 1998; Thoennes, 2003; Trotter et al., 1999). An experienced coordinator may spend as few as 10 hours on average organizing conferences, but the North Carolina study reported an average of approximately 30 hours. In this case the social services offices and their staff were new to the process, and workers tended to need the FGC coordinator's help in reaching out-of-state relatives. The referring workers generally spend an average of six to 10 hours on preparations (Pennell, 2002b; Trotter et al., 1999). Once a family has participated in a conference, they understand the process, and preparations for a follow-up conference can usually be carried out more quickly (Pennell & Burford, 1995).

Family Examples

Preparations for conferences never seem to follow the same route. The following three examples, all from the North Carolina Family Group Conferencing Project, illustrate divergences in the process. Yet each of these conferences adhered more or less to the key FGC principles for preparing participants, and each shows one of these principles translated into action. The first example shows the co-coordinators carrying out extensive preparations with the family group. Here the focus was on making sure that this large white family that involved two fathers would see the conference as belonging to their family group. In the second example, the coordinator did not have the option of working closely with the family to organize their conference. In fact, the African American teenager and child welfare worker were not hopeful that the teenager had any family to claim her. Here, the FGC coordinator worked to foster an understanding of who was family, and moved the conference to the rural community in another state where her family lived. In the third example, the coordinators struggled to bring together a tension-laden, bicultural family group. They held two pre-conference meetings to work through issues of safety.

The preparations for the three conferences, nevertheless, had a number of features in common. The FGC coordinators for the three conferences reported that they had completed the large majority of tasks on the preparation guide for the North Carolina FGC Project. Some tasks did not apply to these conferences, such as arranging for an interpreter or escort from jail or prison. The coordinators worked with family members to develop comprehensive lists of people to invite and then reached out, where possible, to prepare family group members and services providers. They paid careful attention to logistics—where to hold the conference, what food to serve, and how participants would get to the conference. Notably, all three conferences included support people designated for family group members who wanted someone to stay by them during the conference.

At the end of these three conferences, participants were asked to complete the FGC Evaluation form (see Table 2-1), a measure of their satisfaction with the conference. With minimal dissent, the 35 respondents for these three conferences agreed or strongly agreed that their conference had adequate preparations, good

TABLE 2-1
Satisfaction Items on Family Group Conferencing Evaluation Form

1. Preparation for the conference was adequate.
2. I liked where the conference was held.
3. The right people were at the conference.
4. At the conference, I got the information that I needed.
5. I was satisfied with the way the conference was run.
6. The group used effective decision-making techniques.
7. I believe that I had a lot of influence on the group's decision making.
8. I contributed important information during the group's decision-making process.
9. During the group meeting, I got to participate whenever I wanted to.
10. Others members of the group really listened to what I had to say.
11. I felt that I was a genuine member of the group.
12. The group reached the right decision.
13. I support the final group decision.
14. I would be willing to put my best effort into carrying out the group's final decision.
15. I think that the right people were involved in reaching the decisions.
16. I am satisfied with the plan that was agreed upon at the conference.

DeStephen, R. S., & Hirokawa, R. Y. (1988). Small group consensus: Stability of group support of the decision task process, and group relationships. *Small Group Behaviors, 19,* 227–239. Copyright © 1998 by Sage Publications, Inc. Reprinted by permission of Sage Publications, Inc.

facilities, and the appropriate participants. Their views were backed up by the observations of researchers, who, with the permission of all participants, sat in on their conferences, and by the interviews conducted shortly after the conferences with family group members. In subsequent interviews held six months or one year after the conferences, participants reported positive outcomes for their families.

Family Example 1: Understanding the Diagnosis—Have the Conference Belong to the Family Group

"Everyone got along with each other. There were no arguments."

—MIKE, FATHER OF ANNIE,
TWO WEEKS AFTER THE CONFERENCE

On the day of the conference, 11 all-white family group members gathered to determine where their two very young relatives would live. In addition to the family group, two coordinators, a child welfare worker, the children's foster parent, and a research observer were present. At the mother's request, the conference was held in a church hall. The mother began by thanking everyone for attending the conference. Thus, the conference was designed to belong to the family group— *more family group members than service providers attended, and the setting and opening signaled that this meeting was for the family.*

The two tots, Davy and Annie, had been placed in non-relative foster care when their mother was admitted to the hospital for psychiatric care. Because the children had different fathers, there were three sides of the family in attendance. Representation for the different sides, however, was uneven. The young mother, Kim, was accompanied by her support person (a friend) and her own mother, as well as by her mother's support person. Jeff, the father of Davy, had his sister, two aunts, and, as his support people, his girlfriend and her mother. Mike, the father of Annie, was alone. His pregnant sister's delivery date was the day of the conference. Both the fathers and the mother had a history of abusing substances.

On the surface, this conference appears ripe for conflict. In an interview two weeks later, however, Mike stressed that everyone got along well at the conference. Although he wished that his mother and sister could have been there, he still thought that his say at the conference was "just right." He was not alone in his positive view of the conference. Overall, the family group rated the conference favorably. They reached their plans primarily by coming to a consensus and following a trusted leader, Jeff's aunt.

What made for the harmony? One contributing factor is probably the extensive time that the two coordinators spent preparing the family group. Together, these recently hired coordinators devoted a total of 50 hours to preparations. In hindsight, they recognized that the length of time was partially due to their newness to coordination, but it also took a great deal of time simply to connect with the large and not easily reached family. In all, they met with 13 family group members, some on more than one occasion, before the conference. The preparations were prolonged because the conference had to be rescheduled. Originally planned to take place two weeks after the referral, the conference was delayed another two weeks because of the mother's readmission to the hospital to adjust her medication.

Another, and probably the most important, factor responsible for the harmony was the fact that *the family all agreed with the reason for holding the conference.* They recognized that Davy and Annie needed their family to establish where they should live, both in the short term and in the long run. On later reflection, though, they wished that they had known more about the family situation in advance of the conference. As Jeff's aunt noted:

I knew what the meeting was about (the coordinators explained it to me). But I told my niece and my sister about it—showed them a pamphlet—we didn't know that things were as serious as they were. Maybe had we known what was really going on we could have been more prepared. We only knew that the children had been taken away from their mom.

Not until the conference did they learn why Kim had been hospitalized. The child welfare worker revealed this information only after the family's private time in which they developed plans for returning Davy and Annie to their mother.

With Kim's permission, the worker explained that this young mother had been diagnosed with bipolar disorder and might have future difficulties caring for her children. Neither Kim nor her family group really understood the psychiatric diagnosis. The one exception was Kim's mother, who said, "It's heredity," and shared that she had the same condition. The worker apologized for not informing the group earlier and emphasized that, unlike a mother who chose to hit her child, Kim did not choose to become sick. Jeff's sister and aunt worried aloud about Kim being alone with Davy and Annie, and Mike agreed with them. To ease the tension, Jeff joked that it was a shame that Kim had not been diagnosed with something else like "temporary insanity." At this point, the group took a much needed break, but returned with renewed determination to complete a plan for the children.

Although saddened by their new awareness of Kim's situation, the family group held together throughout the day. It helped them to meet the foster mother, who reassured the family, "The children are loved and being well cared for." She added, "It takes all of us to raise these

kids." Their minds were set at ease about the immediate care of the children, but they would have liked to see the children at the conference. In addition, it would have been beneficial to have a mental health and addictions counselor available to provide information. Jeff's aunt later observed, "I don't feel like enough people were there to explain Kim's illness."

The coordinators appreciated how the social worker remained "strengths-focused for the duration of the conference [which lasted for five hours], while honestly confronting some extremely difficult issues." Critically reflecting back on their work, the coordinators wished that they "could have better elicited information about the mother's mental health concerns earlier on in the information sharing. . . . [and] explained to the social worker how taxing the day would be." For her part, the worker admonished herself to "make sure all information is given to the family so that they can make a decision that will not be 'shot' down by the agency."

Six months after the conference, only parts of the plan had been carried out. Nevertheless, Kim and her mother concurred that the family was "better off" because of the conference. Her mother explained, "Before [the conference], Kim was in a totally different state of mind, and she's been doing a lot better. The FGC helped her with ideas on what she could do to get herself together." Likewise, Kim said:

I know that I'm going to get my children back. My lawyer tells me it should take about six months. I am doing all that I am supposed to. I haven't failed drug tests. I have to attend my . . . classes [on mental health and drug abuse] and maybe parenting classes. I go to church with the foster parents and the children.

25

Kim and her mother took ownership of the conference's action plan and were doing their parts. The question is, Can they maintain their momentum against difficult odds?

Family Example 2: The Out-of-State Family Reunion—Foster Understanding of the Family and Creativity in Planning

"My family is a real source of comfort to me."

"I feel like a stranger in my family."

—14-YEAR-OLD TAMEKA, JUST BEFORE FGC

Despite Tameka's misgivings that any relatives would turn out for her, there were 21 family group members at her conference. The FGC coordinator, two social workers, and the research observer were also present. In addition, two family group members and one worker sent messages to the conference. The family group included the mother's, father's, and stepfather's sides of the family, as well as long-term neighbors. As the African American research observer later commented, "Some of the participants were African American, and some were white. But, they considered themselves to be family."

Five weeks after the referral, Tameka, along with her social worker and the FGC coordinator, flew from North Carolina to a small town in another state where most of her family lived. Other out-of-state relatives joined them there. *In its formation, this conference applied a broad definition of family that cut across lines of kinship, skin color, and geography.* How did so many come together for a teenager who was living in a group home far from her home community?

To help 14-year-old Tameka talk about her family in advance of the conference, the FGC coordinator asked her to complete the Index of Family Relations

(Hudson, 1992). On this 25-item instrument, Tameka indicated how she felt about her family. Her responses showed painful fluctuations between close identification with her family and alienation from them. They brought her both "great joy" and a sense of being "left out." Her feelings reflected her history: an adolescent removed from her grandmother, separated from her siblings, and away from her home community for two years.

On the FGC form, the reason for making the referral read, "To attempt to find placement with extended family." The emphasis was on "attempt." As the worker and her supervisor told the FGC coordinator, "Probably the family was not going to come up with any relative placement, but at least [the FGC] would be a good opportunity for the foster child to say good-bye to her extended family and receive some closure." Tameka's family shared these sentiments.

Reflecting on the initial preparations, the FGC coordinator wrote:

> When I began establishing a phone relationship with the family, I soon realized to my dismay that the maternal grandmother, Lilly, was quite hopeless about the purpose of kinship care. I reassured her that if no placement was secured, [FGC] would at least give Tameka an opportunity for some closure. That seemed to be a turning point.

As she continued to contact relatives, the FGC coordinator now described the conference as "a family reunion with a specific purpose." This was a reason with which the family group could agree for convening the conference.

Because the conference took place out of state, this relatively experienced FGC coordinator was unable to work closely with the family in organizing the conference. Her notes show her own education in how family can take charge of the preparations:

> Although over the phone Tameka's two former caregivers had given me only limited interested parties, upon arrival in town, I took them out to eat, and they produced a list of some thirty people they had invited to the conference. Very encouraged, I quickly made plans to enlarge the capacity of the food arrangements and excitedly congratulated them on a job well done. This was a remarkable lesson for me: being out of state, I had much less opportunity to be the true initiator of the invitation list. . . . I had been blinded by my own "professionalism," thinking that only a few people would actually attend because I hadn't been able to meet with them in person prior to the FGC.

Although novel for this urban-based coordinator, her experience is fairly typical of conferences held in small, tightly knit communities (Pennell & Burford, 1995). In these settings, the community network often does much of the organizing. For Tameka, this community included the local social services agency, which assisted with arrangements; the town library, which provided the meeting space; the florist shop, which donated a flower display; and the fast-food restaurant, which reduced the price of the food purchases.

Not only the adults, but also the children ensured that the conference worked. Uncertain about what to do with the four children in attendance, the FGC coordinator designed a child care corner in the conference room. She wrote:

The child care was also a plan out of desperation, yet one which worked very well. The children were quite well behaved, were entertained by the Disney videos, and after I gave older children "duties" to entertain and engage the younger ones, the children did quite well with their families right there in the room with them, close at hand.

The research observer further noted that, as needed, the adults intervened to quiet the children playing in their corner. Despite the family group's extensive involvement, the coordinator still clocked 40 hours in preparation, and the social worker put in 10 hours. Travel time alone was time-consuming for the coordinator and the social worker.

Typical for small communities, the family group did much of their planning in advance of the conference. Sitting in on the family's private time, the research observer listened as the adults developed four possibilities for family placement. She surmised:

> The options had already been decided before the conference, and the participants only tolerated the formalities of the conference for the sake of participating in an FGC. With many of these options, the participants had already conducted a preliminary investigation.

This pre-conference planning helped the participants to proceed even though not all potential caregivers were able to attend and even though Tameka tried vociferously to disrupt the proceedings. As the FGC coordinator commented, "Tameka was continuing to expect rejection." By the end of the conference (which lasted nearly five hours), however, "her countenance lifted, and a number of appreciative statements started edging their way out of her mouth."

Six months later, none of the suggested placements for Tameka had materialized, and she remained in the North Carolina group home. Relatives and friends explained that their local social services office had not completed assessments of potential placements. Her mother's sister, Kitty, who had served as the support person for her lonely and acting-out niece, thought that the conference had left the family "just the same, as far as anything happening." She acknowledged, however, "It made us feel better because we were able to see her. . . . [and] know that she was OK. . . . so far away. It was better being able to see her even if it was just for that little while."

Aware of the benefits to all of the siblings, a neighbor who was caring for one of Tameka's younger siblings observed that the family was better off. She noted that the siblings "got to see each other. They hadn't seen each other in a while. I heard they were all in a group hug, and think that helped them."

In weekly telephone communication with her granddaughter, Lilly thought that Tameka was better off because of the conference:

> She seems to be doing well. Seems like she has adjusted. She's showing improvement to me. [She used to be] rebellious, talked ugly, didn't stay in school—now she seems to have a goal. She is going to school. She wants to be a doctor (I put that in her mind). I'm trying to promote her to be stronger, to do something.

A year later, Lilly died. Tameka attended the service and stayed with her aunt Kitty for a week. This visit gave her an opportunity to reconnect with her siblings and have a "real good time." Returning to the group home, though, Tameka became upset. As Kitty explained, "When she was here, it was chaotic, and I don't think she really had a chance to process losing her grandmother until she returned." After talking with her aunt by telephone, Tameka calmed down. In Kitty's opinion, Tameka seems "OK" in the group home, but should be with family. Not giving up, Kitty is pursuing the possibility of Tameka's living with an older cousin with whom she has "always been close." Wherever Tameka ends up, Kitty said, "We're still trying to keep in contact with her. I got my sisters to call and know that she can call us. We felt that our mother was her lifeline, and we don't want to lose her lifeline."

The conference achieved the family's purpose—holding a family reunion. Kitty and her sisters were making sure that Tameka, even at a distance, would remain attached to her relatives and home community. When she eventually leaves custody, she will have a family.

Family Example 3: Bicultural Communication—Help the Conference Participants Take Part Safely and Effectively

What was this conference like for you?

> *Latoya (mother):* "Really bad at first. They made me so mad. But it. . . really turned out good. We are talking now."

> *Gerald (father):* "I wasn't sure at first. . . . I know how our attitudes can be—me and Latoya. When we get on each other's nerves, we are awful. . . . We accomplished a lot. We're doing great— we talk to each other every day."

> *Helen (Gerald's mother):* "I really had to pray about this before. I was really mad when it started. . . . It was fine once we

got started. . . . We were a tough group, but [the coordinators] handled it well."

—Interviews six weeks after
the conference

Two days before the conference, Latoya reported Gerald to child protective services for mistreating their two-year-old daughter while she was in his care. The parents shared custody, and Briana moved back and forth between their homes. With yet another child protection report against her son, Gerald's mother, Helen, telephoned the FGC coordinator and stated that her family would refuse to attend the conference. In response, the FGC coordinator pointed out that incidents like this were the reasons for the conference. Each parent had repeatedly reported the other to social services. Reluctantly, Gerald's family reconsidered and agreed to attend. When the family group arrived at the conference, the two sides drew up battle lines—Gerald's side white and relatively comfortable financially, Latoya's side African American and lower income.

The purpose of the conference was "to facilitate communication between the parents" and "to promote Briana's well-being." This was a purpose that Latoya and Gerald's families understood and strongly supported. They all recognized that the level of hostility was a major obstacle to the joint parenting. These same tensions, however, made the family group apprehensive about coming to the table. Differences in culture and income heightened the acrimony. For instance, men in Latoya's neighborhood had threatened Gerald and his stepfather when they were attempting to collect Briana for visits.

Each parent had an extensive family network on which they could rely. The mother's closely knit and loyal backing was apparent when she filled out an instrument called People in Your Life that mapped her social network (adapted from Tracy & Whittaker, 1990; see Kemp, Whittaker, & Tracy, 1997). To help the mother make up the invitation list for the conference, the coordinator asked her to complete a chart showing who the important people in her life were and how they related to her. Latoya listed nine people who were either her relatives or friends; none belonged to Gerald's family, and all were African American. According to Latoya, those listed were extremely supportive and closely connected. Furthermore, the relationships were long-term, with contacts on a weekly or daily basis. At the conference, she was accompanied by four of these important members of her network: her grandmother, mother, and two sisters. Gerald was accompanied by his mother, sister, stepfather, uncle, and fiancée and her young daughter. His relatives were white, and his fiancée and her daughter were African American.

The organization of this conference took a long time—three months—largely because FGC was new to the county social services, the original coordinator left during the preparations, and the family group was strongly at odds. Nevertheless, the supervisor and new FGC coordinator persisted, as did the FGC trainer who co-facilitated the FGC. *They planned a number of strategies to ease the conflict both before and during the conference*:

○ *Pre-meetings:* As the FGC coordinator explained:

> There was major conflict between Helen and Latoya because of a power struggle. They were very hostile, mistrusting, angry. . . . We met with both of them separately. We were able to have both make the same promise to cooperate and stay calm.

○ *Support People:* At the conference, these individuals emotionally supported the angry parents while demanding that they contain themselves. Gerald's fiancée served as his support person and, when he started to interrupt, gently reminded him to listen. Latoya's support people were her two sisters, who were fiercely protective of her at the conference while urging her to keep her temper under control and continue with the process. As observed by the researcher, their efficacy was quite evident during an altercation over Briana's medicine:

> Gerald spoke up and stated that Latoya didn't send Briana's medicine [to his house]. . . . Latoya said that she did send it, and Helen shook her head. Latoya jumped up to leave the room, but her sister grabbed her arm and pulled her back down in the chair.

○ *Respected Information Provider:* Briana's well-loved pediatrician attended to describe Briana's needs without appearing to blame either party. The researcher wrote:

> The pediatrician stated that the lack of communication about health issues caused Latoya to take Briana to the ER [emergency room] five times in five days. She spoke to the problems associated with this method of health care. Helen stated that they had no other way to get help after hours if Briana was sick. The pediatrician explained how to reach her after hours. She explained the process she wanted them all to follow concerning health care for Briana. All agreed to try her plan.

○ *Private Space:* The conference was held on the weekend at the social services office. Although the two coordinators had some reservations about the location, the timing made it possible to ensure privacy for the family. The pediatrician and Latoya's mother had difficulty gaining entry into the locked building after the start of the conference, however.

○ *Refocus on the Child:* According to the trainer and co-facilitator, it was helpful to re-center the discussion on the child by pointing to Briana's photos:

> The coordinator asked the family to bring photos of Briana. The photos were placed in front. It really set a wonderful tone. As a co-facilitator, I picked up the photos several times, which is an overt conflict management tactic.

○ *Culturally Representative FGC Coordinators:* For this bicultural family group, it helped to have two coordinators, one African American and the other white. As the county-based FGC coordinator explained:

> Co-facilitation was helpful because one person could do one task while the other supported the task with something else (e.g., talking/writing, observing/engaging). The family could see two different faces and relate to both.

○ *Reframing of the Tensions:* The child welfare supervisor, who had known the family for an extended period, recognized the potential for change in their conflict and reframed the points of tensions as facilitators. This African American supervisor explained, "Interracial family—different cultures, different economic backgrounds—so many things we had to work with. It gave us some momentum to proceed with."

○ *Commitment of Family and Workers:* The supervisor stressed that the most important factor was the perseverance of the family and workers:

> I can't say enough about what [the family] brought to the table. They were looking for a resolution; tired but didn't know how to come together. We didn't give up on the family. No matter how many times the coordinator and I looked at each other with doubt, we never let the family see that. . . . Each time we met with them, we asked them if this was something they wanted. . . . We supported them and believed that they could succeed at it.

At the conference, the family reached their decisions primarily by consensus, and their plan included steps to promote communication and avoid animosities for the benefit of Briana. Reflecting later on the conference, Latoya, Helen, Gerald, and his fiancée all agreed that over the 4½ hours they had "enough supports and protections." Echoing the views of the others, Gerald's fiancée noted, "Everything is fine—they are talking now." Six months after the conference, Latoya said that the family was "better off" and working together with the pediatrician who had attended the conference. Continuing, she explained, "It was worse before the FGC because it was like [Gerald and his family] didn't call, come to visit anything. I couldn't talk to them—that's how bad it was. Now I can talk to them, some."

With preparation and supports, this bicultural family group learned to communicate at the conference and, despite some bumps along the way, continued to work together for the sake of the child that they held in common.

How is the family's leadership promoted in advance of the conference?

Family leadership is a pathway to safeguarding children, young people, and other family members. Family leadership is not about the child welfare worker's turning over responsibilities to the family group. Instead, *family leadership means placing the family group members at the center of the planning process and providing them with the support of community organizations and public agencies.* By assuming leadership, the families of Davy and Annie, Tameka, and Briana were able to develop plans for taking care of their young relatives, as well as their caregivers—Kim, Lilly and Kitty, and Latoya and Gerald. In addition to relatives and child welfare services, a range of community groups supported these caregivers: Kim received help from mental health services and foster parents, Lilly and Kitty from neighbors, and Latoya and Gerald from the pediatrician.

To promote the family group's leadership of FGC from the outset, the following steps are beneficial:

○ Screen referrals on the basis of the case situation rather than the characteristics of individual family members.
○ Encourage referrals from child welfare services, family groups, and community organizations.
○ Make a child welfare referral to develop an action plan after abuse or neglect has been established, not to investigate the possibility that it is occurring.

- Provide sufficient information to the FGC coordinators without biasing them in advance.
- Offer a clear, positive, and compelling reason for calling a conference, and reach an agreement with the family on the purpose of the conference.
- Seek genuine input from the family rather than predetermining the plan.
- Invite—not order—families to participate in FGC.
- Explain the FGC process to the family group members so that they can make an informed decision on taking part.
- Involve family and "like family" and all sides of a family and its different generations, from great-grandparents to children.
- Avoid exclusions of particular family members, except when necessary for the physical or emotional safety of participants.
- Tune into the feelings of individual participants and seek guidance from professional and cultural experts.
- Coach service providers on how to take part.
- Promote networking among the family group members so that they can plan their conference.
- Work with the family group to make travel, food, facility, child care, and other logistical arrangements.
- Develop safety measures such as support people and a private meeting space.

3

At the Conference—
Advancing Cultural Safety

Joan Pennell

At a family group conference, the aim is to develop a plan for safeguarding young and adult family members. The assumption is that, with support, the family group members can apply their insider knowledge and long-term commitment to develop a plan that works. To tap into their understanding and caring, family members need a forum at which they can say what they believe. They need to feel "at home" and to speak in their own words, not those of the professionals. Thus, it is essential to create a culturally safe context in which the family group members can express their mutual sense of identity, uphold their values, and invoke their experiences and traditions to resolve issues. Not all the families that participate in family group conferencing (FGC) feel close, especially given the dislocation, substance addictions, family violence, and other social ills that they may be facing. In these instances, the conference can serve as a means of cultural regeneration. It gives

them an opportunity to identify those values that are important to them as a group, and to assume responsibility for the decisions that affect their young relatives.

Because of its composition and structure, FGC holds out the promise of advancing cultural safety in child welfare planning. As discussed in chapter 2, the family group is both a natural and formed group: it includes family members based on kinship and family members based on relationship. The conference brings together different generations, genders, and sides of the family, as well as "like family"—that is, friends, neighbors, and other close supports. The mix helps to reaffirm family identity, while infusing additional resources and viewpoints. By widening the circle, the conference builds a community that can reinforce positive family customs and counteract harmful ones. Substantiated by research findings discussed in chapter 7, cultural safety goes hand in hand with physical and emotional safety;

it emphasizes simultaneously culture, safety, and their essential links.

Structured so that the family group members can tap into their strengths, FGC is a form of inclusive decision making that encourages positive exchanges across the family group. Family group members of different ages and gender show support for their relatives by coming to the meeting, engaging in planning, and making plans that commonly involve personal contributions. In this setting, the voices of women and young people are more likely to be heard. The product of the meeting—the plan—serves as an agreement to continue the collaborative effort.

What is cultural safety?

As defined in this volume, *cultural safety is a context in which family members can speak in their own language, express their own values, and use their own experiences and traditions to resolve issues.* Any family group has its own beliefs and practices that come from a sense of a shared past. Because of their real and assumed history together, the older family members may (though not always) exercise considerable influence over perceptions of what is customary and normal.

The family group's income, skin color, language, religion, region, and other similar factors affect, but do not determine, cultural identity. The bicultural family example in chapter 2 revealed that the two families' cultures had been formed from multiple factors, including their different neighborhoods. Highlighting what distinguished them from others, particularly when they came into contact with "outsiders," reaffirmed their sense of identity (Green, 1999). Given modern migrations for work and security, what a family group

calls its own is constantly shifting. Upholding a sense of home and familiarity is particularly crucial to family groups disrupted by poverty, war, racism, disease, separation, and abuse. In their engagement with social systems, these families require a culturally safe context in which to connect with their sense of heritage and to find solutions to their problems.

Maori nurses in New Zealand developed the term "cultural safety" in response to institutions that were imposing European culture on indigenous people (Ramsden, 1993, 1997). They identified the bicultural tensions between professionals and indigenous people, and they advocated for a standard of care that respects and protects their culture (Polaschek, 1998). Their aim was to create partnerships between providers and recipients that affirm the indigenous heritage while seeking to change traditions in any culture harmful to women and children (International Confederation of Midwives, 2000). Whatever its background, a family group has its own ways, its indigenous culture. Within a safe context, the members' sense of commonality encourages affirming and challenging their own norms and practices.

Cultural safety looks behind what practitioners do to how clients from a different culture experience the service. It is the outcome against which to measure the worker's cultural competence. For a child services worker, it entails asking both "Is this child safe now?" and "Does that include cultural safety?" (Fulcher, 1998, p. 333). Do these children, young people, or family members feel that they can express their familiar ways of thinking and acting, and that the worker will acknowledge these norms, despite perhaps having only a partial understanding of their meaning?

For marginalized cultures, such safety is a worthwhile goal, but one that requires constant bolstering because of structural barriers to the acceptance of these cultures in our society (Milliken, 2002).

Why is cultural safety important to child welfare?

Cultural safety is especially necessary in the public child welfare system, given its troubled and troubling history in relation to non-mainstream children and their families. Child welfare has protected many children and supported many families, but its record, particularly for people of color and those with low incomes, testifies to their over-representation in out-of-home care (Rangihau, 1986; Roberts, 2002). In the United States, this is evident among American Indian/Alaska Native, African American, and Hispanic families, whose children are far more likely to be removed from their families than those of white families (U.S. Department of Health and Human Services [HHS], 2000).

Increasingly, it has become clear that relying on expert assessment and legal intervention fails to protect children and, conversely, abandoning children to disadvantaged families and neighborhoods is not the solution (Parton, 1997). Promoting child and family welfare requires multiple strategies (Pecora, Whittaker, Maluccio, & Barth, 2000). Like public agencies, families and communities may have practices both beneficial and detrimental to the well-being of their children and young people. Rather than depending on one sector, it is necessary to generate a sense of shared responsibility among families, communities, and public agencies (Adams & Nelson, 1995; Briar-Lawson, Lawson, & Hennon, 2001; Schorr, 1997). In our aging society, a viable route to build community across societal institutions is intergenerational practice.

How does intergenerational practice promote cultural safety?

Intergenerational practice involves "policies and programs that transfer resources and care across age groups, age cohorts, and generations within families" (Cornman, Henkin, & Kingson, 1999, p. 12). It uses various strategies, such as older adults joining with children in learning groups, grandparents caring for their grandchildren, and young people assisting older adults (Kaplan, Henkin, & Kusano, 2002). Other programs, referred to as multigenerational practices, link more than two generations. *Intergenerational and multigenerational approaches such as FGC not only connect generations, but also can connect children and young people to their cultural community and regenerate a sense of cultural identity.*

Maintaining these generational and cultural links is a central principle of the New Zealand (1989) law establishing FGC in child welfare and youth justice programs (Hassall, 1996). At a conference, multiple generations of a family gather to find ways of safeguarding their relatives. To the questions—"Is this child safe now?" and "Does that include cultural safety?"—we can answer "yes" with greater confidence if the family group remains firmly attached to the children and their futures.

Is FGC effective in all cultures?

It is not yet known if FGC is effective in all cultures. So far, *FGC has been well received in a wide range of cultures in the southern and northern hemispheres* (Burford &

Hudson, 2000). Those in urban and rural settings, and those with diverse ethnic backgrounds, have expressed satisfaction with the model. Its appeal is especially evident among historically oppressed groups, as long as attention is paid to their views on how to carry out conferencing (Pennell & Burford, 1995; Waites, Macgowan, Pennell, Carlton-LaNey, & Weil, 2004). The crucial factor seems to be the adaptation of the model to the local context, not the particular culture (Pennell & Weil, 2000).

Are families from some cultures taking part in FGC more than those from other cultures?

As with other child welfare interventions, questions have been raised about whether families from certain cultural groups are more or less likely to be referred to FGC. In particular, will white social workers have better relationships with white families and refer this population more often? Or will they view FGC as a lesser option and refer families of color? Some FGC programs are intentionally designed to divert the placement of children from groups overrepresented in care (Crampton & Jackson, 2000). Most programs, however, do not restrict their referrals to specific cultural groups.

The available evidence indicates that families from a range of cultures are participating in FGC, but not necessarily in proportion to their percentage of their agency's caseload as a whole. A Washington State study found proportionately fewer white families and more Native American families participating in FGC than was representative of their out-of-home placement caseload (Shore, Wirth, Cahn, Yancey, & Gunderson, 2002). In contrast, however, a California study found that white families were over-

represented, and African American families were underrepresented among those taking part in FGC, compared with their representation among the county's total child welfare families (Walter R. McDonald & Associates, 2000). The North Carolina study found in its largest participating county that African American children were slightly overrepresented, and white children slightly underrepresented, among families participating in FGC as compared with their percentages for children entering care. Given the participation of multiple cultural groups and the divergent findings, the studies do not point to certain groups as rejecting FGC. Instead, the findings point to the necessity of designing hospitable programs and training workers to consider a range of referrals.

In child welfare, how does the structure of a conference foster a sense of cultural safety?

When the referral comes from child welfare workers, the family group members know that the authorities exert considerable influence over the children and may even sever their ties to their young relatives. *To develop a plan in this high-stakes forum, the family group members need to know why they are meeting and to have sufficient information on the situation, privacy for making their plans, and affirmation of their competence as planners.* The conference is structured to foster the cultural safety necessary for the family group to engage in planning. A conference has five main phases: (1) the opening, (2) the sharing of information, (3) family private time, (4) the finalizing of the plan, and (5) the closing. Each of these phases is intended to create a context of cultural safety for the family group.

An Opening in the Family's Tradition

At the beginning of most types of groups, participants arrive with a multitude of questions (Shulman, 1999): What is this all about? How will the worker view me? What will the other members think of me? The preparations for the conference help to address some of these questions; these same issues re-emerge as the family gathers, however, and it is a good practice to address them again. The FGC coordinator can help family group members and service providers settle into the meeting by giving them a warm welcome, making sure that everyone is introduced, clarifying the purpose of the group, reviewing the phases of the meeting, and establishing guidelines for group interactions.

For a family group, however, there is an added question at the outset of the meeting: How will others view my family? This sense of family protectiveness is intensified when the family group members and the service providers are divided by culture. On the positive side, such loyalty can energize support for relatives; on the negative side, it can fuel fears and hostilities at the conference. One way to promote family identification and diffuse tensions is to signal from the start that this forum belongs to the family group. As discussed in chapter 2, having the family determine the invitation list, select the conference location, decide on the time, and arrange for the food can help to set this tone during preparations. Another strategy is for the coordinator to ask if the family wants a particular opening for the conference. They may simply choose to have everyone seat themselves in an arrangement that feels comfortable. (The bicultural family group described in chapter 2 had decided preferences on where to

sit; the two families seated themselves on opposite sides of the room.)

Some families may want a more elaborate opening. They may pass around the child's photos, for example. At the out-of-state conference described in chapter 2, Tameka's siblings and cousins sang two gospel selections. At a conference held for an African American family in a white church with eight of its white members present, the opening helped somewhat to rebalance the session. As noted by the research observer (present with the family group's permission), "The African American pastor [from the great-grandmother's church] was volunteered to say a prayer. He readily agreed to do so."

Respectful and Straightforward Information Sharing

Once the group is settled, the FGC coordinator asks the group to share information so that the family group will be able to make a plan. At this time, the family group and the service providers review the facts of the situation, suggest possible resources to include in the plan, and express their concerns for the family and their perceptions of the family's strengths. Commonly, the FGC coordinator uses a flipchart to write down the main areas that the plan should cover. The social workers need to describe clearly the situation and the concerns that must be addressed— without telling the family group what to put into the plan. At times, social workers should set forth "bottom lines," that is, non-negotiable conditions that the plan must meet. Unless these required conditions are clearly spelled out, the family group members remain unaware of the context in which they are making the plan, and are understandably taken aback if the child protection worker later rejects their course of action (Horwitz, 2003). Social workers should limit these stipulations whenever possible, however, to allow greater flexibility for the family group. Examples of such conditions are:

○ The stepfather cannot be alone with the child that he sexually victimized.
○ The mother must be sober when caring for her children.

The information-sharing phase of FGC is usually an emotionally charged time that elevates tensions while firming the resolution to engage in the work. It is painful to hear what has happened under any circumstances, and the fact that this information is shared in front of both the larger family group and the service providers may heighten emotions. The reports may generate a sense of shame among family group members because of their failure to intervene earlier, or they may cause family group members to redirect their anger against the service providers for their interference. Social workers need to anticipate these strong feelings, and to view them as an opportunity to deepen their understanding of, and connection to, the family group.

It is often wise for the FGC coordinator to check with the family in advance on the order of speaking, and to recheck at the conference. Some families feel more in charge if they initiate the discussion; others feel less at risk if the service providers open the discussion of sensitive issues. In cases of sexual abuse or domestic violence, the service providers should usually describe what happened so that survivors are not placed in the position of disclosing their victimization at the conference. Other topics, such as mental illness, may be just too difficult for the family members to raise on their own.

When the problem area is one that needs further explication, the FGC coordinator, in consultation with the family, can invite additional service providers to give presentations. These providers may include substance abuse counselors, public health nurses, domestic violence advocates, and community elders. One particularly helpful information provider was an older substance abuse worker who had worked with the mother on both substance abuse and mental health issues. As described by the research observer, this worker spoke in a "gentle, supportive manner" about his work with the mother:

Next the substance abuse worker reviewed the history of working with the mother. He said that he was impressed recently by how the mother spoke with her doctor, especially her saying that she knows that she needs to stay sober for herself. He identified himself as in recovery from alcoholism and went on to explain that the self-shame is much deeper for women than men. So it is harder for women to reach out for help. . . . He stressed that to be effective, you need to treat simultaneously the substance abuse and the mental health issues.

The substance abuse worker also demonstrated his willingness to work with the family group in supporting the mother's recovery and answered their questions on her condition:

The step-grandfather said that he had a question on accountability. He asked, "How can we know (and want to believe) that she really went to the treatment group meeting?" The substance abuse worker responded that with a signed release from the mother, he could provide this information to others. . . . The substance abuse worker noted that with both the mother's treatment team and her family group, it would be hard for the mother not to take her medication. The mother's friend asked, "What is it [schizophrenia]?" The substance abuse worker described the disease.

If additional information providers are not working with the particular family, they should arrive after the child welfare report, give their presentations, answer questions, and depart. This arrangement helps to protect the privacy of the family and prevents professionals from taking over the group process.

To lend support or offer further insights, family members, community groups, or other workers who are unable to attend the gathering or who feel that they will have difficulty expressing themselves at the meeting may send messages. Sharing these messages is an especially effective way to ensure that children have a voice at a gathering of adults. One research observer described a poignant example at a conference for a boy in foster care:

A letter from the stepfather was read, along with a letter from the mother regarding her [substance abuse] recovery plan. . . . The clinical specialist played a tape he made with the boy in which he briefly explained the concept of FGC. . . . It is a circle of friends. The clinical specialist asked the boy to tell him about people he has called "Mom." The boy listed the foster mother, friend, and mother. The boy said, "Ask [Mother] if she loves me

enough to please stop doing drugs." Everyone in the room (at least those people whose faces I could see) was tearful. After the tape, the maternal foster grandmother comforted the mother and told the mother, "You're doing the best you can."

Taking part in the information sharing gives service providers confidence in the family group. This new confidence makes it easier for them to leave the room and allow the family group the private time necessary to make a plan. A case in point is a guardian *ad litem* (appointed by the court to represent the children's best interests) who originally insisted to the FGC coordinator that she remain with the family throughout the conference and then changed her mind: "The GAL [guardian *ad litem*] wanted to be in the conference family private time but she . . . came to the point of having nothing else to say after all the concerns had been voiced by the family members and others."

Once the family group has sufficient information and moral support, it is equipped to begin the private deliberations. FGC coordinators may suggest that the group designate someone to record the plan. Then they advise the family group that they and the child welfare worker will be in an adjoining room and available as needed. Often, family group members come out of the conference to check a piece of information with the worker. That the service providers stay shows their support for the family's deliberations and ensures that they are present to negotiate and finalize the plan after the private time.

Family Private Time

The coordinators can smooth the transition from the information sharing to the private time by providing refreshments or a meal, depending on the time of day. It is advisable for the service providers to take their food and leave the family group to sit down together. By now, tensions have usually eased, and family members are able to enjoy the food. Eating together is a very familial activity, tightens bonds within the group, and readies them for the planning.

Although the beginning phases of a conference often reflect the style of the FGC coordinator, the private time mirrors the characteristics of the family group. With the professionals out of the room, the group must rely on its own ways of interacting. Some family groups do not know what to do initially, and may appeal to the FGC coordinator to help them. In these instances, the coordinators need to resist taking over and, instead, must reaffirm their belief in the family group's competence. Other groups start by confronting their relatives. The coordinator needs to be ready to comfort or find support for participants emerging in tears from the conference room. With encouragement, most participants will return to the conference room.

The family's culture influences the way that the different generations interact during the private time. In many U.S. cultures, the generations tend to have relatively equal status; in others, however, young people are expected to listen more than speak (Kaplan, Henkin, & Kusano, 2002). A North Carolina example recorded by a research observer shows just how families can ignore children during the private time and how the children can insist on being heard. During a discussion of where the four children wanted to live, the group attended to the views of the three adolescent siblings, but treated the 12-year-old

son quite differently: "Child 4 is sitting beside Mom during this time. Mom does not take his comments seriously. Mom tells him to 'shush,' puts him down. No one makes sure that Child 4 gets to talk." Nevertheless, this young person was undeterred and returned to asserting his wishes later in the conference: "Child 4 speaks up and [says] that he [wants the] order . . . to be 1–grandmother, 2–aunt, and then another aunt." At the end of the conference, he completed the FGC Evaluation, expressed overall satisfaction with the conference, and agreed, "Other members of the group really listened to what I had to say."

Many family groups have a natural leader who emerges, as Jeff's aunt did in the first example in chapter 2. In other groups, the leadership is shared. Support people also have an important role. In her annual report, one FGC coordinator explained that these participants "act as emotional support for people attending the FGC who are in 'vulnerable positions'." She then illustrated this role:

> In one particular case, a mother who gave her children to [child welfare] to be placed in foster care felt very vulnerable attending the FGC, particularly because her family did not understand her actions. She brought a friend as support person, and her role was not to give information, but to act as a silent friend to the mother in this time of great stress.

In another case, a family in which the father had been violent against the mother before they separated was taking part in FGC. At the mother's request, the conference was held in her church with the minister and his wife present. In this instance, the support people simultaneously offered support and kept members under control. Reflecting on the conference, this FGC coordinator wrote:

In planning for the conference I was concerned that the family would not be able to come up with a plan in their private time. I felt that there would be arguing and much disagreement from conversations with family members [during the preparations]. However, the family was able to go into private time with no problems. As soon as I left the room, the family began discussing, and I never heard any raised voices or arguing. I was in the next room and could hear sounds, but could not make out what was being said in order to protect their private time. I felt like the presence of the minister and his wife provided a buffer for the family to reduce the chance of arguments.

Many families develop an increased closeness and informality once the professionals are out of the room—ventilating, joking, and storytelling. The research observer captured the capacity of this group to be honest with each other, confront family members to change, and draw up the plan:

The family first brought their circle in closer together. . . . The grandmother was the first to speak. . . . Her comments were supportive of the mom. The young son (from outside the circle, where he appeared not to be participating) then said that the social worker was a pain in the ****. The grandmother said that she was

only doing her job. . . . The grandmother said that the father and mother needed to "put down the bottles." With the professionals in the room, the mom denied any substance abuse problems, and the family did not speak up about this. . . . The meeting had become much less formal. The two children were joking around with one another. Everybody added comments or responded to statements. They often recalled stories from the past. They would go off on tangents. They avoided addressing the objectives. Grandmother spoke the most and the two aunts the least; they had been given the job of writing the plan down on paper. . . . The grandmother and mom started a side discussion. . . . The two aunts were writing down the plan. . . . The mom, daughter, and one of the aunts took the plan to the service providers.

At times, FGC coordinators wonder if the family time should be more structured to shorten the time and increase the group's efficiency. After a conference, one FGC coordinator reflected, "I am thinking about how to have more specific questions for the family to refer to. . . . maybe on paper that the family can look at in alone time. . . . to keep the goals of the conference in mind. They don't seem to be referring to the flipcharts." At the same time, however, family groups require flexibility to cover areas that they know are important to them as a family and to do so at their own pace. For example, the white coordinator of a conference for an African American family could not have anticipated what the group discussed. This family was not only highly suspicious of the child protection worker and the guardian *ad litem*, but also somewhat disconnected from each other. As the research observer noted, their private time began with the family's history: "The grandmother tells them about her mother's experience as a slave. She has 60 grandchildren and 75 great-grandchildren " From here, they moved into making plans for some of these great-grandchildren.

Affirmation of the Plan

After the family group members have developed a plan, they call back the FGC coordinator, child welfare worker, and other service providers who have been waiting. Back in the conference room, the FGC coordinator asks the family group to review their plan with the child welfare worker and any other remaining service providers. The social worker makes sure that the plan addresses the main child welfare concerns. Whenever possible, workers should commend the strong areas in the plan and be straightforward about any area that needs further attention or approval from their supervisor or the court. Sometimes the plan is in order, and the worker can authorize it immediately—which feels very affirming to the family group. If the worker is unclear or uncertain about an action step, the coordinator may ask the family group to clarify it, or the family group may return to their private deliberations to discuss it further. It is best to resolve the outstanding issues at the time of the conference, or at least to identify them and set a date for reconvening. Whether at the conference or shortly afterward, child welfare workers authorize the vast majority of plans (Anderson, 2003; Cashmore & Kiely, 2000; Marsh & Crow, 1998; New Zealand Department of Social Welfare, 1999; Pennell & Burford, 1995; Thoennes, 2003).

Although in child welfare cases, the social worker and any other involved protective authorities, such as those from the juvenile justice system, are responsible for the final approval of the plan, additional service providers can assist in reviewing and affirming the plan. For example, the substance abuse worker described earlier quietly admonished the group on their plans for the mother: "If I were the mother, I'd feel overwhelmed [by the plan]. The group needs to set priorities and start with what will she do tomorrow."

Often, the family group's initial plan overlooks strategies for making sure that the plan is being carried out and its effectiveness evaluated. The FGC coordinator can help them decide who the monitor of the plan should be, and how they will alter the plan if necessary. The child welfare worker is legally responsible for monitoring the case, but having a monitor from the family group as well can facilitate communication between the service providers and the family group.

A Closing with Appreciation

Once the planning is completed, the FGC coordinator should thank the group for their hard work. Some families have time constraints and want to leave immediately. Such was the case for the family group described earlier; because of concerns regarding babysitting arrangements, the research observer noted, "There was a rush for the door by the family group. The social worker and substance abuse counselor came up with their calendars to set appointment times with the mother. The FGC coordinators shook hands with each of the departing family members."

Other groups welcome a closing activity such as a "final prayer." A research observer summarized the closure of Tameka's conference (described in chapter 2): "The coordinator thanked the participants for their work. She led the participants in a circle exercise during which time they stated their commitment to Tameka. The family ended the conference with hugs, kisses, and tears."

How long are conferences?

Advisedly, conferences do not have a set ending time. Instead, family groups take the time that they need to make a plan and, if necessary, schedule an additional conference for another day to complete the work. *From conference start to finish, reported averages run from 2½ to six hours* (Anderson, 2003; Marsh & Crow, 1998; Paterson & Harvey, 1991; Pennell, 2002b; Pennell & Burford, 1995; Trotter, Sheehan, Liddell, Strong, & Laragy, 1999; Walter R. McDonald & Associates, 1999; Williams & Weisz, 2003). The North Carolina FGC Project found:

○ The opening and information-sharing phases tend to be the longest, averaging 1¾ hours.
○ The family's private time averages 1¼ hours.
○ The last two phases—finalizing the plan and closing—together average a little more than one hour.

Given the unpredictable length of a conference, FGC coordinators need to work out a starting time with participants that will permit the group to complete the work without going too late into the evening, when everyone becomes overly tired.

How do family groups make decisions?

A common fear is that an abusive or manipulative parent, teenager, or other family member will dominate the family group during the private time. The reality is that *conferences are long enough for the family group to use a number of decision-making processes over the course of their deliberations* (Pennell, in press-a; Pennell & Burford, 1995). These may include avoiding a final decision, manipulating the decision process, and ordering what is to be decided. These decision processes would appear to run counter to the FGC value of consensus building. Nevertheless, family groups make their decisions primarily by

○ *Reaching a consensus*—pulling together everyone's ideas and coming up with a plan that everyone is comfortable with
○ *Inspiring*—going along with what a trusted leader says should be in the plan
○ *Bargaining*—having each side say what they want in the plan and then having each side get some of what they want.

The family's culture influences the decision process. White Canadian, white American, and African American family group members ranked reaching a consensus as the most important at their conference, while the Inuit in Labrador, Canada, ranked inspiring first.

What is in the FGC plans?

Family groups share the workers' concerns about their relatives, and their plans address the areas specified by the child welfare worker during the information sharing. The plans state, for example, where the children will live in the short- and long-term, how the parents will get treatment for substance addictions, and what the family members will do to help resolve other issues that led to the conference. Typically, though, the plans cover other issues identified by the family group members and other participants. Families are often more attuned than the service providers are to their relatives' needs for equipment (for example, baby gates) and recreation (for example, family outings), and they look ahead to the children's futures. One FGC plan included the formation of an educational fund for the children. Family group plans do not read like standard service plans and are more likely to include informal, cultural, and/or faith-based supports (Gunderson, Cahn, & Wirth, 2003; Pennell & Burford, 1995; Thomas, Berzin, & Cohen, 2005; Vesneski & Kemp, 2000). *Overall, FGC solutions are more imaginative and wider ranging, and their language more informal and caring.*

A clear plan specifies what is to be done, by whom, and within what time frame. Usually, plans include steps to be implemented by the family group, community organizations, and social services (Merkel-Holguin, 2003). Family group members are generous in offering to donate their time, homes, and resources. They tend to be reasonable in their requests for publicly funded services (Marsh & Crow, 1998). Because it may be necessary to obtain more information before the selection of the final action steps, plans may contain contingency steps. In these cases, it is recommended that a time be set for a follow-up meeting to finalize the arrangements. In addition, it is important to specify who will monitor the plan's implementation and how the group will evaluate its successes and identify areas for refinement.

These crucial features are evident in a plan for a youth with a developmental disability who had exhausted his allotted time for his group home placement and needed a place to live. The plan noted that

the youth "wishes to live with the family friend, who is like a father figure to him" and has a "strong bond" with the son of the family friend. For his part, the family friend would "consider having the youth reside with him if he received assistance in building an additional private room and bathroom to his home." The plan then set forth a series of action steps to be carried out before the group would reconvene in six weeks:

○ Family friend will check with his church and other places for additional resources (financial and human).
○ Social services will also explore options of financial and human resources (for example, Habitat for Humanity, donations from building supply stores).
○ Arc (a resource and advocacy group for people with mental retardation and other developmental disabilities) will provide possible financial and technical assistance.
○ If nephew lives with family friend, his aunt and uncle will serve as respite care during the summer and some holidays.
○ If the nephew cannot be placed with the family friend, the aunt and uncle will take him rather than have him go to another foster home.
○ The aunt and uncle will offer their support and feedback throughout the decision-making process.

This plan's final clause established the aunt and uncle as the monitors. At the follow-up conference, the family friend's wife also attended, and she agreed that the young man could stay with them. Fortunately, the family friend was able to locate the necessary resources and proceeded to build the addition for this young man.

How satisfied are FGC participants with conferencing?

Overwhelmingly, family groups and professional participants report that they like FGC (Anderson, 2003; Cashmore & Kiely, 2000; Merkel-Holguin, 2003; Trotter et al., 1999; Unrau, Sieppert, & Hudson, 2000; Walter R. McDonald & Associates, 1999). Although conferences can be emotionally draining, family group members prefer FGC to other decision-making approaches used by child welfare workers (Marsh & Crow, 1998; Trotter et al., 1999). The North Carolina FGC Project distributed an FGC Evaluation form (see chapter 2) to the participants at the end of the conference to assess their level of satisfaction with the conference. On this questionnaire, family group members reported that they saw themselves as having a say and making plans that they were motivated to carry out (Pennell, 2002b). Likewise, high satisfaction was evident in a North Carolina focus group held with five African American aunts, sisters, and cousins (Henderson, Pennell, & Family Group Members, 2004). They agreed that they liked FGC because the workers gave the information "with compassion and respect" and accorded the "family permission to be involved." This affirmation "gave the kids back to the family."

Both family groups and service providers are enthusiastic about FGC; however, the level of enthusiasm is higher among the family groups (Trotter, 1999). The professionals see the conference as meeting children's needs, but some wonder if other child welfare meetings would produce better plans. This skepticism reflects, in part, workers' concerns about client dysfunction and their personal liability if something goes wrong (Lupton & Nixon, 1999; Sundell, Vinnerljung, & Ryburn, 2002).

Family Example: "We're not stupid"—Tap into the Strengths of the Family Group in Making a Plan

"[The FGC] helped me get my child back. If I didn't have a detailed plan in court, I might not have gotten her back."

—Corey, mother of Kayla, 2 1/3 years after FGC

In the following family example, the family group sensed and productively addressed the service providers' distrust. The family's private time was crucial for advancing cultural safety. In privacy, the family group members said what they truly thought and felt, reaffirming that they know what will work best for their relatives and pledging to carry out the plan of action. A recurring refrain throughout this conference was that the mother and her family group were "not stupid" and knew what the children needed.

Referral and Preparations

Six-month-old Kayla was taken into care after a medical examination found broken bones at different stages of healing. This examination occurred when Kayla was at child care. Kayla's father, Tyrone, was charged with inflicting her injuries. Her mother, Corey, was quite upset and stressed that she had taken Kayla for regular medical checkups without any detection of injuries. Three young sons remained with Corey, who lived apart from Tyrone. The judge permitted Corey to visit Kayla, but denied visitation to Tyrone. Seeking wider input on the situation, the judge ordered the parents to have a conference, and Tyrone and Corey agreed to comply with the order. As Corey later explained, "When I went to court, the judge told me I had to have this conference. And the coordinator told me it shouldn't be mandatory, but I did everything the judge wanted me to so I could get my daughter back."

When questioned on the matter, those at the child welfare agency explained that the judge was ordering a family meeting, not necessarily a multigenerational family group conference, and added that the agency could not have compelled the relatives to participate in FGC. The conference was organized over a two-month period, and preparations took approximately 20 hours for the FGC coordinator and 2 hours for the foster care worker. The conference was scheduled for two weeks before the parents' return to court.

At the conference, Corey arrived without any of her relatives, while Tyrone was accompanied by his mother, father, and grandmother. All were African American. None of Corey's young children attended the conference. Also African American were Kayla's foster parents, foster grandmother, and guardian *ad litem*. The white attendees were the foster care worker, the FGC coordinator, and the research observer. The absence of Corey's kin was in keeping with her Index of Family Relations (Hudson, 1992).

Before the conference, the FGC coordinator had asked Corey to complete the Index of Family Relations to get a sense of family relationships. Corey's Index showed a modest level of intrafamilial stress, except for one item: "I can really depend on my family." Here she had responded, "None of the time." As Corey admitted at the conference, she had been on her own for quite a while, was self-sufficient, and did not like to ask for help. To develop the invitation list, Corey had also filled out a social network map of the important people in her life (Tracy &

Whittaker, 1990). This showed that Corey considered her important family members to be Tyrone, his mother, the children, two younger relatives, and Kayla's foster mother, Bea. No friends were listed. She characterized her relationship with Tyrone, his mother, and Bea as close and supportive, but said that they were "almost always" critical of her. On the evaluation form completed at the end of the conference, all nine respondents, including Corey, strongly agreed that the "right people were at the conference."

Opening

The conference was relatively brief, lasting two hours; this was fortunate because as everyone later commented, the temperature of the room was "very cold." The conference took place in a church basement and started at 1:30 P.M. on a weekday afternoon. Participants were seated in a horseshoe configuration at tables with snack food and beverages available. At the front were the FGC coordinator and a flipchart stand. The research observer, sitting outside the circle, documented the opening of the meeting:

> The coordinator first discussed the purpose of the conference, which was [to ensure] Kayla's safety and to find her a permanent home. The coordinator wrote out on a flipchart that the meeting was to develop a safe and permanent home for Kayla. The parents, Corey and Tyrone, agreed. The social worker added that there should also be a plan for getting support for Corey and Tyrone. The coordinator then addressed the issues of confidentiality. The group felt that confidentiality was not a problem. The coordinator discussed

the FGC process. First, there would be information sharing, followed by family alone time during which the plan would be written down. When the family finished the plan, everyone would meet again to discuss it.

At this point, the foster mother, Bea, asked about the standing that she and her husband were to have at the conference. They noted that they were to become Kayla's godparents and wanted to know if they could stay for the family private time. The other family members gave a resounding "yes." From the outset, the family group welcomed the input of the foster parents and, as became evident over the course of the conference, Bea's leadership. Later, in response to the evaluation form's question "What especially needed to be changed to make for a better conference?" Corey wrote, "Nothing," and then she advised, "Make sure each conference has a 'family leader'."

Information Sharing

The FGC coordinator moved the group into the information-sharing phase. As group members shared their views, she listed them on the flipchart. Tyrone and Corey started by stating what they wanted to happen. Going first, Tyrone stressed that he would like to see Kayla and wanted to "keep himself straight." This young father, barely out of his teens, said that he was dealing with the upcoming court date and lawyers, child support, and a parenting class. He wanted Kayla back with her mother. For her part, Corey said that she wanted more visits with Kayla, whom she was allowed to see for only one hour every other week. She also expressed concern that Kayla did not know her father.

Next, Tyrone's parents emphasized their desire to keep the child safe and offered to watch her until Corey got home from work. Corey said that she was "scared" about Kayla's experience at child care and wanted to watch her daughter herself. Bea responded that Corey needed to use the grandparents as a resource. Relieving Corey's fears, she went on to describe Kayla as a "normal, happy little girl . . . very active." Attuned to Corey and Tyrone's sense of being left out of Kayla's early life, Bea stressed that she wanted Kayla to be with her parents because the baby is a "blessing." On hearing this statement, Tyrone started crying and left the room. Bea then spoke about Corey's potential and supported her attending classes to become a nurse. Likewise, Tyrone's grandmother affirmed Corey as a "hard worker." Thinking about the charges against Tyrone, though, Corey became very angry.

To refocus the group, the coordinator returned the discussion to the purpose of the conference—to ensure Kayla's safety and reunite the family. The social worker, worried that the family group would create a plan that she could not approve, pointed out the agency's bottom line: Tyrone could not visit Kayla until the pretrial release conditions ended on the upcoming court date. Continuing, she said that at the court session the child welfare worker would support Tyrone's visiting Kayla. Likewise, the guardian *ad litem* agreed to support these visits.

The social worker commended Tyrone's display of emotion over his daughter and noted that he had not shown such emotion at the psychological examination. At this point, Bea interjected, "White service agencies often misread the Black male." Sidestepping the "race" issue, the white social worker replied that she really wanted Tyrone to have visits with Kayla, and that the parents should ask for help from the agency when it was needed. Child welfare authorities could return Kayla only when they knew that she would be safe. Outraged, Corey, a mother of four, said that the child welfare workers were assuming that she did not know how to mother her infant. On this note, the family group moved into their private deliberations at 2:30 P.M., one hour after the start of the session.

Reflecting on the conference later, the African American guardian *ad litem* said that the social worker had outlined all of the concerns well, including her own, but wished that Tyrone had been "in touch with his feelings and expressed himself more." Not part of the family private time, the guardian *ad litem* did not observe Tyrone and the other family group members in a more relaxed setting in which they could express their caring for Kayla.

Family Private Time

Describing the reduction in tensions once the service providers left the room, the research observer wrote:

> The family first took a break and relaxed and chatted, laughed and released tension that had been building from the meeting with social services and discussing the issues. It became much more apparent how the family cares for one another. They were much more open with things and discussed that they must abide by the agency's rules.

Next, through a symbolic gesture, the family group members showed that they were now in charge of the conference: "They removed the flipchart with the suggestions that were written up at the beginning. The action seemed to represent that they were going to develop their own plan. They removed the flipchart while joking about not being stupid."

Assuming the leadership, Bea stood next to the flipchart and focused the group on making a plan. She started by addressing Kayla's physical safety. Bea first affirmed that Corey knew how to childproof the house; to help Corey out, she suggested that Tyrone's mother or she would double-check the house. Becoming quite detailed, she proposed to provide Corey with the necessary equipment, including a gate to keep the dog out of some rooms, cabinet locks, stovetop guards, outlet plugs, and a playpen. The discussion then centered on keeping Kayla safe from her brothers' "horseplay." Corey was uncertain that she could count on her active sons to help out, and the group was generally concerned about having the boys "on board" with their efforts to ensure Kayla's safety.

Throughout this discussion, the family group appeared comfortable and talked openly about how the service providers made them feel. Favorably impressed, the research observer commented at length:

> They were doing this mainly by making jokes about how the child welfare worker called the mother stupid. . . . This did not actually happen—but that is how Corey felt when the service providers told her why they had taken her child. . . . The family was finding a way to talk about the problems that the parents were having without getting angry or stressed. They were laughing about some things. This was entirely appropriate laughter. It was not

[that] they were not taking the situation seriously; it was more that they seemed much more comfortable addressing the problems.

Moving the group along, Bea helped the group build a consensus on Tyrone's visiting Kayla. Bea suggested, and everyone concurred, that once the judge had approved visitation, Corey and Tyrone should visit Kayla together at the foster home. By now, Tyrone had become visibly much more relaxed. Reaffirming their connection to Kayla, the group began recounting stories about this well-loved infant: "Now they were sharing stories about the child—sort of like reminiscing, and everyone was enjoying talking about her."

At the same time, they kept to the task and worked out a visitation schedule for Tyrone. Aware that Kayla would need to become reacquainted with Tyrone, Bea asked him how he might handle Kayla's possible rejection of him at first. Not sure, Tyrone was agreeable to Bea's suggestion of visiting with the foster parents while Kayla became accustomed to his presence. Again struck by the family group's continuing good humor and hard work, the research observer wrote, "The family is getting the plan done and talking. . . . They joke about not being stupid—referred to throughout."

Detailing the plan of action, the family group members volunteered to help with specific tasks:

- ○ Grandmother: Will watch Kayla constantly
- ○ Grandfather: Will help with household repairs and cut the grass
- ○ Great-grandmother: Will baby-sit.

Although willing to help, the grandmother noted that these were new roles

for family members, and they would need to adjust to the roles. Bea supported them in this and offered to send all of the baby's things to Corey's house. In her role as godmother, Bea made the following commitment:

- ○ Bea: Will call Corey often, will visit not often (to give them space), and will baby-sit when needed (or wanted)

Recognizing her difficulties in asking for help, Corey promised:

- ○ Corey: Will ask Bea to help me with Kayla's schedule

On further pressure from Bea, Corey gave her word:

- ○ Corey: Will call Bea if I need help paying for extra expenses when Kayla comes home

Then Bea made her final pledge:

- ○ Bea: Going to pray for this situation

With the plan in order, Corey left to bring back the FGC coordinator, the social worker, and the guardian *ad litem*. All of this happened in just one-half hour. From the researcher observer's vantage point, the family group made the plan primarily by following a trusted leader and building consensus, but they mixed in a limited amount of bargaining and ordering.

Finalization of the Plan

With everyone back in the room at 3:00 P.M., Corey took the leadership role and described the plan to the service providers. It showed attention to Kayla's safety and well-being, provided specifics on who was to do what, and included contributions from the parents, family group, foster parents, and social worker. Adding her own contribution by agreeing to help Corey obtain day care and household equipment, the social worker said that the plan was "great." With the court hearing only two weeks away, she would recommend that custody remain, for now, with the agency, but "worded liberally," to keep the parents connected with Kayla.

Closing

At the final phase of the conference, the participants completed the FGC Evaluation form, and the conference ended at 3:30 P.M. The form gave them the opportunity to reflect on the course of events. Their views were uniformly positive. On the questionnaire, the family group members, foster parents, social worker, guardian *ad litem*, and coordinator all "strongly agreed" that they had received the information that they needed at the conference, were satisfied with how the conference was run and with the resulting plan, and would be willing to put their best effort into carrying out the plan. On her evaluation form, the elated foster care worker wrote, "This was a wonderful experience! The coordinator did an excellent job."

Two weeks later, the guardian *ad litem* was asked in an interview if she had any remaining concerns about the conference. Responding "no concerns," she stressed the importance of the family private time and the conference location: "They had privacy. It was in a neutral territory."

Implementation of the Plan

One year later, Corey and Bea were interviewed separately to find out if the family group had carried out the plan and to determine the impact of the conference on the family. Although Corey had not seen the foster parents in a while, both interviewees agreed on developments.

After the court hearing, Corey regained physical custody of her daughter, and Kayla returned home. Kayla was also attending a day care facility that Bea had located. The most important parts of the plan were put into effect, but some parts were not. Tyrone never visited Kayla at the foster home, but later visited Kayla on weekends at his parents' home.

In Corey's view, the main and most regrettable omission was her own failure to follow through on the plans with the foster parents. With remorse, she explained why she had severed this connection for Kayla and herself:

> I decided to stop taking Kayla to her foster parents after she came home because when I used to go visit her, she would want her foster mother instead of me when she got upset. It would have been different if she had been older. They would have been a good influence. . . . It is not that I didn't want my daughter to see them; it is just I couldn't take her there because it hurt my feelings. I didn't mean to hurt their feelings.

As part of the follow-up interview, Corey completed again the Index of Family Relations (Hudson, 1992) and the social network map (Tracy & Whittaker, 1990). Now on the Index, she responded that she could "really depend" on her family "all of the time." Her social network map showed an increase in supportive connections. Tyrone and his parents remained in her network, and her description of them had changed from "almost always" critical to "sometimes" critical of her. Furthermore, she added three friends, an aunt, a pediatrician, and the child care worker to her network.

For her part, Bea was pleased that the baby was back with her mother and very understanding of Corey's feelings:

> Kayla was reunified with her mother. This was a great reunification. The conference was to work out a plan to help out the child's mom. Corey got upset that Kayla was calling me "Mama," and I haven't seen the baby since. . . . I still haven't had any closure. It's just a part of life. I'm not bitter. I pray for the child.

More than two years later, Corey was interviewed again. She was definite that the conference had made the family "better off." She had Kayla back, and she said that she had had "real good foster parents and a good social worker."

How does cultural safety promote carrying out the plan?

In a culturally safe context, the family group can say what they think, challenge members to change, appeal to family and cultural traditions for guidance, and develop plans that fit their family. FGC is structured to foster this cultural safety. The opening signals that the meeting belongs to the family group; the information sharing demonstrates that the service providers want to learn from the group's best thinking; the private time gives the family group the opportunity to take the lead in making the plan; and the authorization of the plan by child welfare workers affirms the family group's efforts. A clear plan lays out who will do what, when they will do it, and how the steps will be monitored, evaluated, and if necessary, revised.

4

After the Conference—
Maintaining Community Partnerships

Gary R. Anderson

The introduction of family group conferencing (FGC) and its adoption and adaptation around the globe placed the initial family meeting at the center of attention. Model descriptions and training initiatives focused on the underlying values and the most appropriate strategies for the first family group meeting. The questions posed for the model included the following:

○ How do you recruit families, extended family members, and community partners for these conferences?
○ Will they participate voluntarily?
○ How should the meeting be structured?
○ Will this meeting result in an acceptable plan that will keep children safe, and be respectful of the family cultural system?

The steps and processes necessary to set up a successful conference also were addressed. The average number of days for this preparation was computed to address

expense, workload, and group process inquiries. All of this attention might make it appear that the conference itself was the desired outcome and that the primary measures of success were the number of participants, the quality of their interaction, and their arrival at an acceptable plan. This emphasis on an immediate goal that focused on the FGC process (that is, conducting the conference), rather than a long-term outcome goal (that is, the safety and well-being of children and families through the implementation of a plan), could be shortsighted. Celebrating the family meeting, as important as the conference can be, may be comparable to judging the success of a marriage based on the tone and meaningfulness of the wedding ceremony. To assess and appreciate the long-term goals of FGC programs requires paying attention to what happens after the conference. After the conference experiences are shaped by the plan and the relationships forged at the family meeting, the structure of the FGC program, the nature of ongoing community partnerships, and the events in the life of the family that test and shape the implementation of their family plan.

How does the plan guide the work after the conference?

The family plan developed at the conference shapes and, to some extent, dictates the activities after the conference. If the family group conference is used in the early stages of a child protective services case, for example, the plan has been crafted in private family time, presented to and negotiated with the FGC coordinator, reviewed and approved by the parents, and accepted by the child protective services worker. If FGC is used at another point in the child welfare or juvenile justice service continuum, the common elements of key family member acceptance and concurrence with the plan by a supervising agency representative will remain. The plan may even have a court official's approval and sanction. The family plan is the guide for family actions and the supporting role of community partners.

Several features of the plan inform this guidance. First, there are the action elements detailed in the plan. Second, there is the assignment of responsibility for the implementation of identified action steps. Third, there are contingencies and other related information included in the plan.

What are the action elements of an FGC plan?

The action elements in the plan vary in number, detail and creativity. Plans are initially crafted and recorded by family members in their private time together. After their presentation to the coordina-

tor and community partners in attendance at the conference, the plan elements are affirmed or modified to provide greater clarity or address elements viewed as essential by a conference participant, and accepted as important by parents, coordinator, and child welfare representative.

The family plan contains action elements, steps that the family group members have decided to take to resolve the issues that brought them to FGC. These steps are typically written down, agreed upon by conference participants, and copied (either at the conference or soon after) so that each person who has a role in the plan has a copy of the plan.

Number of Action Steps

The detail with which the participants described the action steps, the number of participants, and the scope of factors considered by the participants determine the number of action steps in a family plan. The number can vary widely from conference to conference. In some conferences, plans have contained as few as two actions; for example, the mother will get substance abuse counseling, and the children will remain with their maternal grandmother until the mother has successfully completed counseling. Some conference plans have 10 or more actions; for example, the mother will begin substance abuse counseling, the grandmother will care for the children until the mother has successfully completed counseling, the mother will visit with her children each week, the children will receive counseling, the grandmother will transport the children to counseling, an aunt will provide respite care for the grandmother, an uncle will visit the mother weekly to check on her progress, and so on. More detail in the plan may result in more action steps.

The number of action steps may also depend on the number of participants at the family meeting. The family may attempt to include as many conference participants in the construction and implementation of the plan as possible. Community partners in attendance may have a role. Each family member and fictive kin may have something to do. For example, in one case, there were specific tasks for the mother, her ex-husband, and the children. Even the ex-husband's new girlfriend (who was at the family meeting) was designated as a backup driver to get the children to child care.

The scope of factors considered by the participants also shapes the number and, to some extent, the detail of the family plan. Some plans focus on what the family has determined is the primary challenge facing the parent and children at risk, such as substance abuse or the parent's mental illness. Some plans more broadly address family functioning. This broader scope may also reflect a concern for what the family group members perceive as multiple family stressors, particularly in cases of severe child neglect. For example, some plans have addressed the recreational needs of the family, the spiritual needs of the family, and the economic needs of the family, as well as the treatment and psychosocial needs most closely associated with the risk to the children.

Detail of Action Steps

Plans developed through FGC involve multiple tasks. Building on participant introductions, the provision of information by the community partners about the children, and the parents' needs and service histories, family members construct a plan to guide their future steps to ensure the well-being of the children. They must craft this plan and negotiate its action steps with the coordinator and child welfare authorities within a limited amount of time. It is possible that family members have explored action steps before the meeting through their own informal conversations or in direct dialogue with the FGC coordinator during preparations for the conference. Out of respect for the family group process, however, a coordinator would most likely avoid suggesting action steps or negotiating these steps with subsets of family members before the family conference. Consequently, there is much for the family to learn (from each other, from community service providers, and from the coordinator) and absorb at the meeting. Within this context of discovery and the range of emotions that this family crisis may have evoked, the family crafts a plan.

These plans may provide very little detail—the mother will get counseling, the mother will enroll in parent education, the children will stay with a relative. This lack of detail may reflect the limited planning time, the multiple challenges facing the family, the lack of certainty about the details, family ambivalence or desire to avoid conflict, or the existence of few and sketchy options. Key resources or support people may not be available or in attendance at the meeting. Some of the necessary detail may be addressed in the conversation with the FGC coordinator and community resource people after the private family time.

The inclusion of considerable detail in the family plan may reflect the codification of a set of supports that are already in place, a prescriptive response by some family members, or some experience or knowledge of various options. The action steps in the plan may vary in their clarity and specificity. The coordinator, in negotiation with family members at the conference, may need to gently press the family for some details so that the plan is clear and acceptable to the meeting participants. Some of this clarification is likely to take place after the conference, including in follow-up family meetings.

Creativity of Action Steps

One of the features of FGC is that because the family members themselves develop the plan, the action steps match the needs of the individual family and take into account a range of family concerns and aspects of family functioning. In contrast to case plans that are largely generated by individual child welfare workers or by teams in which a family is either not present or outnumbered, FGC plans begin where the family begins, include elements identified by family members as important, and are subject to family approval and, in some cases, veto. In contrast to FGC, typical child welfare case plans have been criticized as "one size fits all," or so established and routinized that they do not reflect differences in families or their resources. FGC family plans usually do not resemble an agency checklist linked solely to traditional agency services (Merkel-Holguin, 2003).

One study that examined more than 200 FGC plans at an early stage in intervention showed both common and traditional service elements, as well as family-specific and seemingly idiosyncratic action elements. The most frequently noted elements in the family plans included counseling for the parent, counseling for the child, child care arrangements, transportation, arrangements for respite care, parenting classes, substance abuse treatment, and plans for visitation when kinship care was a part of the plan. In addition to this array of relatively traditional responses, these plans were characterized by details and provisions that were not typically noted in case plans constructed through traditional service planning and delivery. Such tasks included helping a family assemble Christmas decorations, establishing regular sleep schedules for the children, associating with more "positive" people, instructing the mother to keep a journal, helping a son get properly fitting clothing, instituting a family "movie night," eating three healthy meals a day, keeping swearing to a minimum, praying for a blessing, and counting to 10 and thinking of butterflies as one technique for dealing with frustration. In addition, traditional elements, such as child care, respite care, and transportation are often provided by family members and fictive kin (Anderson, 2003).

This individualized construction of a service plan—with traditional and nontraditional items and service providers— would fit the specifications of the federal Child and Family Service Reviews. This federal audit of state child welfare systems reviews case plans in case records. The goal is to document the connection between the individual family's needs and the elements of the family case plan.

What happens after the conference should be guided, if not determined, by the family plan. The number of plan items, the detail, and the creativity will lay out at least an initial course of action for the family. Although the family plan is the family's responsibility, it will include commitments from the community members and professionals assembled at the conference, or enlisted soon after the conference.

Who is responsible for implementing the plan?

The family plan, as eventually negotiated in the family conference, identifies who is responsible for, or who will accomplish, each task or action noted in the plan. A key person in the family plan will be the person who is primarily responsible for the care of the children. Consequently, in almost all cases, the plan instructions and action elements will include the parents. Often the subject of many aspects of the family plan is the children's mother. She may be asked to attend parenting classes, to get counseling or substance abuse treatment, to attend school meetings or doctor visits, or to seek employment. These actions are designed either to keep the children safely with the mother or to begin the process of returning her children to her home from the care of relatives. In this sense, similar to conventional practice, the mother may be the primary family actor after the conference.

A number of studies have noted the increased involvement of fathers and paternal relatives as a characteristic of FGC plans (Merkel-Holguin, 2003). This attentiveness to all family members and their enlistment in the plan is a hallmark of FGC. The engagement of fathers and paternal relatives should start from the initial referral, go on through the conference, and continue after the conference. In an ongoing Michigan study, almost 50 percent of the plans in some sites assigned responsibilities to fathers. Their tasks included transporting the children; providing respite care for the mother; participating in substance abuse and mental health counseling; attending parenting classes; providing food, clothes, and shelter for the family; and addressing the quality of the relationship between the parents.

There are typically many provisions for other family members as well. A range of relatives has been asked to provide transportation, respite care, kinship care, periodic or regular child care, and emotional support and assistance to the parent. Often, these actions are designed to facilitate the parent's follow-through on designated action items. What happens after the conference is shaped by the family plan that serves as a guide and action plan for the family and community resources. This plan identifies a number of tasks for family members and supporting community members. It also assigns tasks and establishes responsibility for the work that follows the conference.

If the responsibility for item completion is not clear, there may be confusion about who is responsible, and tasks might not be completed. Even with clarity about the items in the family plan, there may need to be some degree of overall coordination of services or some form of facilitation in the face of inevitable obstacles to plan implementation and new challenges posed by dynamics in the family or the community, or both. If there is clarity about plan items and responsibility, but there are no resources for accomplishing the item, the probability of successful implementation is compromised. The development of a family plan, with all of its features, is an important outcome of FGC but does not ensure plan implementation or the safety of the child and the well-being of the family.

How does the plan shape community partnerships?

Several factors influence the family's partnership with community members after the conference. First, the FGC program or agency has become part of the family's formal system of support for the time preceding the conference, during the conference, and for some time after the conference (as determined by the family and program). The coordinator is listening to, working with, and facilitating the design and finalization of a family plan. This family and its plan will be monitored in some manner as designed by the program in a respectful relationship with the family.

Second, community partners, both formal agencies and informal supports, such as neighbors, faith community leaders, and others, have been identified in preparation for the conference. These partners have had varying roles at the conference, for example, providing information for the family's deliberation, offering various forms of support for the family, and participating to some extent in the plan formulation and negotiation. These community partners will either continue their support for the family or modify this support based on the outcome of the family group conference.

Third, the family or a social worker will identify new community partners in response to new challenges or opportunities facing the family. For example, a substance abuse program may be introduced at a later point, as the need for such a program emerges after the conference; a parent aide or friend for the family may be identified.

Some families are very isolated. They may have few resources or relationships before the conference. In fact, the identification and development of formal and informal supports may be one of the goals of the conference. The discovery of these supports and relationship building to connect these supports to the family are primary tasks to be accomplished after the conference.

How can the plan be altered as needed?

The family plan constructed at the conference is the result of a family process at one point in time with a certain set of family members and community members. There is a possibility—if not a certainty—that this guide for what is to happen after the conference will face a number of challenges and obstacles soon after the conference. In addition, some of the actions identified at the conference may prove to be not as relevant or useful as originally thought. Some actions may have been unrealistic or almost unattainable. For example, the substance abuse treatment that was recommended may not exist, or it may not be available or accessible. Referral linkages may have become complicated or ineffective. There are many reasons why a plan may need revision.

With many families, the process of creating an acceptable plan has required much of their energy at a stressful time. A thorough plan anticipates the difficulties that a family may face on implementation of the plan and notes alternative, backup, or contingency features to accompany the action steps in the plan. It may be difficult to anticipate post-conference difficulties, however. Predicting the future may be imprecise, at best. Conference participants may find it unsettling to discuss what the next steps should be if parts of their new plan do not seem to work. The identification of challenges may feel discouraging, or contrary to a desired optimism. There simply may not be enough time or energy to develop contingency plans. Identifying a means of reporting difficulties and seeking additional help may suffice.

The primary contingency feature may be an acknowledgment that follow-up conferences will be necessary to review the plan and address adaptations and revisions. The date and place for this future meeting may be determined at the original conference, or it may be left for the family to request. The responsibility for convening the later meeting may be delegated to a family or community member.

In an Oregon study of family decision meetings (a type of family group conferencing), 35 percent of the cases studied had revisions in family plans. The most frequent reason for a change in plans was an alteration in the circumstances of the case. The second most frequent reason for a revision was in response to a request by a family member. The process by which plans were changed most frequently involved the caseworker revising the plan or a court order. Follow-up meetings and consultation between the caseworker and the family were also cited. In this Oregon study, the process for post-meeting monitoring included the designation of family members, caseworkers, or service providers to review the plan through the use of reports, meetings, and home visits (Rodgers, 2000).

Reconvening conferences is a means of examining the progress of the plan, supporting family and community members, and altering the plan as needed. It seems reasonable that it may be necessary to alter or adapt a family plan constructed at a family group conference, as family situations change with unforeseen events or changes in family landscape resulting from the FGC experience or plan implementation. It makes sense that if the family group constructed the family plan, they would reconvene to review and alter the plan as needed. This is also an opportu-nity to affirm the decisions and actions that have worked and to acknowledge family strengths and steps toward improved safety and positive family life (American Humane Association, 1997).

One of the significant challenges after the conference is to continue to keep responsibility in the hands of the family, and reconvening conferences provides a process for affirming original FGC values and goals. There are several considerations with regard to reconvening conferences:

○ Are follow-up conferences scheduled at the time of the initial conference and, therefore, viewed as normative and routine, or are follow-up conferences convened based on family request or need? If a conference is reconvened based on family request or need, what constitutes sufficient need to reconvene a conference? Are there alternate means of responding to family needs?

○ Who has the responsibility for setting up and facilitating follow-up conferences?

○ What process should precede the convening of follow-up conferences? Is this process identical to the process used to call the first family conference?

○ Who should attend follow-up conferences? To what extent is it necessary to involve the same people who attended the first conference? Are there new invitees? Is inclusiveness still the decision rule with regard to attendance?

○ What should the structure of a follow-up conference be? Should a follow-up conference have all the same stages as the first conference, including private family time?

○ When should the follow-up conference take place?

○ Where should the follow-up conference take place?

○ How frequently should there be follow-up conferences?

The possibility of reconvening conferences underscores the importance of the community involvement and support that becomes available to the family through their participation in FGC. Communication from coordinators and community partners must avoid sending an unintended message that anticipates failure, but prepare for the inevitable challenges following the conference. Even if the family has not planned to reconvene in a follow-up conference, maintaining the spirit of respect, active family involvement and leadership, and community support will be tested after the conference.

Who monitors implementation of the plan?

The nature and structure of the FGC program shape the process after the conference. These structures and strategies are connected to the level of risk in the families served by FGC, other referral criteria, and the point of referral in the child welfare continuum. While sharing values, strategies and goals, individual programs vary with regard to the structures for working with families after the conference. Each of these varied structures poses strengths and challenges for the implementation of the family plan and the ultimate well-being and safety of the children.

The Role of the Family

Consistent with the values of FGC, the primary responsibility for implementing the family plan and monitoring the success of the plan rests with the family. In part, these responsibilities would fit the family's commitment and willingness to extend their own resources to meet the identified family needs. The larger family system may provide child care, respite care, transportation, and recreation for the children and family. Members of the larger family system may provide the meeting of concrete needs such as housing, food, clothes, and assistance with job searching. One of the purposes of FGC is to identify and mobilize this extended family to bring its resources to assist at-risk family members. With the family responsible for resources and monitoring, the independence and responsibility of the family is recognized and reinforced.

This assumption or plan that family members will be responsible for the implementation of the plan, and the resources and monitoring that are required, raises a number of questions:

1. Who in the family is responsible for this coordination and monitoring and is this a feasible role for a family member or members? Has this person or these people been designated at the family conference, and does this designee have the ability to fulfill this role?

2. To what extent is the reliance on the family a cost-saving measure for the agency that unintentionally leaves the family without the resources to implement the family plan? For example, the provision of concrete needs may be beyond the ability of the larger family system and access to professional and community services may pose complicated logistical and financial challenges for family members.

3. To what extent can family members ensure that professional services in

the family plan are provided? Although FGC results in a number of nontraditional, family-centered activities, there remains a significant percentage of tasks that require professional involvement. These tasks include the provision of counseling for children, parents, and couples, substance abuse treatment for adolescents and parents, and parent education. For example, as already noted, access to these services may be difficult due to hours of operation, transportation, waiting lists, or eligibility requirements.

4. What happens in the event of a family crisis? To what extent can family members effectively assist if there is a mental health, financial, housing, substance abuse, domestic violence, or other life crisis?

Several studies have indicated that a number of family plans have not been implemented in part or in full (Merkel-Holguin, 2001; van Beek, 2004). With inadequate resources, the ability of family members to follow through on plan elements is compromised. With unclear or insufficient monitoring, the ability to follow through with a plan, particularly in times of crisis, may be threatened. Reliance on a larger family system to provide the resources and the monitoring of the family plan corresponds with the values of FGC and recognizes the strengths and abilities of the family. However, there may be challenges and a need for alternate forms of assistance to families.

The Role of Child Protective Services

In some programs, the responsibility for following up with the family falls to the child protective services worker or another child welfare worker who was involved with the family before and during the conference. Assigning responsibility for monitoring to a child protective services worker after the conference provides some assurance that the child welfare system will remain involved and available to assist families. As the family may still be on a child protective services worker's caseload, having the worker maintain a continuing relationship with the family fits into the worker's ongoing responsibilities. This approach may simplify decision making, as there is one primary agency person to whom the family relates. However, this additional duty of working with families after a conference may substantially increase the workload of a child protective services worker. Furthermore, new abuse and neglect cases may command a higher priority, and these other duties may prevent the worker from providing ongoing attention to the family. A positive side effect of this situation is that the responsibility for the plan and the safety and well-being of the child rests with the family.

In addition to workload issues for the child welfare worker, assigning the follow-up responsibility to the worker may raise issues with the family. If family members have had a stressful relationship with the child welfare agency, they may be hesitant to continue a relationship with the agency. Part of the motivation for the family to engage in FGC initially may have been to minimize exposure to and experiences with child protective services. This multiplicity of roles for a child protective services worker—helper and investigator—produces a complicated relationship. Regardless of the structure of the program, this duality of roles—support person and monitor—is part of the continuing dynamic involvement between the agency and the family, and to some extent, between family members.

*Other Potential People with
Roles After the Conference*

In some programs, the FGC coordinator may have a continuing role with the family for a specified period of time after the conference. This role could be defined along a continuum of time and responsibilities. A coordinator might not have ongoing responsibility, but would be involved in convening and facilitating follow-up conferences. For ongoing involvement, the coordinator must have a workload that allows additional duties, a willingness to commit the time necessary, and an appropriate level of skill. Given the potential level of intensity required to convene an initial meeting, a coordinator's primary attention may be focused on setting up the initial conference, rather than following up after the conference.

As with a child welfare worker, the continuity of an FGC coordinator's relationship and knowledge of the plan, the family, and community members are valuable attributes after the conference, as well. If the coordinator is an employee of the child protection agency, however, the coordinator's continuing involvement may complicate the relationship. On the other hand, just as they do with a child welfare worker, limits on the coordinator's time and energy for involvement with the family may reinforce the responsibility that the family has to implement its own plan.

With varying degrees of formality, programs may designate a follow-up worker to be involved with the family and other community supports after the conference. This worker will face a number of challenges. The family members may feel connected to the FGC coordinator and may initially be reluctant to share their experiences with a new person. The follow-up worker will be entering a process that is already under way, and learning about a plan that has already been negotiated. Administratively, a new position requires funding, recruitment, training, and supervision. However, working with the family to achieve its plan and working with community members to continue their support requires time and attention that a designated follow-up worker can invest. One of these program variations—designating a worker to follow up with the family after the conference—is the creation of the "advocate" position in the FGC pilot programs in the state of Michigan.

What is the role of the advocate?

In Michigan, the advocate is a professional person employed by the FGC program who is responsible for working with the family from the end of the conference through the end of the service period. In Michigan, families served by FGC are referred early in the child protection process and have relatively high levels of risk and substantiation of child maltreatment. The program generally accepts a broad range of child protective service referrals, including cases in which there is sexual abuse or domestic violence if the perpetrator is not in the home. The service period post-conference in Michigan may last for up to 12 months.

This advocate will receive the family plan, meet with family members and community partners involved in the implementation of the family plan, and assist the family and community partners in successfully implementing the plan. The advocate will also convene future family conferences to review and adapt the family plan. These meetings are routinely scheduled at the initial FGC meeting for three months following this initial conference.

What are the qualifications of the advocate?

Like the FGC coordinator, the advocate in the Michigan pilot program is a private agency program employee who has a social services background and education, who has training in FGC, and who endorses the values of the FGC program. This professional must be committed to empowering families and respecting their decision-making processes so that the actions that follow the conference are informed by the same values that were used before and during the conference. As the advocate is working with family members and community partners in home visits and community settings, a flexible, collegial work style is required. An advocate must also be aware of cultural and family dynamics and must be able to understand and appreciate a family's traditions, patterns of communication, and values. Other programs, outside of Michigan, may use paraprofessionals and community resource people to serve in this follow-up role with families.

When does the advocate meet the family?

The advocate's formal responsibilities typically begin with the conclusion of the first family group conference. In Michigan, in some cases, an advocate may meet the family at the family meeting as the advocate works with the coordinator to facilitate the meeting. For example, the advocate may assist the coordinator with preparing and serving the food, taking notes, or group facilitation. In conferences with multiple family members (some have more than 20 members in attendance), the assistance provided by the advocate is very helpful.

The advocate's presence at the conference also provides an opportunity for family members and community partners to meet the advocate so that the transition from a relationship with the coordinator to a relationship with the advocate is less abrupt. The advocate also has an opportunity to observe the family, receive firsthand the information provided to the family by community service providers, and to at least witness, if not participate in, the crafting of the family plan. If the advocate is not present at the family conference, it is important that the coordinator apprise the family of the advocate's role. A joint meeting with the coordinator, advocate, and key family members after the conference can also facilitate the transition.

What does the advocate do in relation to the family and their plan?

In the advocate role in Michigan, the primary responsibility of the advocate is to assist the family in the family's implementation of its plan. The advocate's role and activities require balancing this respect for the family's strengths and capabilities and planning with forms of assistance that are supportive to families. The advocate is not to "take over" for the family. The advocate role is designed to assist with resources and support of the family plan. Although not conceptualized as a task-centered role, this assistance can include a number of activities. Advocates identified these broad categories of service:

○ *Risk assessment:* these activities include attentiveness to the well-being and safety of the child, identifying and/or being aware of circumstances that may precipitate a crisis, working with the family to address

63

particular stresses that could escalate into a crisis, and identifying resources to prevent or assist in a crisis. Risk assessment also includes attentiveness to potential domestic violence, suicide threats and risk, and other dangers.

○ *Linkage with social supports:* assessing and aiding in the enlistment of kinship child care providers (either identified at the conference or after the conference) for either primary care or for respite care; helping the family maintain ties to school staff, to family friends, and to faith-based communities. Frequently, these are identified in the family plan, but new information or challenges may arise. This activity may include working with primary family members to affirm and strengthen general relationship-building skills so that family members discover and craft these linkages.

○ *Advocacy:* intervening on the family's behalf with other social service agencies, the mental health, education, or court and law enforcement systems. In addition to formal human service systems, advocacy, in conjunction with the family, may target utility companies, landlords, and employers as identified by family members. As needed, the advocate would work with family members to acquire the resources identified in the family plan and support family efforts toward self-advocacy.

○ *Concrete services:* providing transportation; helping to locate or secure housing; providing clothing, food, financial assistance, furniture and household items, and toys or supplies for the children. Family members may be able to assist with many of these needs, and the advocate is available to provide support for the family in acquiring necessary concrete resources.

○ *Referrals to other sources:* facilitating the connections to or identifying additional services as the family's needs become clearer, or change. Referrals parallel linkage to social supports to some extent. The advocate may assist in gaining professional social supports such as counseling, substance abuse treatment, or mental health services.

○ *Safety planning:* educating the family members about the effects on children of experiencing violence or witnessing family violence, planning safety measures for mothers and children as identified at the conference or as risks are identified after the conference, planning with family members to identify appropriate caregivers, providing information about the legal system, and discussing visitation procedures.

○ *Substance abuse services:* identifying resources, making referrals, and helping the family to obtain services. In addition, the advocate provides education to the family members about substance abuse, information about the effects of substance abuse in the family on children, and, if appropriate, relapse planning.

Again, the advocate's role is to assist families in the accomplishment of the family's plan through assessment, listening, and supporting the family. These activities assume that the primary work related to the implementation of the plan lies with the family, with the advocate helping to locate specific assistance, advocacy, and referrals as needed. The nature of these activities also reflects, in part, particular challenges such as lack of public transportation, the rural and isolated locations of some families, and the level of poverty of both individual families and larger family systems that may pose an obstacle to plan implementation.

How frequently does the advocate meet with the family?

More generally, how frequently and to what extent would an FGC professional remain involved with the family after the conference? The number of actions and extent of involvement may be noted in the family plan. Specific tasks may be assigned to family members, community professionals, and the follow-up FGC worker, and it may be assumed that the worker will assume some level of supervision or monitoring responsibility.

One would expect that the assistance provided by any professional after the conference would be shaped by such circumstances as time after the conference and family crises. One would expect that there might be more activity immediately after the conference, as various forms of assistance are put into place and resources are mobilized by and for the family. With the establishment of service relationships—such as counseling—or the provision of various forms of assistance by family members, the need for professional involvement and support would diminish over time. The exception to this reduction of activity would be if a crisis presented itself that overwhelmed the resources of the family and the extended family. During such a

crisis, one would expect that professional assistance would increase to assist the family and ensure the safety of the children.

In the work of the Michigan advocates, which was reviewed at three-month intervals until case closure at 12 months after the conference, there was a marked difference in the frequency of advocate activity with the family after the conference. The number of contacts made by the advocate with the family in the first three months ranged from four to 111 contacts (with an average of 31 contacts). Contacts were defined as either face-to-face meetings with family members or telephone calls to family members.

In those cases with 10 or fewer contacts in the first three months, the children were placed with or remained with highly competent relatives whose care for the children had been affirmed at the family conference. Family problems in the cases with the most contacts required active child protective services involvement to reassess the safety of the children, make a decision about their placement, and in some cases, move them to an out-of-home placement with a relative or other foster care parent. In the case with 111 contacts, the parent with primary responsibility for the children had a substance abuse problem ("hit rock bottom"), and the children were moved to the care of a relative. In other families with more than 50 contacts in three months (four cases), there were fairly significant issues of substance abuse and/or mental health concerns about the parent who had remained the primary caregiver of the children after the conference. In one case, a close relative of the parent died, and the parent had a serious automobile accident during this time of grief. The accident and recovery resulted in a loss of transportation, followed by a loss of employment, precipitating a housing crisis. For the majority of families, the family addresses the family plan with some measure of assessment and support from the advocate. Given the initial high risk of child maltreatment in a few of these cases, however, a parental crisis precipitates considerable activity to stabilize the family and ensure the safety of the children.

In the second quarter, the average number of contacts dropped to 26 contacts (with a range from one to 71 contacts). In families with fewer than 10 contacts, the case was moving toward successful closure, the family continued doing well, and the children were safe. Several families moved outside of the state. The family with 71 contacts was the family with which there had been 111 contacts in the first quarter, so worker activity was still frequent, but significantly reduced from the first quarter. Other higher contact cases reflected continuing efforts to assist families with substance abuse and mental health concerns, but the number of contacts also decreased from the number in the first quarter.

In the third quarter of activity, the average number of advocate contacts with family members was 21, ranging from two to 90 contacts in three months. In the case of 90 contacts, more than six months after the conference, the family decided that the grandmother rather, than the mother, should have custody of the children.

By the ninth month after the conference, fewer than one-third of the families were still involved with the FGC program. For those families that continued in the program, there was an average of 15 contacts over a three-month period. The highest number of contacts was 50, with one family in which there were concerns about

the physical and mental health of the children's primary caregiver.

Overall, there was a consistent pattern of moving from high to low numbers of contacts over the months following the family group conference. Each quarter showed a decline in the number of contacts from the previous quarter. In cases in which the number of contacts remained high or increased from one quarter to another, there were instances of substance abuse relapse, a family crisis, or a change of custody in relation to the children (Anderson, Hodge-Morgan, Snyder, & Whalen, 2001).

One could reasonably ask, How frequently should there be contact with a family after the initial conference? How much is too little, and how much is too much? There are dangers on both ends of this continuum—too little contact fails to support a family in which there is at least initially some measure of risk to child safety, and too much fails to develop or support other natural helping systems for the family and does not foster family responsibility. The amount of follow-up activity should correspond to the level of risk, the family plan, family capacity, and the family circumstances. However, it may be difficult without a family-by-family assessment to know if an advocate is filling a vacancy for these families (particularly in rural or underserved areas), or becoming more extensively involved with the family than intended. Clearly, uneventful, uninterrupted positive adaptations with effortless plan implementation are unlikely for vulnerable families. It seems reasonable to expect that a plan developed within 30 days of referral would require modification, and that new information would emerge after the conference that would have implications for that plan.

How is the advocate's role different from that of a family preservation worker or other child welfare or juvenile justice professional who is working with the family?

There are a number of similarities between the actions of an FGC advocate and those of other community or child welfare professionals who serve the family. For example, the identification and assessment of concrete needs, such as food, transportation, or safe housing, are within the range of activities that may concern a number of professionals. Some less conventional activities, such as securing music lessons for children or celebrating a birthday, may also fall within the range of recognized activities of some family preservation workers.

The distinctive aspect of the advocate's role lies less in the activities performed than in the values and approach used. First, the advocate is guided by, supports, and works to assist with implementation of the case plan that the family crafted through the family group conference. The family designed this plan, and family members or community partners that participated in the conference have the primary responsibility for its implementation.

Second, the advocate engages in processes and actions that are consistent with the philosophy of FGC. The central values of respecting the family group members' capacity to make decisions, engaging family members in the work to support the safety and well-being of their children, and empowering the family to decide and act are an advocate's crucial considerations. The advocate must be vigilant and self-assessing to ensure that she or he does not take over responsibilities and actions that belong to the family. The advocate must support the capacity of the family

to achieve its goals and implement and adapt the family's plan. This respect for families is paramount—and it stretches to include respect for the formal and informal support systems that are available to families.

Third, the advocate's assessment of a family, understanding of family functioning, and relationship with a family must be informed by knowledge, understanding, and appreciation for the family's culture and traditions. These patterns may reflect the family's ethnic, racial, and/or geographic heritage, as well as the styles and habits that have specific meaning to the family. Cultural competence is an important quality in all work with families; in FGC, cultural competence is a central tenet for working with families before, during, and after the conference.

When is the advocate's work finished?

Although the advocate should not prolong contact with the family unnecessarily, the termination process should not be precipitous. The advocate stops working with the family when one of several outcomes has been reached. The family may have substantially achieved its goals through the completion of the action steps identified in the family plan. This achievement may not include the successful implementation of all aspects of the plan but, rather, a substantial portion of them such that the children are safe and their well-being is ensured. Successful implementation of the family plan does not mean that there is no continuing need for support. Appropriate referrals and engagement with community resources may facilitate this ending of the family's formal involvement with the FGC program. In rural or small towns, there is the possibility of ongoing informal contact between family members and advocates. A re-referral to FGC may also be offered if a family requests one at a future date.

The family may end its involvement with FGC by moving away or by refusing ongoing contact with the advocate. The FGC program maintains a delicate balance between the advocate's authoritative role based on affiliation with child protective services (and the possible role of the court) and the family's voluntary participation in the program. In cases of child abuse and neglect, family involvement with the child protection system may not be voluntary, although participation in FGC is voluntary. If a family withdraws from the program without successfully implementing the family plan, the advocate must make a decision about the level of continuing risk in the family and the need for ongoing services. The result may be a re-referral to child protective services, a referral to another agency, or communication with an agency that has ongoing contact with the family (such as a school counselor) while closing the family's case.

In the Michigan FGC pilot program, there is a limit of 12 months for service provision. This length of time is sufficient for the advocate to work with the family and for the family to mobilize the necessary resources to ensure the safety of the children. It also is long enough to test the stability of a child's placement with a parent or relative or to effect a needed move, either toward reunification with the parent or to a relative's home that is identified as a backup placement for the child. The longer the advocate is involved with the family, the more difficult it may be for the advocate to get out of the family system and to support the family's primacy in decision making and planning. A time limit also provides some measure of mo-

tivation for family members and advocate to achieve the steps and goals identified in the plan. If there is a sufficient measure of safety at the end of the specified time, ending involvement with the program is a reasonable step.

Conclusion

The outcome of FGC requires considerable attention to what happens after the conference. The family and supportive community have actions to perform that are guided or prescribed by the family plan. The successful implementation of these actions will significantly contribute to the safety and well-being of the children and the family. In this implementation effort, the family and supportive community will face a number of challenges. New problems may arise, old and persistent obstacles may interfere with implementation, and some plan items may prove to be not as relevant or helpful as when they were originally conceived.

The continuing role of FGC professionals after the conference may take multiple forms. The Michigan program designates an advocate for the family, but other programs may have different people take on some of the same responsibilities identified for the advocate. It seems beneficial to designate someone to work with the family after the conference and to make sure that this person has gained some relationship with the family during the FGC process. Budgets, available community resources, and program needs are likely to determine the identity and affiliation of this person. Designating the child protective services worker as the follow-up worker seems to have inherent complications because of the demands of that position and the potential conflictual relationship with the family. Regardless of who works with the family, the central concern should be the preservation of FGC values and approaches after the conference.

The examination of what happens after the conference remains an opportunity for FGC programs to move past the conference to describe the subsequent process and outcomes. The need for and ability to address outcomes has moved the discussion from intermediate outcomes—such as the convening of the conference and the successful crafting of a family plan—to outcomes that focus on the safety and well-being of the children and family. Consequently, there needs to be an increased focus on the "weakest link in this family-centered process"—the follow-up stage after the conference (Merkel-Holguin, 2001, p. 215). To understand the challenges and achievement of longer term outcomes, and to fully support family responsibility, an understanding of what happens after the conference is essential.

Initiating and Sustaining Conferencing

Joan Pennell and Gary R. Anderson

As discussed in section I, the model of FGC follows good group work practice in organizing meetings and supporting the efforts of its participants. By placing the family and their close supports at the center of decision making, FGC encourages respecting cultural diversity, attending to the self-knowledge of families, and forming partnerships to safeguard children and other family members. This is an alternative to conventional approaches to planning in public child welfare. Sustaining such an innovation over time requires supportive organizations, communities, policies, and legislation. This second section of the book enlarges the focus from the family group to the community and the broader society in which conferencing takes place. It takes up the challenge of examining the conditions that make it possible to carry out enduring FGC programs.

How can a hospitable context be developed for an FGC program?

Developing a hospitable context for an FGC program requires efforts not only in an agency and its local community, but also at the state and national levels of social services. The two chapters in this section focus on these efforts. Chapter 5 looks at local planning efforts needed for starting and maintaining an FGC program and the ongoing training needed for effective delivery by the FGC coordinators, the referring social workers, and community partners. Chapter 6 examines developments in U.S. federal legislation that are likely to support the use of FGC and other partnership approaches to child welfare, and it addresses the question of whether to pass legislation explicitly ensuring families' access to FGC in resolving child protection issues. These two chapters are concerned with the implementation of three FGC principles:

1. Build broad-based support and cultural competence.
2. Enable the coordinators to work with family groups in organizing their conferences.
3. Change policies, procedures, and resources to sustain partnerships among family groups, community organizations, and public agencies.

At the local level, planners need to take an inclusive and partnership-building approach that brings together diverse groups in developing the FGC program. Together, they need to develop the human and material resources required for implementing the model and evaluating it. In Chapter 5, Joan Pennell emphasizes that this work should be both collaborative and ongoing, and that it relies on building the community's capacity for FGC work. This entails four capacity-building strategies: (1) leadership development, (2) organizational development, (3) community organizing, and (4) interorganizational collaboration. Using four community examples, chapter 5 demonstrates how to undertake each of the strategies; it also shows how the work with individual families guides the program development.

Moving to the national level, Gary Anderson, in chapter 6, reviews recent developments in U.S. child welfare legislation. Chapter 6 considers how specific legislation, such as the Adoption and Safe Families Act (ASFA) of 1997 and Indian Child Welfare Act (ICWA) of 1978, shares the same values as FGC, and sets forth general approaches that are parallel to, and supportive of, FGC. Turning from legislation to child welfare audits, chapter 6 points out that the federal Child and Family Service Reviews (CFSRs) mandate the states to involve families in service planning and, thus, implicitly encourage the development of FGC programs. The federal legislation and reviews create a context in which FGC is viewed as a way to advance child safety, permanency, and well-being.

5

Collaborative Planning and Ongoing Training

Joan Pennell

Laying the groundwork for family group conferencing (FGC) requires orienting key participants to the model and then engaging them in planning the means for initiating, implementing, and sustaining the FGC program. Given the importance of community partnerships for successful FGC, a collaborative approach to planning is essential from the outset of an FGC program. To carry out this joint planning, stakeholders require training in FGC, preferably as a group so that they learn about the model together and hear each other's views on how to make it work in their community. Launching a program, however, is only one part of the task at hand. Once conferencing has started and new issues emerge (as they always do), the program must continue to offer opportunities for collaborative planning and ongoing training.

For many, FGC as a way of involving families in decision making is a relatively simple concept to grasp. What is often much more complicated is determining how to set up this program and keep it going, especially if it goes against the grain of "normal" practice. Reflecting on a particularly conflictual, but eventually successful, conference, an FGC trainer wrote:

> It is so clear to me that as natural a process as FGC is, it is so foreign in a traditional child welfare setting. It absolutely requires a lot of community development and training. . . . The system and the workers are not trained and brought up in an agency culture that supports FGC.

At heart, FGC as an intervention is about building a community that cares. To be successful, FGC as a program must be based in a community that has the capacity to carry out conferencing.

What is community capacity? How is it built?

Community capacity refers to the individual abilities, organizational strengths, and social bonds within a community that can be applied to resolving collective concerns and advancing the welfare of the whole (Chaskin, Brown, Venkatesh, & Vidal, 2001). For an FGC program, the individuals may come from the family groups, community organizations, or public agencies. The underlying assumptions of conferencing are that families and their communities have assets, even those that appear exceptionally deprived, and that those cases with the fewest apparent resources most require collective rather than individual action to effect change. By starting with the family group and "building communities from the inside out" (Kretzmann & McKnight, 1993), there is hope not only of addressing current problems, but also of building the capacity to prevent future ones.

Initiatives to build community capacity typically use some mix of four main approaches:

○ *Leadership development*—heightening the competencies and commitment of individuals so that they can catalyze and guide the involvement of others in community building;
○ *Organizational development*—generating new organizations or strengthening existing ones in order to advance collaboration;
○ *Community organizing*—building associations and mobilizing key stakeholders to promote change; and
○ *Interorganizational collaboration*—advancing partnerships across organizations to carry out an initiative together (Chaskin et al., 2001, p. 25).

To establish, maintain, and renew an FGC program, each of these strategies is useful, especially as applied in combination with the other three.

Who needs to offer leadership to an FGC program? How is this capacity developed?

An FGC program needs leadership that will, in turn, support the families' leadership in making and carrying out plans. *It is important to strengthen the competencies of the FGC coordinators, preferably by interweaving on-the-job training and formal training events.* To learn the necessary skills and to maintain their leadership, coordinators need more than a written manual or an oral introduction to organizing and facilitating conferences; they need far more active training and consultation to carry out their tasks each step of the way (Mayer & Davidson, 2000).

Training may take place in formal sessions on such matters as ensuring that children's voices are heard at conferences or preparing parents who have cognitive limitations. Training may involve bringing together coordinators for informal lunchtime exchanges, giving a quick telephone consultation on organizing conferences complicated by factors such as the need to move them out of state, or having a trainer co-facilitate a conference. Beyond training, it also helps if coordinators can draw on prior experience that supports their current work. One new FGC coordinator noted:

The trainer/co-facilitator said I was a good coordinator, but I think why is because I've received training . . . [as a family preservation worker] for 10 years. FGC fits with this. I have a good understanding of families and can engage and relate with them.

FGC coordinators, however, cannot work in a vacuum. *They need leadership that supports conferencing at all organizational levels of the hosting agency:* on the front line where agency and families meet, among supervisors who offer guidance to workers and protect their time so that they can take part, and among senior administrators who develop the policies, provide the training, and find the resources to sustain conferencing. As a matter of policy, for example, agencies must allow workers to have flexible hours so that they can attend FGCs scheduled around non-business hours, when families are available to meet.

In addition, FGC relies on community partnerships; thus, *it is essential to draw on the history of partnership building in the locale and, as required, to develop the leadership of other participating organizations.* Noting the need for further orientation to FGC, a community participant wrote on her evaluation form at the end of a conference, "I would be interested in receiving a description of the whole conference process. I need to understand my role in the conference so I can enhance my contribution."

To exert leadership, *individuals need support within their particular context and at their stage of development.* As one planner of a local FGC program explained, "You don't see all the benefits of what you learned until you do a conference. Coming back to the table and talking about tools and preparation issues, everything, would be more beneficial now."

Some training happens spontaneously as service providers observe each other in action. For instance, at a conference held for a sexually abused girl, the child welfare worker had difficulty presenting the girl's history. Fortunately, the mental health worker was present and clearly outlined the child's symptoms and issues.

One way in which the North Carolina FGC Project provided on-the-job training for FGC coordinators and referring social workers was to hold joint debriefing sessions after a conference. At the end of one seven-hour conference with 24 participants, the FGC coordinator welcomed the opportunity to talk through what had happened: "I feel as though because the conference was not only very long, but also very intense, each one of us needed some time to process and have some closure."

Similarly, a large conference with three sides of the family in attendance, and strong tensions evident between the family group and the foster parents, warranted a post-conference discussion. As later noted by the FGC coordinator, the social worker had hesitated to set forth all of the reasons that the children were currently in foster care. The result was that the family group had to revise its plan after the private time, when the social worker finally relayed the events leading up to the seven children's placement. In the debriefing session held three days later, the FGC coordinator acknowledged to the social worker that she should have given the social worker more direction. She recommended that FGC coordinators "prompt the social worker for *all* that needs to be shared prior to the family alone time, i.e., mental health concerns."

In this same county, a different social worker's behavior at another conference led to the decision to hold formal training of referring social workers on a regular basis.

Community Example 1:
The Social Worker and the Cell Phone

A county advisory council had been created to offer guidance to a recently established FGC program. In order to keep abreast of FGC developments, the council received reports from the FGC coordinators on conference developments. To maintain the families' confidentiality, the coordinators did not share identifying information and case details; instead, they reviewed patterns and emerging issues. One such issue was a social worker's behavior at a conference.

The council learned that an unnamed social worker had spent a large portion of the conference on her cell phone rather than taking part in the proceedings. As the FGC coordinator reported, "The most frustrating aspect of the conference was the social worker's disengaged attitude. For the first 45 minutes of the conference, she was on the cell phone [for personal reasons]." The research observer noted that as a result, "the coordinator had to skip around to cover for her absence." Because the social worker had missed the information sharing, she was ill prepared to take part on her return. The FGC coordinator wrote, "The . . . social worker was very hesitant with any type of commitment of any sort, and in fact did not approve the plan the day of the conference, even though the family had met the criteria of the bottom line."

On hearing this report, the FGC advisory council recognized that training was necessary for all referring social workers. Until this stage, the focus had been on orienting key stakeholders to conferencing and providing more in-depth training to the FGC coordinators. Subsequently, training of social workers was scheduled every six months to ensure that newly hired social workers understood how to engage with the family group. The social workers welcomed this training. In fact, a focus group with social workers who had taken part in conferencing independently reached the same conclusion.

All eight social workers in the focus group saw FGC as beneficial: it encouraged collaboration within families, let the workers see the family at work, built understanding and trust between workers and clients, educated the family group through hearing presentations on issues such as substance abuse, and reduced the "leg work" of social workers because they could confer simultaneously with the family group members. At the same time, the participating social workers agreed that they needed further training on FGC. They wanted to know more about when to refer families, how to frame the purpose of a conference, and what they should do in the sessions.

How is an organization's capacity for implementing an FGC program developed?

Strengthening the organization so that it can effectively carry out conferencing comes from internal development, often pushed by advocates outside of public child welfare. The initial drive to start an FGC program may spring from the outside. Advocacy has come from groups that are external to public child welfare, including indigenous populations, family rights groups, and national child welfare associations or foundations (Hudson, Morris, Maxwell, & Galaway, 1996). National/international standards, professional associations, and schools of social work that are encouraging family participation in service planning can further propel these efforts.

Unless development within child welfare agencies accompanies the external push, however, FGC flounders. A community organization can volunteer to organize and facilitate conferencing for families involved with child protective services. This program, though, stalls without child welfare workers making referrals, taking part in conferences, and following through on the FGC plans. In addition, these outside organizations usually depend on public child welfare to finance their FGC programs.

Workers inside public child welfare agencies can initially push through some conferencing by donating their time and money. Such was the case in one North Carolina county where highly motivated staff members paid $60 for the conference refreshments out of their own pockets to hold their first conference. Such enthusiasm has an impact on senior administrators. A social services director in another county commented that he supported FGC because for once, he did not need to drag his staff into a new program.

Nevertheless, these ad hoc arrangements can make for shortcuts. For instance, in yet another county undertaking its first conference, a child welfare supervisor volunteered to serve as the FGC coordinator. In this case, the mother initially thought that no family member would agree to attend, but to her surprise, six relatives joined her at the conference. After the conference, the FGC coordinator was highly satisfied with the resulting plan, but continued to have strong reservations about the preparations. On her FGC Evaluation form (see chapter 2), she wrote:

> Full-time supervisory responsibility with vacant caseloads prevented optimal preparation time. . . . I was able to meet with [the mother] and the children in the office and make a home visit and have 2 telephone calls prior to the conference. Spoke with other familial support (relatives) via phone only. . . . More family members could have been available.

Although a community participant gave a more favorable rating to the conference preparations, she concluded, "More information needs to be given to group members prior to conference."

Legislation paves the way for child welfare agencies to establish FGC programs on a firmer footing (see chapter 6). As described earlier, technical assistance from external training groups can also reinforce local FGC implementation. Nevertheless, *in order to maintain an FGC program, the child welfare agency and its community partners should create a plan attuned to their local cultures and conditions* (Burford & Hudson, 2000). Bringing together a mix of participants with strengths in direct practice and community development safeguards against the FGC program being abstracted from practice demands or shifting from a planning forum into a therapy session. Significantly, if workers take part in the decision to start an FGC program, they are more likely to make referrals to the program (Sundell, Vinnerljung, & Ryburn, 2002).

Optimally, the planning group includes family representatives to offer guidance and to urge continuation of a program that they like. However, in the majority of early initiatives, family representatives remain "virtually invisible partners" (Merkel-Holguin, Nixon, & Burford, 2003, p. 5). The North Carolina FGC Project struggled with this same issue and used a variety of strategies to amplify the voices of family representatives: having them on its statewide advisory council, holding focus groups with people from many walks of life to guide the development of the project, and seeking out feedback on conferencing from FGC participants.

In developing an organization's capacity for an FGC program, participants should consider the following activities:

○ Establishing an advisory body with agency, community, and family representation

○ Funding FGC coordination and conference expenses

○ Deciding whether to locate FGC coordinators inside or outside the public agency

○ Training FGC coordinators, social workers, and other participants

○ Supervising and providing consultation to FGC coordinators and social workers

○ Scheduling workers to attend conferences outside of regular work hours

○ Referring families to FGC

○ Developing a policy on how to share confidential information

○ Approving FGC plans or presenting them to court for authorization

○ Incorporating FGC plans into agency service plans

○ Developing procedures for placing children with relatives across state lines

○ Following through on FGC plans and reconvening family groups

○ Evaluating the implementation and outcomes of FGC programs

For many programs, especially in jurisdictions where FGC is an optional service, referrals pose a challenge (Merkel-Holguin, 2003). They never seem to flow in a steady, predictable manner. Initially, programs may have a dearth of referrals, but as word spreads about a successful conference, the number of referrals suddenly jumps. If the FGC program cannot handle the increased demand, the social workers may become discouraged, or simply focus on other matters and cease to refer families for FGC. The high turnover rate of FGC coordinators on time-limited projects aggravates the situation (Horwitz, 2003). A Michigan study found that a minority of workers repeatedly referred families, but that the large majority of eligible workers made only one referral or, even more often, no referrals at all (Anderson, 2003).

The following community example looks at efforts by the county advisory council to establish a systematic process for increasing the number of FGC referrals while regulating their volume. The multiple strategies that they developed for raising social workers' awareness of FGC helped to increase the number of referrals. At the same time, these efforts demonstrated the need for extensive marketing in a system where legislation does not grant family groups the right to take part in decision making.

Community Example 2:
The Young Person at the Training Camp

Before the county advisory council was founded, a well-attended planning session was held with representation from public child welfare agencies and community organizations and technical assistance from the North Carolina FGC Project. Right from the outset, the planning focused on the referral process and populations for referrals. The group established that "families identified as high risk for placement and/or child abuse and neglect" were to receive priority. This decision was dictated not only by the particular federal funding source for the FGC program, but also by the concerns of the planning group. Not wanting the FGC program to be limited by funding constraints, however, the committee members agreed to search out alternative funding sources so that they could later expand FGC into the schools and the juvenile justice system. In order to expedite planning, the group agreed to establish a more compact, but still representative, FGC advisory council.

This county advisory council met first on a monthly basis, and later on a bimonthly basis. The council had a balance of representatives from child welfare agencies and community organizations, and they were able to consult with those at the North Carolina FGC Project. In addition, they tried to recruit parent representatives. As is often the case with new programs, this proved problematic. They had not yet developed a pool of family members who had taken part in FGC, and who had sufficient distance from it and from the child welfare system to feel comfortable serving on an advisory body. Nevertheless, this omission remained of concern.

In its first meeting, the FGC advisory council set up two committees: one on the referral process and the other on expansion into other possible populations. The first committee, within several weeks, developed a referral form, process, and tracking system, and it scheduled an informational session to show social workers how to make referrals. The committee sought to streamline the referral process by having workers refer families directly to the FGC coordinator, rather than to an intermediary. This procedure allowed workers to discuss with the coordinator the appropriateness of referrals. A month later, the new FGC coordinator reported that she had accepted two referrals and was organizing the conferences. It became clear that a brochure to inform families about the program and an informational packet for participating service providers would be necessary.

The council also posed the question of what its lone FGC coordinator would do if she "reaches capacity and people still want to refer." Although they found no immediate answer, they agreed that the FGC coordinator should "not create a waiting list," which "could result in FGC happening too late in a case and [cause] confusion." Looking ahead to the next fiscal year, the agency advised that its federal funds could be used to secure a second FGC coordinator. The advisory council unanimously voted to hire a second coordinator for child welfare cases.

On recommendation from the expansion committee, the council agreed that any expansion should not take resources away from the current FGC program, but interest in including other populations remained high. At the very next meeting, a council member reported that negotiations were under way to adopt a modified form of FGC in the school system (and these plans eventually came to fruition). Expansion of the program into the juvenile justice system was held in abeyance. Over the next few months, the advisory council continued to develop ways of reaching out to child welfare workers to refer cases before they entered the court system and, with the advent of the new FGC coordinator, just to increase the number of referrals. These strategies included having the FGC coordinator attend case staffings, incorporating FGC referrals into the process of transferring families from investigations to treatment, featuring an article on FGC in the agency's newsletter, leaving flyers in workers' mailboxes, raising the profile of front-line (as opposed to senior) staff on the advisory council, and as previously discussed, scheduling regular social worker training sessions.

Still concerned about juvenile justice cases, the advisory council recommended expansion into other agency units, including those whose workers received referrals from juvenile court counselors. These were cases in which the young people who had committed offenses were out of their parents' control and at risk of entering the child welfare system. This effort opened the way for the first referral of a juvenile justice case. It concerned an African American young man, James, who was at a training camp, and his two younger brothers, who were residing with relatives. In preparation for the conference, the FGC coordinator worked with James so that even though he was unable to attend in person, his voice would be heard. During the information-sharing time of the FGC, the coordinator read out an extensive letter that James had written. The following is the research observer's summary:

> In the letter, he talked about how when he "was on the run," he enjoyed living with his grandparents, but that the best thing would be for him and all of his siblings to live with Mom. He stated that he would go back to school; would like to learn more about his family; would know not to get into trouble; would help keep his younger siblings out of trouble and in school; wants Mom and Grandmother to know that he loves them a lot.

Later by cell phone, James joined the group for the family's private time and shared his thoughts further on where he wanted to live once he was discharged from the training camp. About six months later, James joined his brothers at the home of a relative.

Afterward, in her reflective notes, the FGC coordinator observed that James' involvement was welcomed not only by the family group, but also by the child welfare agency:

> The . . . supervisor was delighted that the family could speak with

James, and [she] then told me that she would write to the training camp. Because in the future, she would like the officials out there to understand how important the FGC [program] is for the future well-being of the children involved.

With this successful experience, referrals originating from the juvenile justice system quickly caught up with or exceeded those from other units. It was found that, in general, families dealing with a troubling young person were relieved to have this intervention.

How is the community's guidance of an FGC program mobilized?

In various countries' legislation, policies, and standards, there has been a converging agreement in principle, though not necessarily in practice, regarding child welfare. They stress that the child welfare system alone cannot protect children; the system must have family and community partners (Berg & Kelly, 2000; Briar-Lawson, Lawson, & Hennon, 2001; Connolly & McKenzie, 1999; Crozier, 2000; Parton, 1997; Pecora, Whittaker, Maluccio, & Barth, 2000). *FGC is an effective strategy for mobilizing a wider spectrum of community resources around a family—as long as the child welfare agency welcomes these groups as partners in finding solutions.* Ways of mobilizing these partners include informing them about the model and asking for their commentary, including them in program-planning committees and advisory bodies, seeking their help in organizing a conference, inviting them to give information and lend their support at the conferences, writing them into the FGC plans, requesting their evaluative feedback on the FGC program and individual conferences, asking them to serve as advocates for FGC funding, and incorporating their input into legislation and policies.

As is the case elsewhere in the United States (Crampton, 2001), the North Carolina FGC Project found that many of its referred families were facing issues of substance abuse. In effect, the child welfare referrals became a means of outreach to those with addictions and their social networks. Because U.S. federal law protects the confidentiality of information related to addictions to alcohol and other drugs, the participating North Carolina counties had consent forms already available, or quickly drafted such forms, so that individuals could give permission to share information on their substance addictions with the family group.

The question requiring greater thought was how to structure the FGCs so that they would be a productive experience for those with addictions their family groups. To address this question, the North Carolina FGC Project facilitated focus groups with individuals with substance addictions (Pennell, 2001a).

Community Example 3:
"This Wasn't a Time to Bash Mom"

A community-based center that provided services to adults with substance addictions agreed to host two focus groups. The center invited clients who were receiving methadone treatment for intravenous heroin use and, like most of the agency's clientele, tended to have multiple addictions. One group had six female clients and two female interns, and the other group had seven male clients and one male counselor. The volunteers were nearly evenly split between white and African American.

At the start of the group sessions, the university researchers welcomed the volunteers, stressed that their participation was voluntary and that no identifying information would be gathered, and explained that the purpose of the group was to gain their views on the best ways to carry out and evaluate FGC. Because the group members were unfamiliar with FGC, the university facilitator provided an overview of FGC and then showed a videotaped dramatization of a conference regarding a young Maori mother with an addiction and her family group, *Mihi's Whanau* (New Zealand Department of Child Youth and Family, 1995). Next, the participants were asked six questions on FGC and substance abuse. The sessions took about an hour and a half each, and refreshments were served.

After viewing the videotape, both the men and women were impressed that so many family and friends had attended the conference, and they appreciated the compassion shown. The two groups, however, thought that Mihi's three children should also have been present at the conference. In their discussion of the model, the men focused primarily on the parent with an addiction, while the women gave answers related mainly to the children. The men agreed that FGC would make the parent feel more accepted and, thus, more motivated to change. In such a loving group, they believed, the parent would choose the family over the substance. They also realized that FGC would be most effective when the parent was ready to "get clean," but anticipated that if the parent remained in denial, someone in the family would recognize that and refocus the discussion.

The women surmised that FGC might stop substance abuse only if the parent had hit "rock bottom." They appreciated that even if the parent denied the addiction, there would still be a plan for the safety and well-being of the children. The women believed that if parents knew that the children were safe, they would have more time necessary for recovery. The women stressed that it was important for the conference to be a family meeting rather than a meeting with a therapist.

Both groups emphasized that the model would be more effective if not linked with the child welfare system. The men saw the child welfare system as politicizing the conference environment by creating a power struggle between the agency and family, and the women thought the presence of child welfare would elevate fears about losing the children. A report of the discussion was shared later with the focus group participants and informed the North Carolina FGC Project's training. Repeatedly, the words of these men and women rang true at conferences.

The truth of their words was particularly evident at a conference convened to "plan for a safe and healthy home" so that one-year-old April could stay with her mother, Karen. The conference included only three family members—Karen, her mother Nancy, and April—who were all white. Because of Karen's long-term substance addiction, also invited were her 12-step sponsor and a friend, both of whom had struggled with addictions. Joined by the family's pastor, the family group was as much constructed as related by blood. On the day of the conference, Karen and Nancy arrived at the church with a wide array of refreshments to express their gratitude to social services for holding the conference and to the participants for attending.

The conference opened with the Serenity Prayer said in unison by the group.

Throughout, the conference had the tone of an Alcoholics Anonymous 12-step program for individuals with addictions. As anticipated by the focus group participants receiving methadone treatment, compassion was evident in the social worker's remarks from the outset: "The group [needs to] use 'I' rather than 'you' statements in order to avoid pointing fingers and avoid dwelling on the past and instead look towards the future."

Karen responded that she was familiar with this approach from her 12-step program. In her personal statement to the group, Karen asked the participants to remain open-minded and acknowledged that she isolated herself, knows that she is not doing the right thing, and therefore, is embarrassed.

The social worker listed her concerns about April and Karen, but also pointed to the mother's strengths—her love for April and her greater willingness to care for herself and her child. As if at a 12-step meeting, the friend then gave a testimonial about her own experiences with addictions and depression. Joining in, the sponsor caringly confronted Karen on putting her strengths to good use: "Karen has all the tools she needs, but just needs to put them in action."

On entering their private time, Nancy was too emotionally wrought to take the lead, and the sponsor and the friend stepped in. They immediately confronted Karen on her intentions. They asked if she was willing to take action and said, if not, there was no need for them to make a plan. Karen reviewed the reasons that she finds it difficult to make decisions. As the focus groups had anticipated, the sponsor jumped in to confront Karen's denial: "We need to make a plan, not analyze why things won't work."

The friend reached out to the grandmother, Nancy, who was in obvious distress, and urged her to go to Al-Anon, a national organization offering mutual support groups for relatives of alcoholics. Gradually, the family group developed a plan under the leadership of the sponsor: "The sponsor teases out the details—checks to make sure all on the [social worker's] chart is covered." Then the sponsor invited the social worker and the FGC coordinator to return and discuss the plan, which included addictions treatment for Karen, day care for April, and new housing. After refining the plan, the social worker affirmed the family group's work, stated that it was a good plan, and immediately approved it.

A few weeks later, the sponsor and the friend were separately interviewed about the conference. The sponsor wondered if she had acted appropriately in taking leadership, but recognized that she had avoided "bashing Karen" and provided support and guidance throughout the session. Like the women in the earlier focus group, she realized that the meeting needed to be about family connections, not about therapy:

> Was it right for me to take charge and tell people what to do? . . . Everyone participated, but I personally felt like I was pulling teeth. . . . I got a call before [the conference] telling me that this wasn't a time to bash Karen, but I don't know if Karen's friend got that call because she treated it more like an intervention.

Following similar lines, the friend did some self-reflection: "I think I could have used a different tone with Karen or been a bit more gentle. . . . The sponsor did an excellent job. Karen listened to her."

Thinking back to her own experiences, the friend wished that she had had a conference, something that a number of the focus group participants probably wanted in their own lives: "[The conference was] a wonderful process. The social workers and others getting together to make a plan is very positive. Back when I was going through my bad times. . . it could [have made a difference]."

The friend also remained steadfast in her support and hopes for Karen: "I'm still going to be there for Karen, because I know that she can change and one day she'll see the light."

For her part, Karen wished that more people had come to the conference and that experts could have been present to explain her mental condition. Overall, however, she agreed with the plan and was willing to carry it out. As the focus group participants expected, the caring helped to motivate Karen to want to change.

How can organizations be connected to sustain an FGC program?

An FGC program relies on community partnerships to make it work. *Their history of relationships and state-level influences shape the way that organizations relate to the local program.* Many of the counties would have been unlikely to adopt FGC if the North Carolina Division of Social Services had not promoted FGC as good practice and if the North Carolina FGC Project had not offered training on the model.

One effective strategy for connecting organizations is having them join advisory bodies for initiatives that they all support. The North Carolina FGC Project adopted this approach and invited a broadly representative group to serve on its statewide advisory committee. Over time, the membership included state- and county-level social services representatives, parents who had been social services' clients, disability advocates, court officers, police officers, representatives from the attorney general's office, domestic violence and drug addiction counselors, juvenile justice system workers, women's prison officials, and the representatives of the involved universities.

The purpose of the statewide advisory committee was to guide the North Carolina FGC Project. One of its earliest tasks was to formulate the project's mission statement, which would then serve as a reference point in assessing whether FGC training and evaluation was consistent with the project's mission. Because FGC raised numerous policy questions, the North Carolina Division of Social Services established a policy subcommittee composed of representatives from social services and the involved universities. By maintaining a dialogue between the statewide advisory committee and the policy subcommittee, it was possible to ensure that the state Division of Social Services authorized and announced FGC policies. This worked particularly well in establishing new county recruitment and funding mechanisms.

Another strategy for building interorganizational collaboration is to assess together what factors facilitate, and what factors impede, such collaboration. As defined by Gray (1989), "Collaboration is a process through which parties who see different aspects of a problem can explore constructively their differences and search for (and implement) solutions that go beyond their own limited vision of what is possible" (p. 5). The North Carolina FGC Project gathered this information through a survey and later re-examined the findings with advisory committee members (Pennell, 2001a; Weil, 2002).

Community Example 4:
Bills, Rides, and Mentors

Early in the North Carolina FGC Project, a survey was disseminated to those active in its planning. The intent was to stimulate interest in the project, document the respondents' prior experiences with interorganizational collaborations, and identify those factors that were likely to help or hinder community and family partnerships. For the most part, the survey respondents saw the climate as hospitable for collaborations, but noted a number of factors that were likely to be helpful, unhelpful, or both. Among the helpful factors were the agencies' history of collaboration, service networks, and training. Unhelpful factors were issues in transportation, regional geography and economy, and the culture of particular organizations. The factors given mixed reviews included the policies of other agencies, interagency protocols, and the availability/accessibility of services. All these factors were later rechecked, first with the county advisory council, and then with the statewide advisory committee. Both groups reaffirmed the survey results and expanded upon them.

The individual conferences showed that the unhelpful factors often played a significant role for the families who were impoverished and isolated. This was quite apparent at a conference held for an African American great-grandmother and her two teenaged great-grandchildren— Sabreena and Zachary. They and Sabreena's infant daughter were residing at the grandmother's home in a rural community. Just before the conference, Zachary had made a transition from house arrest to probation because of his drug use.

Not only the immediate family, but also many of their relatives, lacked transportation, and the FGC coordinator had made arrangements to get them to the conference. It was held at a church selected by Zachary, and with which he was affiliated. Entering the church, the research observer was immediately struck by how the "white" setting did not seem to fit the family, and the seating arrangement further highlighted racial separations:

Upon arrival, I was struck by the fact that the church seemed like a very "white" church (all of the family were African American). The room—a Sunday school room with countertops and sink along the wall—was set up with tables in a horseshoe shape. . . . The room was small for the large crowd. The [six] family members sat on one side of the room. The child welfare worker and the juvenile court counselor were on the opposite end of the horseshoe from the family. In between the two of them and the other service providers sat eight white church members from the host church and two African American clergy [a pastor and deacon] . . . from a different church that knew the great-grandmother. The mental health case manager and Zachary's mentor sat clustered together. Zachary sat beside his mentor. The maternal outreach worker, Susie, sat beside Sabreena and was very supportive of her throughout the conference.

The FGC coordinator stated that the conference was convened in order to arrange supports so that the teens and the baby could continue to live in the great-grandmother's home. Immediately, the great-grandmother's pastor questioned the purpose of the conference: "The pastor asked if the purpose of the conference was to remove the children. If so, he said, it should be temporary. They need support systems; the family should be kept intact." The research observer noted that the opening then reaffirmed the family's cultural community: "The African American pastor was volunteered to say a prayer. He readily agreed to do so."

The FGC coordinator helped the group to move to information sharing and, to keep the family group in the forefront, asked them to share first "the strengths in your family and concerns you may be having." With some encouragement, Sabreena spoke up: "I have to do most of the bills. I need help. I have to find rides. . . . It is hard during the school year."

Afterward, the social worker spoke sympathetically about the burden on Sabreena and commented: "Transportation is a problem. It limits the activities that the kids can participate in."

To assist the family group in drawing up its plan, the providers present described various services; letters from the lawyer and the school social worker also addressed several options. Throughout the discussion, the pastor re-emphasized the importance of keeping the children with their great-grandmother and strengthening the community supports to make this possible: "Pastor begins talking about how foster homes and adoption are not the best things for the kids. He says we need to make sure there is a support network to prevent out-of-home placement."

At the start of the private time, the FGC coordinator and most service providers left the room. Remaining were nine people of color—the six family members, Susie as support to Sabreena, and the two African American clergy—and the eight white church members. As described by the research observer, the white church group became much more vocal and took the lead, with some input by the African American clergy:

> The church people . . . grill Zachary about opportunities for him to work. . . . The head church member, Henry, asks great-grandmother for her input. . . . She talks about the children staying with her until they are gone. . . . The pastor 'interprets': Now they stay at home with support.

The white participants also iterated that the church and social services could not work in collaboration:

> Henry says, "If you choose other services without God, you'll get nowhere. You must choose God to change.". . . Another church member adds, "Every single service or resource mentioned today can be offered by our church.". . . Henry says, "Today, [the coordinator] mentioned two services (church and formal human services) working together, but in my opinion, it's not possible. We don't have the same goals. Great aunt and Deacon readily agree. . . . Great Aunt talks about the importance of God's presence. . . . The cousin and Sabreena are quiet and do not participate.

When Henry called on Sabreena to speak, she presented her own goals: "She says that the family needs help with transportation, to pay the bills, to go to the grocery store. . . . The church members offer to help with transportation. . . . White and Black church members appear to be working OK together."

Turning to Zachary, the white church members stated that he had to replace his current mentor with a church-based one:

> The white church members want him to switch mentors—quit working with current mentor and work with a "spiritual mentor.". . . Zachary speaks up and says that he does not want to switch mentors. Susie speaks out and defends the county . . . -based mentor program. . . . Susie challenges the church members: "Sounds like the church is taking over everything and eliminating the use of other services." Henry says, "That's exactly the idea. This is a new area for us, but it may develop into a new ministry for us."

At the end of the private time, the other service providers returned, and the coordinator asked for someone to review the family group's plan. Once again, Henry assumed the lead, but this time the social worker moved in on the discussion and reasserted public control:

> Henry volunteers to present the plan. He talks about placement, structure for the children at home. . . . The FGC coordinator interrupts Henry and asks the social worker to provide feedback on what has been presented thus far. The social worker is concerned about day-to-day [happenings] and gives examples: Who will help make sure Zachary gets home from school? Who does the social worker call when she gets a call that Zachary has climbed out the window? The social worker says that the reality is that if Zachary messes up,

juvenile justice will take placement into their hands.

When the coordinator asks Zachary what he wants, he immediately raises the issue of the mentor: "Zachary says he doesn't want to lose his current mentor. The mentor is upset and confronts Henry about his being cut out of Zachary's service plan."

At the end of six and a half hours, a plan was finally written. It included day care for Sabreena's daughter and transportation for mother and child. As for Zachary, there was a mix of social services and church programs with Zachary's mentor continuing in his current role.

Six months later, neither teenager was with the great-grandmother, but she was receiving help from her deacon in handling the bills. Sabreena had moved in with a guardian and continued her education with her child in day care. Still in contact with his church, Zachary was now living in a group home, attending school, receiving drug treatment, and seeing his same mentor. According to Zachary, the family was "better off" because of the conference: "The church tried to do more stuff with the family. The family came together more."

As seen in this community example, organizations must agree on goals and philosophy to collaborate. From the outset of the conference, the pastor from the African American church stressed that children should not be taken into state care, and that they should remain with their families and communities. During the private time, Henry, who was from the white church, maintained that the goals of his church and those of social services conflicted. The churches and social services established an uneasy alliance, however, because all wanted Zachary to stay

out of trouble, and the young man insisted on retaining both secular and faith-based services in his life. Sabreena declined the white church services and opted for just those from social services.

Over the course of this intense and protracted session, the conference benefited from the leadership offered by the FGC coordinator, social worker, Susie, and other service providers. FGC was not a new program in this county, and the conference effectively mobilized a wide array of services around the family. This experience reinforced the FGC program's commitment to reaching out to people of different cultures, while at the same time creating boundaries as to who should be considered part of the family group and who should not.

How is an FGC program sustained?

Outside influences—a statewide training program, foundation support, national advocacy groups, and others—can propel a community into undertaking an FGC program. *For an enduring program, though, the community must have developed the capacity from within to implement the model and must renew on an ongoing basis its commitment to and competency for delivery.* Each of the four major strategies of capacity building—leadership development, organizational development, community organizing, and interorganizational collaboration—benefits from a close intersection of frontline practice and program development. Much too quickly, the program can fall out of step with what is happening in conferences and communities. To stay on track, planning and training need to pay close attention to the events that occur in conferences while at the same time offering a vision of where the program should go.

6

Family Group Conferencing and Supportive Legislation and Policy

Gary R. Anderson

A number of features of family group conferencing (FGC) have inspired advocates of FGC to consider developing policies and laws to define and support conferencing. In addition, the congruence between FGC and a number of child welfare laws and policies may support conferencing. Whether or not specific laws are considered, and congruence with existing law and policy highlighted, the value of drafting laws and state policies that specifically address FGC is debatable.

Why should there be laws and policies specific to FGC?

Proponents of FGC may have good reasons to consider FGC-specific legislation. *The authorization or support for a strategy or intervention model through legislation provides some assurance that the model will be put into practice and maintained over time.* Without such support, a reform effort like FGC could fail to gain sufficient notice or

acceptance to demonstrate its potential impact. Also, legislation and policy may ensure the preservation and strengthening of essential intervention elements. For example, there may be an effort to build community partnerships that recognizes the need to use family networks, friends, and other informal supports in developing a new vision for child protection—but fails to explicitly include family members in case planning and decision making (Farrow, 1997).

One of the earliest locations for FGC was New Zealand. After a number of years of experience with the program, the use of FGC became national law. This law described FGC and required that it be used routinely in the child welfare system and in the juvenile justice system. Laws and state policies have the potential not only to ensure the continuing practice of conferencing, but also to build its practice into the continuum of services for children and families.

Defining and supporting FGC through policy and law could potentially protect several key features of FGC, including confidentiality, cultural responsiveness regarding the conduct of conferences, and entitlement of the children and their family group to take part.

The central role of confidentiality in FGC requires protection through law. In many instances, states are using FGC at stages of the child protection process in which information shared at a conference would have consequences for conference participants. Program guidelines or policies may affirm the confidentiality of the content of the conference, but a law affirming confidentiality (and inadmissibility of conference information in court proceedings) would provide uniform assurances for family members and professionals involved in conferences. The lack of such assurances jeopardizes the attendance and the genuine and open participation of family members.

Designing and implementing programs that are culturally responsive and that incorporate cultural considerations and cultural safety should not be optional. As is the case in New Zealand, the development of laws and policies to support culturally responsive practices, such as FGC, seems both justified and necessary. If FGC values are essential for successful intervention, preserving and ensuring the primacy of these values through formal agency policy, if not legislation, make sense. If FGC can demonstrate its effectiveness in keeping children safe and in gaining the support of family members and professionals, then there should be policies that affirm the place of FGC values and program features.

Agency and state policy and federal and state law help to maintain the values and features of programs and practices. Policies reinforce best practices and institutionalize the programs and initiatives that they are designed to address. The advantages to using nonadversarial approaches, such as FGC, are so significant that agency policies and state laws should promote their use.

How does family conferencing fit with existing child welfare legislation?

FGC has emerged as a promising practice for child welfare in the context of existing federal legislation that defines and informs child welfare practice. These laws and regulations have taken shape over the past 30 years and include a number of provisions and principles that directly or indirectly impact FGC.

Child Abuse Prevention and Treatment Act

Issues of child abuse and neglect were originally highlighted in federal law through the Child Abuse Prevention and Treatment Act of 1974 (CAPTA) (P.L. 93-247). This legislation followed a decade of research and program development informed by the "World of Abnormal Rearing" and the "Battered Child Syndrome" pioneered by Drs. C. Henry Kempe and Ray Helfer (1972). The purpose of CAPTA was to provide federal funds for states to develop systems designed to prevent, identify, and respond to child abuse and child neglect. This legislation also created the National Center on Child Abuse and Neglect and addressed national standards for receiving and intervening in reported cases of child maltreatment. Demonstration grants were incorporated into the funding to train professionals in law, medicine, and social work. There was also financial support for developing innovative projects designed to prevent or treat child abuse and neglect (CAPTA, 1974).

In the legislation, Congress noted the high incidence of abuse and neglect and stated that the problem of child abuse and neglect required a comprehensive approach. This approach had a number of features: (1) the integration of social service, legal, health, mental health, education, and substance abuse agencies; (2) coordination among all levels of government and with private agencies and civic, religious, and professional organizations; (3) recognition of the need for prevention, assessment, investigation, and treatment to take place at the community level; (4) the provision of proper training for child protection staff; and (5) emphasis on sensitivity to ethnic and cultural diversity.

The law underscored that all elements of U.S. society have a shared responsibility in responding to child abuse and neglect. It stated that national policy should strengthen families to prevent child abuse and neglect, and this policy should support intensive services designed to prevent the unnecessary removal of children from families. Policy should also promote the reunification of families (CAPTA, 1974). The child protection system was intended to be comprehensive, child centered, family focused, and community based.

Originally, CAPTA established an advisory board, a national clearinghouse, research and evaluation activities, citizen review panels, and demonstration programs and projects. It provided grants to public and private nonprofit agencies that demonstrated innovativeness in responding to abuse and neglect. There were also provisions to award a limited number of grants to states to assist in the development and implementation of procedures

using relatives as the preferred placement for children who were removed from their homes due to abuse and neglect (CAPTA, 1974). Additional grants to states included support for programs that developed and enhanced the *"capacity of community-based programs to integrate shared leadership strategies between parents and professionals to prevent and treat child abuse and neglect at the neighborhood level"* (CAPTA, 1974, section 106, 8; italics added).

There were a number of revisions and amendments made to CAPTA. It was rewritten as the Child Abuse and Prevention, Adoption and Family Services Act of 1988 (P.L. 100-294) and amended by the Child Abuse Prevention and Treatment Act amendments of 1996 (P.L. 104-235). These amendments rewrote Title II of the act, named Community-Based Family Resource and Support Grants. The purposes of this Title were (1) to support state efforts to develop, operate, expand, and coordinate a broad network of agencies and fields of practice to address child maltreatment, and (2) to "foster an understanding, appreciation, and knowledge of diverse populations" to effectively respond to child abuse and neglect (CAPTA, 1996, Title II, section 201, a2).

To be eligible for these grants under Title II, the chief executive officer of the state had to make a commitment to parental participation in the development, operation, and oversight of the state's resource and support programs. Under the definitions of terms used in Title II, family resource and support programs were programs that provided "services characterized *by relationships between parents and professionals that are based on equality and respect"* (Title II, section 209, 3.A.i; italics added). Extended family members are recognized as potential resources to parents, particularly in the provision of respite care services.

In summary, CAPTA outlined a series of federally supported efforts to strengthen state responses to child abuse and neglect. Relevant to FGC, this legislation highlighted: (1) the need for sensitivity to ethnic and cultural diversity, (2) the role of extended family members as potential providers of out-of-home care and respite care, (3) collaboration between service providers and community and civic organizations, (4) community-based/ neighborhood-based intervention, (5) shared leadership between parents and professionals, and (6) relationships between professionals and parents that are based on equality and respect. Thus, this federal legislation introduced and supported a number of the values and strategies that are integral to FGC.

Indian Child Welfare Act

In 1978, the federal Indian Child Welfare Act (ICWA) (P.L. 95-608) was passed. This law granted extensive jurisdiction to Indian tribes in child welfare cases that involved Indian children. The law noted that "there is no resource that is more vital to the continued existence and integrity of Indian tribes than their children" (section 1901). The law stated that the number of Indian families broken up by the removal of their children was alarmingly high, and that this removal was often unwarranted. The percentage of Indian children placed in non-Indian foster and adoptive homes was also alarmingly high. Consequently, minimum federal standards with regard to the removal and placement of children were crafted to promote the stability and security of Indian families. These placements of Indian children were intended to protect and preserve Indian cultural values.

The provisions of ICWA included construction of a state plan, family service plans, and annual progress reports to be developed in consultation with tribal organizations (Brown, Limb, Munoz, & Clifford, 2001). The tribes were to determine who would speak for them, and ICWA required face-to-face contact between state administrators and tribes and tribal organizations. The goal of providing an opportunity for everyone to speak was viewed as the optimal format for the construction of a state plan. ICWA program instructions noted that plans must allow flexibility to meet individual situations. If there was no federally recognized tribe in the state, other resources, such as urban Indian organizations and national organizations, were to be consulted. The state plan was expected to include a description of the consultation process and procedures for addressing cases, and it was required to include all areas of concern raised by the tribes. In addition to the state plan, there could be memoranda of understanding to document agreements or unresolved issues.

Major ICWA requirements included (1) identification of Indian children by the state child welfare agency; (2) notification rights for Indian parents and the right of Indian parents and tribes to intervene in child welfare proceedings that involve Indian children; (3) special preference for placement of Indian children with members of the child's extended family, other members of the child's tribe, or other Indian families; (4) active efforts to prevent the breakup of Indian families, including the use of the tribe's community services and culturally appropriate programs; and (5) use of tribal courts in child welfare issues involving Indian children (Brown et al., 2001).

Because ICWA predated the development of FGC in New Zealand by at least a decade, it did not identify FGC as policy or practice. However, a number of its provisions are congruent with FGC. For example, the initial process and annual review for states' responses to ICWA parallels the stages of FGC: (1) identifying the participants (in this case, tribes and tribal organizations) and, if they are not readily available (no recognized tribes in the state), identifying alternate, relevant participants (urban tribal organizations or national tribal organizations); (2) meeting face-to-face to share information, such as a description of the Indian population; (3) providing an opportunity for everyone to speak; (4) constructing a plan that is led by and responsive to the concerns expressed by the tribes; (5) documenting the plan and sharing this document with all participants; and (6) implementing the plan and having a procedure for reviewing the plan and assessing the progress made toward addressing tribal concerns. Furthermore, there was an overall principle of flexibility to meet individual situations in preparing this state plan.

Foreshadowing FGC's central theme of cultural responsiveness, ICWA directed that state policy and practice reflect the unique values of Indian culture. Tribal community services and culturally appropriate programs were identified as having key roles in preventing the breakup of the Indian family. The primary roles of the family, the extended family, and the tribal community and the central focus on the child's well-being parallel FGC's broad definition of family and prioritization of family leadership and responsibility.

Adoption Assistance and Child Welfare Act of 1980

Congress enacted the Adoption Assistance and Child Welfare Act of 1980 (AACWA) (P.L. 96-272) in response to the research and practice experience that decried the hasty placement of children in out-of-home care and the length of time that children and youths remained in out-of-home care without a plan that ensured a stable, potentially lifelong relationship for children and youths. Although some features were noted earlier in CAPTA, this law codified "permanency" planning—that is, ensuring that "a child has a safe, stable, custodial environment in which to grow up, and a lifelong relationship with a nurturing caregiver" (Duquette & Hardin, 1999, p. I-3).

The law provided for foster care maintenance payments, state agency management responsibility, state agency reporting to the federal government, establishment of standards for out-of-home care and their periodic review, and adoption assistance. It also addressed reasonable efforts to keep families together or reunite families once children were removed, and case planning. A number of principles were outlined in this 1980 federal legislation:

○ The child welfare authorities were to make reasonable efforts to keep children with their biological parents by extending a number of services to the family.
○ If the child could not remain safely with the parents, the child was to be placed in the least restrictive setting.
○ This placement was to be close to the child's home, and the foster parents were to possess or have acquired the ability to address the special needs of the child.
○ Reasonable efforts were to be made to reunite the child with the parents.
○ If it was not possible to return the child to the parents, timely efforts were to be initiated to terminate the parents' rights, and arrange for an adoptive home.

The physical safety of the child was to be ensured. The child's best interests were to be served by child welfare decision making that reduced the separation and trauma for the child and prioritized a permanent home and relationship for the child.

Several provisions associated with the Adoption and Safe Families Act of 1997 (ASFA) revised the AACWA. A number of these revisions addressed the "reasonable efforts" requirements to preserve and reunify families. For example, the law now states that in determining reasonable efforts, the child's health and safety shall be the paramount concern. The 1997 law also identifies a number of circumstances in which reasonable efforts are not required (for example, the parent's felony assault history toward the identified child or another child of the parent).

FGC shares this primary commitment to the safety of children. When conferencing takes place relatively soon after a child protective service referral and early decision making includes the family and extended family or fictive kin, the FGC coordinator and the child protective services worker assess the safety of the child. For the FGC-generated family plan to be accepted, the child protective services worker must agree that the family's plan ensures the physical safety of the child. The motivation for and the context of the information sharing, plan writing, and negotiations are to focus on the well-being of the children—to consider and plan for what is best for the children. The AACWA law introduced this child-focused decision making, and FGC is congruent with this act. A commitment to permanency planning, and the legislated principles and steps in this law, support family conferencing.

Family Preservation and Support Services Program

The federal legislation addressing family preservation and family support was part of Title IV-B of the Social Security Act. This subpart, called the Family Preservation and Support Services Program (P.L. 103-66), was established in 1993 and amended in 1997 (renamed the Promoting Safe and Stable Families Program). The aim of this program was to promote services, including crisis-oriented services, that would prevent the removal of children at risk of child maltreatment and out-of-home placements from their families.

The federal government required that the design and implementation of this program in each state take place through an active, collaborative process involving a broad range of community stakeholders, not just child welfare agencies. (Duquette & Hardin, 1999). This law's focus on a collaborative process (including a planning process in which parents and consumers of service participate) on creating a family preservation and support plan, on the prevention of children's removal from their families, on an expansion of the child welfare services continuum, and on respect for the strengths and resources of families reinforced the values and processes used in FGC.

Adoption and Safe Families Act

The three federal child welfare principles of safety, permanency, and the well-being of children and their families were explicitly affirmed in the ASFA (P.L. 105-89). Central to ASFA were efforts to ensure child safety, decreasing the time to reach permanent placements, increasing the incidence of adoption, and improving states' capacity and accountability for reaching these goals (U.S. Department of Health and Human Services [HHS], 2000). Changes at the practice level were considered essential to reach safety and permanency goals.

Institutionalizing a safety-focused, family-centered, and community-based child welfare approach was described as the "cornerstone of service delivery" (HHS, 2000, p. 15). The ability to connect families to resources, work with community-based formal and informal supports, and collaboration among components of the community were identified as necessary steps to successfully address ASFA provisions and timelines. One of the principles central to good practice affirmed, "The best care and protection for children can be achieved when service delivery focuses on developing and using the strengths of nuclear and extended families and communities" (HHS, 2000, p. 25). One element considered good practice in child welfare was described in the statement, "Children, parents, and extended family members are involved as partners in all phases of engagement, assessment, planning, and implementation of case plans" (HHS, 2000, p. 25). Another element stated, "Problems and solutions are defined within the context of the family's culture and ethnicity" (HHS, 2000, p. 25).

Consequently, a critical question for planning was, How involved are families in determining how, when, and where services are provided? Although FGC was not identified as a specific strategy for achieving this result, a family plan that reflected good child welfare practice was "child-focused, family-centered, strengths-based, individualized, culturally competent, comprehensive, reflective of community partnerships, and outcome-based" (HHS, 2000, p. 35). The central commit-

ment to a child's safety, permanency, and well-being and the endorsement of a family and community-centered planning process underscored that the successful implementation of ASFA required an approach that was congruent with FGC (HHS, 2000).

Are there laws supporting family group conferences?

Although not common, the laws addressing FGC serve as detailed examples of supportive legislation. FGC originated in New Zealand. The experience of New Zealand, convening family meetings at an early stage of the child protection process, was defined, supported, and promoted through federal legislation: New Zealand Children, Young Persons and Their Families Act of 1989. This act addresses many aspects of child welfare and youth justice, and it mandates that when the state becomes involved in child abuse and neglect cases the family has a crucial role in decision making through family group conferences. Furthermore, it contains detailed provisions about almost all aspects of conferencing: the designation of a coordinator, the people entitled to attend, the information to be made available to families, the need to ascertain the views of those unable to attend the conference, notification procedures, issues related to privilege and confidentiality, follow-up conferences, decision-making processes, record keeping, and more. In sum, the act requires conferencing and addresses a broad range of policy issues and practice guidelines (Statutes of New Zealand, 2004).

Appreciating the support and direction provided by the New Zealand act, some advocates have recommended that FGC in the United States be authorized and supported through state legislation, as well as agency policy. In 1998, a cross-disciplinary group of experts in child welfare developed wide-ranging and detailed guidelines reflecting their best thinking about existing and desirable child welfare policy frameworks. This group, which included administrators, lawyers, judges, advocates, and frontline workers, identified what they believed to be better approaches to achieve permanency and highlighted the relationship between policy and critical implementation issues. The federal Administration on Children, Youth and Families/Children's Bureau supported their work (Duquette & Hardin, 1999).

The resulting guidelines for public policy focused on two forms of non-adversarial case resolution (NACR): mediation and FGC. They recommended that (1) state law authorize various forms of NACR to be used by child welfare agencies and the courts; (2) state statutes, child welfare agency policies, and court rules structure NACR programs to support child safety, permanency, and well-being as their principal goals; (3) state law facilitate the development (and evaluation) of child welfare-related NACR models, including FGC pilot projects; (4) state law ensure that statements made within the NACR process are confidential and inadmissible in any court proceedings (with the exception of new allegations of abuse or neglect subject to mandatory reporting laws); and (5) legislation and policy ensure that information about the child and family can be shared with extended family members during the conference process as appropriate, with the duty of participants to treat this information as confidential (Duquette & Hardin, 1999).

The rationale for extensive state legislation and policy support for FGC high-lighted the advantages for the child welfare system, the courts, the child, and the family when (1) there is shared responsibility among families, community, court, and agency; (2) parents are empowered in the decision-making process; and (3) those with a strong interest in the child have a forum for expression. This approach helps to ensure parental compliance with plans, avoids conflicts and delays associated with more adversarial processes, reduces crowded court dockets, and circumvents the need for expensive and contentious trials and case review hearings.

Existing State Legislation in Support of FGC

At least two states have taken legislative action to address and support family conferencing: Kansas and Oregon.

KANSAS. The Kansas legislation passed in 1994 adds a supplement to the Kansas Code for the Care of Children that addresses several elements, including the placement of a child with a person other than the child's parent, relative conferences, and immunity. Before a child is placed with someone other than the child's parent, the state is authorized to convene a "conference of the child" that includes grandparents, aunts, uncles, siblings, cousins, and other relatives determined by the state to have an interest in the child's well-being. In these kinship conferences, relatives are to receive relevant information concerning the needs of the child and other information that would be helpful in determining the child's placement. After they have been given this information, "the relatives of this child shall be permitted to discuss and decide outside the presence of any other persons, the family member or members with whom it would be in the child's best interests to be placed" (Kansas Code for Children, 1994, section a). The relatives then make a recommendation to the state's representative. Unless there is "good cause to place the child with someone other than the relative recommended by the child's relatives, the child shall be placed in accordance with the recommendations of the relatives" (Kansas Code for Children, 1994, section a). This provision grants immunity from any civil liability to conference participants.

The Kansas legislation clearly recognizes the use of a kinship conference, although it does not require such a conference. Under this act, the relevant participants are identified by a state convener. This identification could take place in consultation with family members, but the legislation does not specifically require it. Providing information to a broad range of relatives (fictive kin are not listed) and setting aside private family time are supported. The family's decision identifying a relative who will care for the child is to be respected unless the state convener has sufficient cause to identify a different caregiver. The decision making appears to be limited to determining the child's placement with a relative; a plan for family preservation or reunification is not noted (Kansas Code for Children, 1994, section b).

OREGON. Legislation in Oregon (House Bill 2787) enacted in 1997 begins with a preamble affirming that "family groups are experts on themselves; they hold information that no one else can access; and . . . families have wisdom and solutions that are workable for them" (Oregon, 1997, p. 1). Section one defines *family group decision making* (FGDM) as a "family focused

intervention facilitated by professional staff that is designed to build and strengthen the natural caregiving system for the child." In Oregon, FGDM includes FGC, family unity meetings, family mediation, or other similar interventions. The purpose is to establish a plan that provides for the "safety, attachment and permanency needs of the child" (Oregon Bill 2787, 1997, p. 1).

Section two states that the public child welfare agency shall consider using FGDM in each case in which a child is placed in substitute care for more than 30 days. It is recommended that the meeting take place before the child has been in care 60 days. If the agency chooses not to have a family decision-making meeting, the reason for not having a meeting must be documented in the case service plan.

Section three provides further direction for the meetings. First, if a meeting is to be held, there is to be documentation of efforts to locate and identify parents, grandparents, and any other relatives who had significant direct contact with the child in the year prior to placement. Second, all notified members may attend the meeting unless their attendance compromises the safety of another family member. Third, an excluded family member may provide a written statement addressing the issues to be discussed and determined at the meeting. The statute defines *family member* as someone who is over the age of 12 years and is related to the child by blood, marriage, or adoption. Children under age 12 can be included in the meeting when appropriate.

Section four states that the family meeting should result in the development of a written plan addressing placement and service recommendations. The family plan should include expectations of parents and other family members, services that the agency will provide, timelines, benefits associated with compliance, consequences of noncompliance, and a schedule of subsequent meetings, if appropriate. Family members are directed to sign the plan. The family plan is to be incorporated into the agency's service plan for the child provided that it protects the child, builds on family strengths, and focuses on timely permanency. If the plan is not included in the agency service plan, the reason must be noted.

The *Client Services Manual I* extensively describes other aspects of the process and specifies the rules and policies associated with the legislation (Oregon State Office for Services to Children and Families, 1998). For example, the policy states that family member participation should be voluntary, and that family members should be "prepared prior to the meeting to increase the likelihood of a safe and productive meeting" (p. 3). Also, it states that a written copy of the plan is to be sent to all participating family members within 21 days after the meeting. The original Oregon legislation does not appear to address confidentiality.

The Oregon bill provides considerable direction for the provision of family meetings and conferencing. Although a family meeting is not mandatory, the exclusion of some form of family meeting must be explained and documented in the case service plan. Closely following the stages and practices associated with FGC, the Oregon bill provides strong support for FGC implementation.

Child and Family Service Reviews

Although there are few examples of laws that specifically support FGC in the United States, the recent introduction of federal reviews of state child welfare systems has introduced a process with a number of standards and considerable authority. This review process affirms central child welfare outcomes. Empowered by federal law, these reviews have implications for the use of FGC in the United States.

There is no U.S. legislation establishing FGC that is comparable to the New Zealand Children, Young Persons and Their Families Act, nor is there any federal legislation that describes family group conferences in as much detail as the Oregon statute, or even as briefly as the Kansas statute. However, since the passage of ASFA in 1997, federal outcome standards for U.S. state child welfare systems have been identified, and state programs have been evaluated based on these standards. So federal standards derived from federal child welfare legislation have begun to significantly shape state policy and child welfare practice.

These outcome standards address child safety, permanency, and child and family well-being. With regard to safety, the outcomes examined include protection from abuse and neglect and maintaining children safely in their homes when appropriate and possible. With regard to permanency, the standards support stability in the child's living arrangements and continuity of family relationships and connections. Well-being is primarily concerned with meeting the educational, physical, and mental health needs of the child (HHS, 2003).

Although the federal standards do not explicitly mention FGC, they have implications for the practice of FGC. In addition to these primary standards, seven systemic factors are included in this federal review. Several systemic factors, in particular, can be linked to FGC. For example, the state case review system is one of the seven systemic factors. This federal systemic factor specifies that parents participate in the development of a child's case plan and are engaged in case planning process, and that the case review process reflect a family-centered approach to child welfare and identify family strengths. Periodic case review and support for relative caregivers are also noted in this systemic factor area. Although primarily addressing families with children in foster care, these principles are extended to children at risk of placement and to all families served, regardless of their circumstances. (HHS, 2003).

The combination of principles and practices from existing federal legislation and the policy ramifications related to child and family service reviews support the development of FGC. The general absence of specific federal or state laws delineating FGC may reflect many factors, including the possible adequacy of existing policies affirming family-centered practice, the newness of the model, or the existence of a range of obstacles to such legislation.

What are the complications or cautions associated with legislation and policy supporting FGC?

Legislation appears to be a means of ensuring support for FGC, but there are a range of complications associated with such a strategy. Although significant elements of federal legislation support the strategies and practice of FGC, some have called for legislation directly authorizing FGC. They argue that the only certain means to have FGC included in agency policy is to enact legislation that would then prompt or require corresponding agency policy and rules.

With relatively compelling reasons to support FGC, why not make extensive efforts for all states to have supporting legislation? Or, why not consider national legislation? There may be a number of reasons to be cautious about pressing for legislation, however.

FGC builds on a foundation of values that are difficult to legislate: respect for families and for extended families, a commitment to sharing responsibility and power with families, cultural sensitivity, and community inclusion. Family meetings that are not grounded in values tied to respect for families, family strengths, culture, and resiliency may not produce the intended results and benefits of FGC. Respect cannot be legislated, and FGC could be reduced to a mechanical formula rather than genuine involvement with families and communities.

Crafting legislation may require either generalizations broad enough to encompass a number of family involvement strategies and nonadversarial models, or the endorsement of more specific strategies and procedures deemed to constitute FGC. Broader generalizations may provide insufficient guidance, and it may be difficult to reach agreement on specific program features.

There are practical difficulties in legislating a program model. For example, are legislators qualified to be the best judges or arbiters of good practice? It may set a precedent—should all intervention models be supported through legislation? What if certain models do not gain legislative support, and others do? Is a legislative process the proper means to affirm good practice? What standards of evidence are required to gain sufficient approval? What if there are measured and reasonable adaptations over time?

There is a risk that these tools and program features will be perceived as sufficient to address the challenges facing the child welfare system. This could lead to the replacement of system review and reform with legislated programs, or a reduction in the impetus for system change and improvement.

It may not be feasible to have supportive legislation for all innovative, effective, or promising programs.

Although evaluations in progress or completed examine the elements of FGC and its outcomes, few studies involve an experimental design with sufficiently large samples over time to make indisputable claims about the effectiveness of FGC. It may be difficult to persuade a more skeptical audience of the advantages of FGC without such evidence.

The crafting of legislation and the sustained advocacy required to move a program and set of principles into legislation may be too time- and energy-intensive for providers and advocates of FGC. The time and resources required for this effort would compete with the time and resources needed for program development, implementation, and expansion. In the end, supportive legislation might not translate into supportive funding.

What is the best course of action with regard to legislation and policy?

With a number of powerful reasons for that legislation supporting FGC as a needed step in the evolution of this promising practice but with serious concerns about and potential limitations to such legislation, other means for supporting FGC should be explored. The best course of action may be to adopt an approach such as one or more of the following:

○ Even though the fundamental values that inform FGC cannot be fully legislated, they can be articulated and affirmed in preambles to legislation (such as in the Oregon statute) and in the discussion accompanying legislation (such as in CAPTA), and they can be incorporated into agency mission statements, administrative and practice visions, the articulation of values, worker orientation, and training.

○ Although agreement on program features may be elusive, agencies can affirm broad principles or multiple strategies, and they can conceptualize and identify the varied points in the child welfare continuum where FGC can be implemented.

○ Agency policy can affirm the authorization for FGC. State law is not required to provide permission or support for the piloting and provision of FGC, which is clearly congruent with decades of federal policy. Agency policy—at the state or local level—may be easier to design and adapt.

○ The identification of best practices in family conferencing can lead to the affirmation of values, principles, strategies, and skills that can inform the way that an agency does its business through FGC and other avenues of service to children and families.

○ As FGC pilot efforts become more established and programs mature and expand, the efficacy of FGC can be more widely and strongly demonstrated.

The place and the importance of state and federal legislation dedicated to supporting FGC can and should be re-evaluated at future points in time as knowledge about and experience with FGC further develop in the United States.

Conclusion

In its development, FGC quickly moved from agency practice to supportive legislation in New Zealand. In the United States, the growth of FGC has not been accompanied by widespread supportive legislation dedicated to advance FGC. However, FGC in the United States can flourish in a legislative and policy environment shaped by federal legislation and guidelines. Child welfare laws over the past 25 years have laid a foundation for the development of FGC in the United States. By affirming family involvement in case planning and decision making, the importance of cultural sensitivity, and a family and community perspective on practice that is dedicated to the safety of children, federal policy underscores many of the central tenets of FGC.

Evaluating Conferencing

Joan Pennell, Carol Harper, and Gary R. Anderson

When family group conferencing (FGC) coordinators invite families and service providers to a conference, they are usually asked, "What happens at a family group conference?" When social workers discuss a referral with a family, they are often asked, "Does it work?" And when administrators seek funding for FGC programs, they are invariably asked, "How much will it cost, and are the results worth it?" In answering these questions, it helps to point to studies carried out in other places, and useful compendiums are available (for example, Burford & Hudson, 2000; Hudson, Morris, Maxwell, & Galaway, 1996; Merkel-Holguin, 2003). It helps even more, though, to point to evaluation carried out in one's own program.

This three-chapter section answers these commonly posed questions. Chapter 7 addresses the question, What happens at a family group conference? In response, Joan Pennell sets forth means of measuring whether a conference has ad-

hered to the key FGC principles. Chapter 8 examines ways of determining, Does it work? First, Gary Anderson looks at the policy context that shapes an FGC evaluation and then discusses a range of outcomes from the short term to the long term. And in chapter 9, economist Andy Rowe sets forth ways of calculating costs and benefits to answer the question, How much will it cost, and are the results worth it? In an appendix to chapter 9, Joan Pennell summarizes findings on FGC costs.

What inhibits and what facilitates carrying out an FGC evaluation?

Carrying out program evaluation raises a host of questions: How much time and money will it take? Does the program's staff have the expertise for this? How will the results be used? The last question is particularly worrisome for new programs such as FGC. *They are typically held up to* high standards, while practice as usual proceeds without the same level of scrutiny and justification. At the same time, the demand for evaluation offers an opportunity to examine the strengths and challenges of a program and to seek additional resources for carrying out a more extensive study.

The aim of program evaluation is to gather knowledge to improve social programming (Shadish, Cook, & Leviton, 1991). Evaluating practice and programs is an ethical standard of the National Association of Social Workers (2000): "Social workers should monitor and evaluate policies, the implementation of programs, and practice interventions" (p. 25). To gain support for an evaluation, it helps to set forth a clear reason that makes sense to others. One response is simply to say that it will help to answer the questions on the minds of family members, social workers, administrators, and community partners. It also helps to present a guiding framework or theory of change for FGC. In this volume, the guiding framework is that FGC widens the circle of those committed to safeguarding children, young people, and other family members. *A guiding framework serves to focus the evaluation on what is important; it also allays suspicions that the evaluation is about terminating a program rather than about trying to make it work well to achieve its goals.*

What is a guiding framework or map for an FGC evaluation?

For an evaluation, the key principles that describe the practice of FGC can be organized into a logic model or series of guideposts linking each aspect of a program (Alter & Egan, 1997; McLaughlin & Jordan, 1999; Milstein & Wetterhall, 1999). The logic model for FGC can be ordered from its resources through to its long-term outcomes.

Resources

Build capacity for FGC service delivery and its evaluation. As discussed in section II, capacity should be developed within the program and its community, but it should be supported at the federal and state levels by legislation, reviews, and training. Building capacity can be documented through a number of means, including surveys of community strengths and challenges in carrying out FGC, focus groups with important constituencies on progress achieved, and minutes of planning forums or advisory committees.

Inputs

Include culturally diverse groups in FGC. As discussed in sections I and II, strategies for including culturally diverse groups may take the form of consulting with a broad spectrum within the community in designing the program and organizing conferences, selecting and training FGC coordinators who are sensitive to and able to reach out to local communities, developing referral policies that include a wide spectrum of families, and translating FGC materials and using interpreters as needed. The inclusiveness of an FGC program can be monitored by comparing the families that are referred to those that are not and tracking which families proceed to a conference.

Activities

Advance the family group's leadership in making a plan. As discussed in section I, the leadership of the family group is fostered by inviting and preparing family members and other participants; assessing the safety of every family member and building in supports and protections, if necessary; structuring the conference in a way that recognizes the family group's knowledge and customs; and giving the family group members the information, time, and privacy to develop their own plan. These steps can be monitored by having the coordinators complete checklists of the preparatory activities (see chapter 2) and notes on what happened before and during the conference. The extent to which the process remains faithful to the FGC model can be assessed by administering a questionnaire to the participants (chapter 7).

Immediate Outcomes

Reach agreement on a plan. As discussed in section I, the coordinator reviews the family group's plan to make sure that it is clear about what is to be done, by whom, at what time, and with what supports in place. The referring social worker and other involved protection authorities must approve the plan in terms of meeting safety considerations and allocating public resources. The plan is an immediate outcome of the conference. Satisfaction with the process and its resulting plan can be assessed by distributing a questionnaire to the participants at the end of the conference (see chapter 2 for an example). The content of the plan can be examined in regard to the extent to which the maternal and paternal sides of the family agree to contribute to the plan, the distinctiveness of the items as compared with standard child welfare service plans, the wide-ranging nature of family group plans, and the costs of carrying out the plan.

Intermediate Outcomes

Coordinate the work of the family group, community organizations, and public agencies in implementing the plan. As discussed in section I, the work of carrying out the plan after the conference is crucial. The law mandates that the referring child welfare workers continue to monitor the protective interventions, but now they have a means of partnering with the family group and other services. The plan includes a monitor from the family group to facilitate this collaboration and may have a set time for reconvening the parties. In some places, an advocate works with the family to make sure that all family members are carrying out their part of the plan (see chapter 4). An evaluation can assess how many parts of the plans are implemented and whether they are revised as needed. It can also look at the impact of affirming the family on the partnerships developed at the conference, the enhanced knowledge of community and family resources, and the guidance provided by a clear and consensually developed plan (chapter 8).

Long-Term Outcomes

Promote child and family safety, permanence, and well-being. The aim of FGC is to safeguard child and adult family members. This means ensuring that all family members are safe, that children have stable homes and remain connected with their families, and that families are better able to care for their children and to meet their children's physical, mental health, educational, cultural, and other needs. These outcomes can be measured in a number of ways, including family or worker interviews, reports from schools and other involved services, and an analysis of child welfare records before and after FGC (chapter 8). The outcomes of FGC can be compared with those from other services (for example, casework) and their costs examined to determine the cost-effectiveness of FGC (chapter 9).

In practice, the FGC steps are not undertaken in a consecutive manner and instead circle back on each other. Nevertheless, the logic model offers guidance on both implementing an FGC program and evaluating its processes, results, and costs.

7

Checking for Model Fidelity

Joan Pennell

Translating an intervention model into practice is not easy. In training, practitioners quickly grasp the steps of family group conferencing (FGC), but when faced with real families in complex situations, they often have questions about whether their practice sufficiently approximates the model to be called FGC. However, conforming rigidly to the model inhibits the good practice of an intervention like FGC, which requires responsiveness to families. Without such flexibility, FGC suppresses the constructive leadership that families can exert, reduces the capacity of the group to foster a culturally safe context, and lessens the likelihood of creative and productive community partnerships.

The use of a model's key principles and practices is a way to specify what the model is without making it rigid. Thus, programs can adapt an intervention without compromising its nature and outcomes. These same principles and practices can be used to evaluate the implementation of the model. Such an assessment measures model fidelity, the extent to which practice stays true to the model's essential features and carries out its important activities in a flexible manner. As described in the introduction to this section, the FGC logic model places these important practices or activities at its central point: They link an FGC program's resources and inputs with its different levels of outcomes. The FGC model is made up of these activities, and the FGC *logic model* is a map of the way in which an FGC program achieves a range of desired outcomes—from reaching agreement on a plan, to coordinating the response of family group and service providers, to realizing child and family safety, permanence, and well-being.

What does an FGC look like that deviates in part from the model's key practices?

This chapter starts with an example of a conference that diverged from some of the key FGC practices, particularly with regard to clarifying purpose and preparing participants. In this instance, *the FGC coordinator was trying to follow the model but could not because of various obstacles*. Thus, it provides an example of a deviation from the model, rather than an effort to replace FGC with an alternative.

Family Example: "Everyone had a different idea why we were having it"

"It is the opinion of the coordinator that this meeting is a classic case of poor communication and preparation prior to the meeting."

—EXPERIENCED COORDINATOR, TWO WEEKS AFTER THE CONFERENCE

A first meeting with an all African American family had gone smoothly, with a preliminary plan drafted to keep the two young sisters, Twanda and Chandra, with their great-grandmother, Rose, at least for the time being. This gave the mother, Crystal, time to receive treatment for both substance addiction and mental health issues. Six months later, a second conference was called to make a permanent plan for Twanda and Chandra, and the worker anticipated closing the case at that time. In the first meeting, the family group members' ability to use their private time and to produce a sound plan had impressed the worker and supervisor, and they saw this follow-up conference as a way of acknowledging the family's progress and efficacy.

During the period between meetings, Crystal had decided to transfer the children to her father, John, because of Rose's advanced years. In the reflective notes, the coordinator recorded the reason for the referral:

The conference was planned by the referring social worker as a cut-and-dried meeting in which Crystal was to sign relinquishment of Twanda and Chandra to John per Crystal's request. . . . Referring social worker informed that family understood the purpose [of the conference] and were in agreement. This preparation eliminated the coordinator's need to address the issues for the meeting as [the coordinator] was assured that all knew and were ready for the meeting.

Nevertheless, the coordinator attempted to telephone Crystal, but her line had been disconnected. Her worker observed that, in general, Crystal was "very hard to locate." The coordinator succeeded in speaking by telephone with Rose and later with John: "Questions were asked of family if there were any areas of the upcoming meeting that the coordinator could help explain. There were no questions from the family, and it was stated they were looking forward to the meeting." As is the case with many reconvened conferences, preparations took limited time; the coordinator devoted three hours to preparing for the conference, and the referring worker spent six hours on preparations.

To the coordinator's dismay, attendance was lower on the day of the conference than at the previous meeting. Rose arrived first, but without her husband; Crystal followed shortly with a white male friend who was unknown to the other family members; and John delayed the conference for half an hour until he finally appeared with his wife. Crystal's mother never arrived, and Twanda and Chandra were not in attendance. All four of the service providers, including the coordinator, were white. During the waiting period, the white research observer asked family members to sign a consent form permitting her to sit in on the session.

The session was held in the social services building and lasted 45 minutes, with 10 of these minutes used for the family's private time. According to the research observer's notes, the coordinator at the outset of the meeting asked the family to sign a confidentiality form, reviewed the conference guidelines, recapped developments at the earlier meeting, and read a letter stating:

> It is the agency's hope that Crystal will continue substance abuse treatment and drug testing. Twanda and Chandra are currently in a safe and stable placement with Rose and her husband. It is the agency's understanding that Crystal is seeking permanent placement for the children with John and his wife.

The referring social worker and Crystal agreed that the letter was correct. At this point, Crystal started explaining the children's transfer to a very surprised Rose. Interrupting this tense exchange, the coordinator suggested that the service providers leave so that the family could talk among themselves. They departed, as did Crystal's friend.

The research observer's notes reflected the "stress and confusion" during the family's private time:

> The conversation took off very fast. Rose was not aware that Crystal wanted Twanda and Chandra to go live with John and his wife, who lived two hours away. John and his wife were expecting to take Twanda and Chandra with them when they left

the conference. . . . Crystal began to get very upset. She raised her voice and began to cry and talk very loudly. Crystal told Rose that Rose was old and she didn't want the children to have to move again if anything happened to Rose and her husband.

In turmoil, the family gave up on reaching a plan, left the room, and brought back the service providers. The "very short and aborted" family alone time, the coordinator explained, was a result of misunderstandings among the family and between Crystal and her social worker. The worker and John thought that Crystal had completed the legal paperwork necessary for finalizing the permanent placement with John. In separate interviews three weeks after the conference, Rose and John elaborated further. For her part, Rose knew before the conference that Crystal was contemplating moving the children, but "not that she was going to." John described the conference as a "big disappointment," adding that "everyone had a different idea why we were having it." In a post-conference interview, the coordinator laid out four lessons learned from this session:

1. To continue to educate the social workers and supervisors referring cases on the process of FGC.
2. To assume nothing in the assessment and preparation stage of a conference by reviewing carefully the knowledge already provided by social workers to family members.
3. To be more diligent in family contact and discussion before the meeting, preferably by face-to-face meetings and careful discussion over the telephone.

4. To caucus with the family member groups at the beginning of the conference. . . . [and] address the gaps created by the absence of members of the group.

The conference adjourned on the understanding that the children would transfer to their grandfather's home, and the case was closed. Six months later, Twanda and Chandra continued to live with their great-grandmother, and their mother moved away. Rose explained:

> John told Crystal after the conference that he thought it would be better for Twanda and Chandra to stay with me. So we changed the plan—Crystal wanted the children to go live with John and his wife, but John said he wouldn't take them without legal papers because he is afraid Crystal will change her mind all of a sudden and decide to move them again.

In effect, the family group reconvened the conference and came up with a workable plan. Remaining connected with Twanda and Chandra, John frequently visited his grandchildren, and their grandmother (who had not attended the conference) took care of the girls every weekend. In the event that Rose could no longer take care of her great-grandchildren, Twanda and Chandra would have caring adults in their lives. Asked overall how the conference affected the family, Rose replied, "Better, because everything got out in the open. After the conference changes were made—wouldn't have been made had there not been a conference." In conclusion, Rose proudly exclaimed, "I wish you could see the children now—they're so smart!"

Despite the confusion about the purpose and the abbreviated preparations and conference, the aftermath testifies to the caring and resourcefulness of family groups in planning for their young relatives. It also testifies to the faith of the service providers in the family's capacity to plan for the children. This faith was not misplaced. By convening the conference, social services helped the family group members to sort out their misunderstandings so that later they could make arrangements for the children on their own. Without legal transfer of custody, however, these arrangements were not binding and may later lead to disruption in the lives of Twanda and Chandra. With adequate preparation, the family group might have reached a decision that was formally authorized. This raises questions about model fidelity and the impact of deviations from key FGC practices.

What is model fidelity?

Model fidelity means an intervention is carried out in a manner that is true to its key principles and their practices. In the case of FGC, these principles and practices are the means for putting into action FGC's theory of change—widening the circle to safeguard children, young people, and other family members. Unfaithfulness to the FGC model lies in the agency taking the lead, not the family; professional culture dominates in such a case, and the agency works in isolation from community partners.

At Twanda and Chandra's conference, two key practices were notably in question: (1) giving reasons for holding the conference that the family group and service providers can understand and agree with, and (2) preparing the family group and service providers. The social services agency for this family believed in the model of FGC and sought to carry it out. The departure was not in a change to another model but, rather, in the omission of some key FGC practices.

Why should model fidelity be checked?

Checking for model fidelity makes it possible to determine how to improve practice and what areas to concentrate on in program planning, training, and policy. The coordinator for Twanda and Chandra's conference demonstrated honesty and integrity in assessing what happened, and used this experience constructively to develop "lessons" for future FGC implementation and worker orientation.

Assessing model fidelity is essential as a precursor for outcome evaluation (Rossi, Freeman, & Lipsey, 1999). To evaluate the outcomes of FGC, it is necessary to know if the model was carried out properly. Otherwise, the evaluation may be focusing on the outcomes of some intervention other than FGC. The finding of weak outcomes of an intervention may be the result of a failure to consistently carry out the model (Henggeler & Randall, 2000). Some adaptation of a model helps to promote its use and success. For example, some programs add new components to a model, but do not modify its original features (Mayer & Davidson, 2000). Thus, *along with constructive adaptation of an intervention to the organizational setting, faithful replication of a tested service intervention is correlated with effectiveness.* In the case of Twanda and Chandra, their conference contravened some key principles and, as a result, left the family and workers disappointed and the plans in disarray.

How is a valid check on model fidelity carried out?

An assessment for model fidelity requires some agreement on what the model is. Without this blueprint, agencies have no standard for implementation against which to compare their actual practice. As discussed in section II, agencies too often start new programs without the planning, training, and policies in place to inform and sustain good practice. To explain the model to conference participants, FGC coordinators need an operational definition that has the sanction of their employer and the agreement of their community partners. The operational definition sets forth the specific activities or practices necessary for putting the "widening the circle" theory of change into action and lays the foundation for a theory-based evaluation (Weiss, 1997). This operational definition makes it possible to evaluate the extent to which a program succeeds in implementing its intervention model (Scheirer & Rezmovic, 1983).

For a model that seeks to advance family leadership, it is essential to pay close attention to the views of the family group. Leaders, though, require strong supporters, so *the views of all key stakeholders—family, community, agency, and evaluator—should be taken into account.* Asking just for the opinions of the grandparent or the FGC coordinator or the referring worker ignores an opportunity to learn about other viewpoints, either different or similar, and to build an understanding of developments before, during, and after conferences. Looking at FGC from many directions gives a clearer picture of what is happening, and allows greater confidence in the validity of conclusions.

If research conclusions are to be valid, *research participants must understand what is being asked of them, and they must feel safe enough to say what they think, rather than what they think others want to hear.* Thus, researchers must explain why they want to gather data and how they will use what they learn, ask permission to include family members in a study, word questions clearly, refrain from asking questions that could set people at risk, and respect the privacy of the family. People are more willing to take part in research if their consent is requested at the same time that they are invited to take part in the intervention, if they are informed that they can drop out of the study at any time without repercussions and will be paid for any completed interviews, if they develop a sense of rapport with the interviewer, and if the interviewer comes across as caring and interested (Gondolf, 2000). To develop an as-safe-as-possible evaluation design, it helps to seek guidance from children's and women's advocates (Shepard, 1999). In the case of Rose and John, they appreciated being interviewed after the conference and being asked for their views. John explained, "It lets you be more informed on how to train coordinators—communication is very important."

Practice does not hold still. As a consequence, it is necessary to evaluate model fidelity at multiple times. Ongoing assessment reveals variations and helps to ensure that workers are on track with the goals for FGC. If not, they can alter their direction. The coordinator for Twanda and Chandra's conference was an experienced and competent meeting organizer and facilitator; nevertheless, this conference offered yet one more opportunity for refining practice.

FGC takes place in a context. To understand findings, *workers need to know about the cultures and resources of the community, host and partner agencies, and participating families.* They also need to know how familiar the community is with the FGC process. The social services worker hosting Twanda and Chandra's conference was committed to including families in decision making and stayed with an at times difficult process.

Including a range of people in interpreting them and translating them into action plans further validates research results. For instance, the findings can be presented to an advisory group with a request for their thoughts on what the results mean and how to use them to guide practice (see chapter 5). Later, this same group can reflect on the outcomes of their action plans and revise them as needed. In general, a partnership approach strengthens program evaluation (Shadish, Cook, & Leviton, 1991). The involvement of a range of partners helps to ensure not only the validity of the findings, but also the likelihood that the findings will be used (Patton, 1986) and that the participants will feel empowered by the process (Fetterman, Kaftarian, & Wandersman, 1996; Parsons, 1998).

What are ways of assessing model fidelity?

Preferably, a program assesses model fidelity in a number of ways. Such an assessment makes for a fuller picture of how FGC is being implemented. *The most important assessment method is the use of ongoing checks by the FGC coordinators, referring workers, and other service providers on their practice.* They must remain vigilant in determining whether they are carrying out the necessary steps in preparing for, facilitating, and following up after conferences. For example, a checklist serves as a reminder of preparation steps, especially for those new to coordination (see chapter 2). Monthly gatherings of FGC coordinators to discuss their progress, exchange ideas, and reflect on ways to enhance their work are helpful (see chapter 5). The coordinators also check their practice by asking the FGC participants for feedback; they should do so frequently throughout all stages of conferencing. For example, the coordinator for Twanda and Chandra's conference did this informally by asking participants if they were unclear about the process before and during the meeting and formally by distributing the FGC Evaluation form at the end of the session (see chapter 2).

Structured ways of assessing practice—such as questionnaires, interviews, file review, and observation—provide information in a more uniform way. This approach permits coordinators to document their practice from multiple perspectives over the course of the work, to compare findings, and to share the results with others.

What is the Achievement of FGC Objectives?

The North Carolina FGC Project designed a questionnaire called the Achievement of FGC Objectives as one means of measuring fidelity to the FGC model.[1] *To measure model fidelity, the questionnaire translates key FGC principles and practices into*

---

[1]The original Achievement of Objectives had 25 four-point Likert scale items (Pennell, 2003a); a factor analysis reduced the instrument to 14 items forming three subscales (Pennell, 2004). Participating county Social Services referred families for the research, and a university interviewer completed a consent form with each participating family group member. The sample for the factor analysis consisted of 111 respondents with complete data on the 14 items. The respondents came from 30 conferences and included 65 family groups, 31 FGC coordinators, 14 research observers, and one service provider. A Varimax rotation extracted three factors with eigenvalues of 3.67, 3.48, and 3.46. The three factors each had total Cronbach coefficient alphas ranging from .754 to .782.

"objectives" (Figure 7-1). As discussed in chapter 1, the FGC principles are based on empowerment theory and the study of conferencing in diverse cultural contexts. This mix of sources strengthens the conceptualization of the model (Trochim, 1985).

The questionnaire operationalizes FGC principles for activities before and during the conference (see chapter 1). For each of its 14 items, the respondent is asked to give an answer of "strongly disagree," "disagree," "agree," or "strongly agree," with the option of answering "don't know" or "not applicable."

Who completes the questionnaires?

Family group members, FGC coordinators, and research observers can all fill out the questionnaire. It is completed on a specific conference, preferably by more than one participant to obtain a wider perspective. It is not intended for children who are under the age of 12 years or individuals who are experiencing dementia. Because of time constraints and difficulties in accessing people, usually not all family group members are asked to fill out the form. Instead, it is recommended that the program leaders select family group members who are central to the situation and likely to have a range of viewpoints. The North Carolina FGC Project commonly interviewed mothers, fathers, grandparents, aunts, and young people for whom the conference was held. In the case of Twanda and Chandra's family group, their great-grandmother and grandfather were interviewed.

How are the questionnaires administered?

With family group members, the questionnaire is administered in an interview. In this way,

FIGURE 7-1
Achievement of FGC Objectives (Pre-conference and Conference)

INSTRUCTIONS: Beside each of the statements listed below, please indicate whether you strongly disagree, disagree, agree, or strongly agree.

OBJECTIVES	Strongly Disagree	Disagree	Agree	Strongly Agree	Don't Know	Not Applicable
1. Each service provider was clear about their role (ex., child protection, counseling).	1	2	3	4	7	8
2. The FGC coordinator was respectful of the family group.	1	2	3	4	7	8
3. The only job of the FGC coordinator was to organize the conference. He/she did *not* have other jobs to do with the family.	1	2	3	4	7	8
4. The family group understood the reasons for holding the conference.	1	2	3	4	7	8
5. The conference was held in a place that felt right to the family group.	1	2	3	4	7	8
6. The conference was held in a way that felt right to the family group (ex., the right food, right time of day).	1	2	3	4	7	8
7. More family group than service providers were invited to the conference.	1	2	3	4	7	8
8. People at the conference were relatives and also people who feel "like family" (ex., old friends, good neighbors).	1	2	3	4	7	8
9. The family group was prepared for the conference (ex., got enough information on what happens at a conference).	1	2	3	4	7	8
10. The service providers were prepared for the conference (ex., got enough information on what happens at a conference).	1	2	3	4	7	8
11. The conference had enough supports and protections (ex., support persons).	1	2	3	4	7	8
12. Service providers shared their knowledge, but they did not tell the family group how to solve the problems.	1	2	3	4	7	8
13. The family group had private time to make their plan.	1	2	3	4	7	8
14. The plan included ways that the family group will help out.	1	2	3	4	7	8

Additional Explanatory Comments: (Please put the number of the corresponding objective beside each comment) the interviewer can clarify items and inquire further into the reasons behind the responses. The interviewer should be someone with whom the family group member can speak relatively openly without fear of repercussions. Often, family group members need some time after the conference to reflect on what happened, but the time between the conference and the interview should not be so long that they begin to forget what happened. For this reason, it is advisable to conduct the interview about two to four weeks after the conference. The research observer interviewed Rose and John separately approximately three weeks after Twanda and Chandra's conference.

These interviews can be conducted either in person or by telephone. To ease administration by telephone with people as young as 12 years and well into old age, all items are worded in a positive manner; there are no reversed items (for example, the family group did *not* understand the reasons for holding the conference). The available scores are limited to four choices, which likewise simplifies administration by telephone to people of a wide range of ages.

It is better to include the Achievement of FGC Objectives as just one part of an interview. The interviewer should first ask open-ended questions about the conference process, such as, "What was the family group conference like for you?" and "How could the family group conference have been planned and organized better?" Such questions give the family group members the opportunity to reflect on their conference and tell the story of the conference in their own words. Asking broader questions shows an interest in the family group members, readies them to answer the specific items on the Achieve-

ment of FGC Objectives, and enriches the understanding of the questionnaire scores. Expanding on his scoring of the Achievement of FGC Objectives, for instance, John stated that he "disagreed" with item 7, that "people at the conference were relatives and also people who feel 'like family'." Referring to Crystal's friend, he explained, "The one guy that they let sit in... we don't even know him." Rose and John's interviews took 20 and 26 minutes, respectively. These figures are consistent with the average of 26 minutes for 93 of the 98 after-the-conference interviews for which length was recorded (they ranged from a low of five minutes to a high of 60 minutes).

Once oriented to the questionnaire, the *FGC coordinators and research observers can complete the Achievement of FGC Objectives on their own*, or the researchers can interview the FGC coordinators and research observers about their choices. To provide a better picture of their views, the FGC coordinators and research observers should add reflective notes on the conference to their completed questionnaires. In these notes, they can discuss what happened at the conference, what worked well, and what should be done differently in the future. These reflections gave Twanda and Chandra's coordinator a forum in which to articulate the list of four lessons learned.

How was the questionnaire tested?

The North Carolina FGC Project tested the Achievement of FGC Objectives questionnaire by administering it to 151 respondents from 30 conferences, among whom family group members were in the majority (Pennell, 2003a). The family group members were interviewed, on average, a month after their conference. Compared with the FGC coordinators and the research observers, the family group members most often gave an opinion rather than answering "don't know" or "not applicable." This result shows their understanding of the FGC process at their conference and reflects well on the care with which coordinators explained the process and prepared participants.

Overall, the responses on the Achievement of FGC Objectives were positive, although they were not uniformly positive across the items. All respondents were in agreement that the FGC coordinator was "respectful of the family group" (item 2), but sizable minorities disputed items on participant composition (item 7) and preparations (item 9). A case in point originated in Twanda and Chandra's conference where the questionnaire scores revealed disagreement with the statement that the "family group was prepared for the conference."

The original questionnaire included 25 items, but this number was reduced to the 14 items in the current version of the Achievement of FGC Objectives. The selection of items for retention was based on two criteria. First, priority was given to items that, for the most part, were scored by family group members, because their views were of greater concern than those of the FGC coordinators and research observers. Second, a factor analysis of the 111 questionnaires with complete responses found that groups of objectives tended to be scored similarly by respondents, these formed three reliable subscales, and the 14 items in the three subscales were retained (Pennell, 2004).

What are the three subscales of the Achievement of FGC Objectives?

Each subscale or group of objectives serves as an indicator of one of the three pathways to *safeguarding children, young people, and their families.* The subscales for cultural safety, community partnerships, and family leadership are shown in Figure 7-2.

The first group has four objectives that all point to the conference being held in a way that felt right to the family group and is an indicator of the cultural safety pathway. Three of the items relate to the family's culture: where and how the conference was held and who was in attendance. When achieved, these objectives heighten the family members' sense that the proceedings are appropriate and set them at greater ease. The fourth item, "enough supports and protections," is about ensuring that the family feels the physical and emotional safety required to participate. Its inclusion demonstrates the link between cultural safety and physical/emotional safety.

The second subscale likewise has four objectives, each relating to the community partnerships pathway. These objectives emphasize that service providers must be clear about their role at the conference, the family group must understand why the conference has been convened, and both service providers and family group must be prepared to take part. Being clear about role, purpose, and process helps the partners carry out their distinctive tasks in a local collaboration to achieve shared goals.

The third and last subscale includes six objectives, all about empowering the family group to make a plan, and each integral to the family leadership pathway. Three sets of two objectives frame, respectively, the relationship of the FGC coordinator to the family group, the relationship of the service providers to the family group, and the relationships among family group members. The first set highlights the respect that the FGC coordinators demonstrate toward the family group and the capacity of coordinators to focus on organizing and convening the conference, rather than counseling, policing, or judging the family group. This pair of objectives lessens role confusion and supports the family group members as competent decision makers. The second set is about balancing the power between the service providers and the family group and affirming the efficacy of the family group; simply having more family group members than service providers present helps to achieve the first objective, and having the service providers offer information, rather than dictate solutions, helps to achieve the second objective. The third set of objectives in this subscale places the family group at the center of the search for solutions to family problems during the conference (the family's private time) and after the conference (their contributions to the plan). With the service providers outside the room, family groups can use the private time to ventilate, confront, sympathize, reminisce, and take charge of making a plan (see chapter 3). They can tap into their knowledge of their family and determine ways to help out after the conference. As a result, the plans include their commitment to donate their time and resources to their relatives.

How is the questionnaire interpreted?

First, it is helpful just to scan the questionnaire and look for convergences and discrepancies between the scores and the comments made during the interview or in the reflective notes. Scanning can be useful both for questionnaires from participants at the same conference and for questionnaires across multiple conferences. It is an important step in identifying patterns grounded in the data. Taking those from Twanda and Chandra's con-

ference, all data sources concurred that preparations were insufficient, and their observations and reflections highlighted the resulting confusion at the conference.

A next step is to look at the scores on each of the three subscales, as they can point out pathways that require particular attention. Figure 7-2 shows the aggregated and then averaged responses of the four individuals who completed the Achievement of FGC Objectives on Twanda and Chandra's conference. Among the three subscales, the one for community partnerships, not surprisingly, has the lowest subtotal average. Its average of 2.25 falls between the scores 2 (disagree) and 3 (agree), but is closer to disagree. This low subtotal is in keeping with the feedback that participants were unclear about what they were expected to do at the conference. The second lowest subtotal average is 2.8 for cultural safety. Again this average lies between 2 (disagree) and 3 (agree), but in this instance is closer to agree. It reflects the unease experienced by participants at the conference. The family leadership pathway has by far the highest subtotal average of 3.4, which is between agree and strongly agree. This testifies to the competence of the coordinator in dealing with a confused situation and to capacity of the family group members to make their own plan after the conference.

Do participants in different roles give the same scores on the questionnaire?

For the most part, family group members, coordinators, and research observers at the same conference score the questionnaires differently. To check whether participants at the same conference gave different scores, an independence test for small samples (Cochran-Mantel-Haenszel statistic) was applied to

FIGURE 7-2
Subscales of Achievement of FGC Objectives (Pre-conference and Conference)
for Twanda and Chandra's FGC

Cultural Safety: Conference held in the right way for family group.

11	5.	The conference was held in a place that felt right to the family group.
11	6.	The conference was held in a way that felt right to the family group (ex., the right food, right time of day).
8[a]	8.	People at the conference were relatives and also people who feel "like family" (ex., old friends, good neighbors).
12	11.	The conference had enough supports and protections (ex., support persons).
42		**Subtotal 42/15 = 2.8**

Community Partnerships: Family group and service providers clear about what doing.

10	1.	Each service provider was clear about their role (ex., child protection, counseling).
9	4.	The family group understood the reasons for holding the conference.
7	9.	The family group was prepared for the conference (ex., got enough information on what happens at a conference).
10	10.	The service providers were prepared for the conference (ex., got enough information on what happens at a conference).
36		**Subtotal 36/16 = 2.25**

Family Leadership: Family group empowered to make a plan.

15	2.	The FGC coordinator was respectful of the family group.
14	3.	The only job of the FGC coordinator was to organize the conference. He/she did *not* have other jobs to do with the family.
10[a]	7.	More family group than service providers were invited to the conference.
13	12.	Service providers shared their knowledge, but they did not tell the family group how to solve the problems.
13	13.	The family group had private time to make their plan.
10[a]	14.	The plan included ways that the family group will help out.
75		**Subtotal 75/22 = 3.4**

[a]One missing datum.

Source: Pennell, J. (2003b, June). FGC key principles—Are we following them in practice? Paper presented at the Pathways to Permanence: 2003 Family Group Decision Making Conference and Skills-Building Institutes workshop, Minneapolis. Reprinted with permission.

the Achievement of FGC Objectives. For this test, a significant finding is interpreted to mean that the answers were dependent, in other words, that the respondents tended to concur in their scoring of an objective. The data come from the 21 of 30 conferences for which questionnaires had been completed by a family group member, a coordinator, and a research observer, making a total of 63 respondents. Where feasible, the mother or primary caregiver was selected as the family representative.

For each of the 14 objectives, the scores were compared for the coordinator with a family group member, the coordinator with the research observer, and the research observer with a family group member, resulting in a total of 42 comparisons (14 objectives × three matched pairs). Among the 42 comparisons, only three significant correlations ($p < .05$) were found to support the conclusion that the respondents held similar views on the achievement of the objective:

○ Coordinator by family group member: objective 11 (the conference had enough supports and protections). Although family group members and coordinators agreed on the rating of only one objective, it is the one for which disagreement would have raised the greatest concern. This result shows that coordinators were aware of the extent to which family group members felt supported and protected at the conference.
○ Coordinator by research observer: objectives 7 (more family group than service providers were invited to the conference) and 9 (the family group was prepared for the conference). A possible explanation for these two

convergences is that the researcher would have been able to observe directly or infer with relative assurance the attainment of these two objectives at the conference.
○ Research observer by family group member: none. Strikingly, there was no overall agreement between the views of the family group representative and the research observer who sat in on the conference.

With these three exceptions, the matched pairs generally diverged on whether the FGC objectives had been achieved. This finding makes sense in that the 14 objectives are largely about how the family group members experienced the conference. In item 5 (the conference was held in a place that felt right to the family group), for example, a program evaluator should not assume that the views of an FGC coordinator or research observer can represent those of the family group. Thus, an evaluation should include a consultation with the family group as to whether the model was faithfully enacted.

What does the Achievement of FGC Objectives leave out?

The current questionnaire includes at least one item related to each of the FGC principles 2 through 7, but does not encompass all of their stipulated key practices (see Pennell, 2003a). For example, none of the objectives reference "building in monitoring and evaluation of plans and follow-up meetings." The original questionnaire included 11 more objectives than those presented in Figure 7-1. Perhaps with simpler wording, some might be re-incorporated into the questionnaire.

Other omissions reflect the fact that the family group had no way of knowing how to answer questions in certain areas. For example, an item asking if service providers agreed with the reasons for holding the conference was removed, because family group members frequently responded that they did not know. On the one hand, deleting the objective helps keep the focus on the areas where the family group members can make a judgment; on the other hand, however, it directs attention away from an important aspect of community partnerships—agreement on purpose. As a consequence, the questionnaire fails to signal an important issue for FGC implementation. In the future, more items may be added to the current subscales to enrich understanding of the three pathways.

The questionnaire has a Likert scale of only four possible choices and only positively worded items. As previously noted, these features ease administration of the questionnaire by telephone with respondents of wide-ranging ages. At the same time, the positive wording of all items increases the tendency of respondents to give one answer across the questionnaire rather than thinking through their scores, as they must when some items are reversed. Having limited choices in scoring prevents respondents from giving more qualified answers, and it is likely that the distance between a "disagree" and an "agree" is far greater than that between these responses and their "strongly" version. For instance, the respondents for Twanda and Chandra's conference all concurred that family private time had taken place, even though it was only 10 minutes in length and the family group was unable to make a plan together. Perhaps if they had had the options of "slightly disagree" or "slightly agree," they might

have selected one of these rather than simply answering "agree." Nevertheless, the advantage of the four-point scale with each point labeled is that it encourages the respondent to take a stance on whether they agree or disagree.

It is likely that more than three subscales are required to encompass a full range of FGC objectives. An intriguing possibility is a fourth pathway—inclusive planning. A further analysis of the Achievement of FGC Objectives points to such a possibility (Pennell, in press-b; see chapter 10).

The Achievement of FGC Objectives covers only key principles encompassing preparation and conference activities. Separate measures should be used for the post-conference activities (fulfill the purpose of the plan), for the community building (build broad-based support and cultural competence), and for organizational development (change policies, procedures, and resources to sustain partnerships among family groups, community organizations, and public agencies).

What are the strengths of the Achievement of FGC Objectives?

The North Carolina FGC Project tested the Achievement of FGC Objectives with families from varied backgrounds. The specific family example in this chapter shows that the Achievement of FGC Objectives can signal areas requiring changes in implementation. *As a measure of model fidelity, the questionnaire has a number of strong points*:

○ The FGC key principles and practices are based on empowerment theory and the study of FGC implementation in different cultural contexts.

○ The Achievement of FGC Objectives operationalizes the FGC principles and practices and makes possible an evaluation of the extent to which implementation occurs.

○ The questionnaire can be administered in person or by telephone.

○ Family group members usually are able to complete all or most items.

○ The responses point to areas for improving practice, training, and policy.

○ The scores reveal differences in views on model fidelity at the same conference.

○ The scores fit with the comments that participants make in describing the conference or explaining their answers on the Achievement of FGC Objectives.

○ The questionnaire has three reliable subscales—cultural safety, community partnerships, and family leadership—that are congruent with theory on widening the circle to safeguard children, young people, and other family members.

The Achievement of FGC Objectives is a tested questionnaire for measuring whether an FGC program carries out its essential practices or activities. Thus, it serves as a way to establish the central link in a logic model between an FGC program's resources and inputs and its desired outcomes.

8

Identifying Short-Term and Long-Term FGC Outcomes

Gary R. Anderson and Peg Whalen

Gaining an understanding of family group conferencing (FGC) requires an exploration of both the processes and the outcomes associated with this innovative practice. As with any innovation, but particularly with those involving child welfare services, it is necessary to link interventions with outcomes; with FGC, it is necessary to connect the conferencing interventions to improvements in the child and family outcomes of safety, permanency, and well-being.

The achievement of, or failure to achieve, outcomes occurs at multiple levels. Therefore, it is critical that advocates of FGC understand and evaluate the various aspects of FGC outcomes for individual children, their families, and their communities. Successful outcomes are essential to demonstrate the benefits of FGC. Accountability for cost-effectiveness is an important consideration, as well.

Outcomes may be short or long term. Short-term outcomes, as discussed in this chapter, include immediate outcomes—

what is expected or aimed for and achieved at the time of the intervention or action—and intermediate outcomes—what is achieved in an extended time span following the intervention and that contribute to long-term outcomes. Immediate outcomes address questions such as the following: Did the family participate? Was it possible to construct an acceptable plan? Was the family group satisfied with the process and the resulting plan? Intermediate outcomes focus on such issues as whether family members and service providers carried out their parts of the plan, whether conferences were reconvened as necessary, and whether plans were revised. Long-term outcomes address the ultimate goals in child welfare systems: safety, permanency, and child and family well-being.

Why is it important to measure both FGC processes and outcomes?

The focus on the processes associated with the implementation of FGC has merit and value. The ability to describe the activities associated with FGC informs training, program improvements and modifications, and replication. Describing how FGC operates is necessary to understand this relatively new model of practice. As part of the examination of the processes, it is also necessary to describe how well the design was followed and the extent to which FGC accomplished each of the tasks and activities that comprise the model.

As a new model of service delivery, the activities and process elements of the model must be identified and described. For example, the length of time between referral and the first family conference, the nature and extent of a coordinator's activity in preparation for the conference, the number of family members in attendance at the conference, and the length of time required both for the conference as a whole and also for the family's private time provide useful descriptive information. This type of information not only helps FGC programs maintain some measure of model fidelity, but also has implications for training and replication. Without a thorough understanding of FGC and how it unfolds, it may be difficult to ascertain what specific aspects of the model make a difference for families and result in positive outcomes. Also, a well-defined system of intervention is an essential early step toward developing a successful outcomes-based, decision-making model (Casey Outcomes and Decision-Making Project/American Humane Association [CODMP/AHA], 1998).

Description of the process does not establish that FGC has positive results for families. Process evaluation is, however, a necessary starting point for outcome assessment. Assessing the implementation of the service makes it possible to reason-

ably demonstrate that FGC was delivered in the manner in which it was intended and designed. It also provides an estimation of effort, for example, the nature and intensity of coordinator activities. These activities can be clearly and systematically examined.

In addition to the assessment of processes that determines what program activities are the means to achieving desired ends, the assessment of program outcomes in child welfare and child protective service delivery is essential. As interesting as the FGC process may be, the ultimate goal is not simply to convene a family meeting or to construct an acceptable plan. The successful convening of a family group conference and the development of a detailed plan reflecting the leadership of the family are objectives that may have multiple positive features and results for a family, and it is these results that must be considered when evaluating the success of FGC. A focus on the outcomes of FGC identifies the actual impact and effect of the conference activities on the family, and others, as well as on the problems that brought the family to the attention of the child protection system.

How do federal initiatives frame the context for FGC outcomes?

Stakeholders, consumers, and funding bodies ask human service organizations and the programs, strategies, and intervention models that they employ to demonstrate that their programs and actions achieve desired and expected results. This emphasis on program and intervention outcomes is evident at the national level with the Child and Family Services Reviews (CFSRs) of the U.S. Department of Health and Human Services (HHS) and in the resulting reports to Congress and the public.

The Social Security Act Amendments of 1994 and the Adoption and Safe Families Act of 1997 mandate the evaluation of systemic and programmatic outcomes of child welfare interventions in the United States. With respect to this legislation, HHS has established seven child welfare outcomes as a basis on which to judge a state child welfare system's performance: the child welfare system's ability to

1. Reduce recurrence of child abuse and/neglect
2. Reduce the incidence of child abuse and/or neglect in foster care
3. Increase permanency for children in foster care
4. Reduce time in foster care to reunification without increasing reentry
5. Reduce time in foster care to adoption
6. Increase placement stability
7. Reduce placements of young children in group homes or institutions (HHS, 2000, pp. I-2–I-4).

The federal government collects information from each state to measure outcome achievement. Information is gathered from case record reviews, interviews with stakeholders, and statewide administrative data collected by the states and reported to the federal government through the Adoption and Foster Care Analysis and Reporting System (2001) and the National Child Abuse and Neglect Data System.

There are a number of ways to determine whether a desired outcome has been attained. In one method, it is necessary to compare the child welfare system's performance in one year with its performance in prior years. For example, a comparison of the number of children who have a re-currence of abuse in one year to the number of such children in a prior or subsequent year provides some measure of a state's progress toward reducing the recurrence of abuse. National standards provide another point of comparison. The average or median experience of other states can be contrasted with a state's rate of child abuse recurrence to determine if the state's rate is either higher or lower than that of other states. Also, the state's rate or experience with the seven basic child welfare outcomes, for example, the length of time in foster care until adoption, can be compared to an established federal standard.

The federal CFSRs address outcomes that parallel the seven HHS child welfare outcomes:

○ With respect to safety:
1. Children are, first and foremost, protected from abuse and neglect;
2. Children are safely maintained in their own homes whenever possible and appropriate;

○ With respect to permanency:
1. Children have permanency and stability in their living situations;
2. The continuity of family relationships and connections is preserved for children;

○ With respect to child and family well-being:
1. Families have enhanced capacity to provide for their children's needs;
2. Children receive appropriate services to meet their educational needs;
3. Children receive adequate services to meet their physical and mental health needs. (HHS, 2000, p. 47)

The CFSR also examines seven systemic factors that are known to have a direct impact on the state's ability to deliver the services that will achieve these outcomes and substantially meet or exceed federal standards with regard to the primary HHS child welfare outcomes. The following seven systemic factors inform one or more of the outcomes enumerated by the CFSR. Reviewers determine if there is

1. A statewide information system that makes it possible to readily track the status, characteristics, location, and goals for children in foster care;
2. A case review system that provides a written case plan for each child, developed jointly with the child's parents, and that supports required reviews and timely hearings;
3. A quality assurance system that addresses the quality of services and includes an evaluation of and report on these services;
4. Adequate staff training to address the state's child welfare goals, including on-going worker training and training for foster and adoptive parents;
5. A service array that provides a range of services that can be individualized to meet the safety, permanency, and well-being needs of the child and family;
6. Evidence of agency responsiveness to the community and consultation with major stakeholders;
7. A set of standards for foster and adoptive parent licensing, recruitment, and retention. (HHS, 2000, pp. 47–48)

Within this federal emphasis on outcomes, FGC operates and shares multiple features.

What are the expected short-term outcomes of FGC?

Although a number of prominent features associated with FGC support the systemic factors that are examined in the CFSRs, FGC encompasses a broader range of desired immediate and intermediate impacts. FGC should result in an experience and a plan that family members find to be *culturally appropriate and sensitive.* The family conference, through sharing information with family members and placing decision-making opportunities in the hands of the family, supports a sense of *family responsibility* for its members, particularly its children. The involvement of extended family, significant friends and advisers, and community professionals promotes *family and community connectedness.* The respectful provision of information, a private family meeting to make a plan, its successful negotiation with the coordinator and child protective services staff, and the implementation of the plan can promote *family pride and esteem.* These factors are intended results of FGC and comprise an aspect of FGC evaluation, along with traditional child welfare outcomes.

Immediate Outcomes

Family group conferencing aims to encourage a truly equal partnership between professionals and family members, and to give families a greater say in decisions that affect them and their children (Burford & Hudson, 2000; Lupton & Stevens, 1997). Consequently, the identification of FGC immediate/short-term outcomes addresses such questions as,

○ To what extent are family members included in the conferences, and do family members report that they are taken seriously (have a "real say") and participate actively in this conference?

- To what extent do family members and professionals have a genuine partnership in the decision making? For example, do the professionals unduly influence the decisions made by family members and the resulting family plan?
- To what extent are family members provided with adequate information before and during the conference?
- To what extent do professionals and family members view the conference as productive and positive in creating an acceptable family plan?

FAMILY PARTICIPATION. One of the objectives of FGC is to encourage the participation of family members in the planning process. In FGC, the role of family members is more extensive and intentional than that found in other models, as FGC seeks to include a high number and broad range of family members. It also includes and values the participation of fictive kin and community members who have a strong connection to the child and family.

This wider approach extends not only to family members' participation, but also to their leadership—particularly evident in respect for the family's private time. Consequently, counting the number of participants and identifying the range of participants provides a perspective on only one aspect of conference success. Although measuring attendance is quite discrete and concrete, measuring participation presents a greater challenge. The primary means used to determine FGC attendee participation has been coordinator observations and satisfaction surveys.

FAMILY PLAN. In addition to a respectful, collaborative process, an immediate outcome of a family group conference is the development of a family plan. The FGC objective is to construct a family plan, guided by the family's leadership, that ensures the child's safety and well-being. This plan must be acceptable to the child's parents, to the FGC coordinator, and to the child protective services agency. In fact, many programs require written approval of the plan from the child protective services agency when the FGC has been convened based on an agency's referral (typically at an early date in the child welfare intervention process). This approval and agreement may require additional negotiations between the family members, coordinator, and the CPS worker. Consequently, the fact that a conference results in such a plan provides a potentially useful indicator for assessing the conference. The overall rate of acceptable plans reached through FGC provides some measure of the program's success.

In addition to ensuring the safety and well-being of children, the FGC family plan should have a number of features. As described in chapter 3, the plan should reflect the diverse input of family members and input from attending (or corresponding) professionals. Plan content and wording should contain sufficient detail to guide the family's work after the conference. Several people should share responsibility for implementing the plan. Overall, the plan should be respectful of family leadership and responsibility. A plan crafted in such a manner will be individualized to meet the unique needs and resources of a child and the family.

Consequently plans should contain details and provisions that case plans constructed through traditional service planning do not typically have.

Some of these elements might reflect attentiveness to daily living and the perspectives of family members that may be overlooked in professionally guided case planning. The presence of nontraditional, family-specific items is a process outcome that demonstrates the individuality of family plans and attentiveness to the family's responsibility for planning (Gunderson, Cahn, & Wirth, 2003). The nature of the family plan may indicate whether family leadership has been evident through the conference. Other studies have also found that FGC plans go beyond standard service plans (Gunderson, Cahn, & Wirth, 2003; Pennell & Burford, 1995).

Even when the plan items are fairly traditional—such as arranging for transportation or respite care—the family plans are innovative in the responsibility assignments. For example, in one case, one of the child's aunts volunteered to provide child care while another aunt provided transportation for the mother to get to counseling. In one program, 50 percent of the plans included tasks to be done by fathers or paternal relatives. This increased attendance and participation by fathers and paternal relatives is cited as a positive process outcome associated with FGC (Gunderson, Cahn, & Wirth, 2003; Merkel-Holguin, 2003). The individualized, family-involved, and detailed nature of the family plans matches the distinct objectives of FGC.

PARTICIPANT SATISFACTION. Family member and professional satisfaction with FGC provides useful data beyond process description. If the measurement of satisfaction is framed as a means to obtain a range of feedback from stakeholders, its value in understanding FGC is increased beyond simply learning family members'

level of satisfaction with the FGC experience. Short-term goals of FGC—that is, engaging family members in the problem-solving process, respecting family participation and leadership in decision making, and the participants' assessment of the viability of the family plan with respect to child safety and well-being—are measures of success in relation to the aims of FGC. Measuring satisfaction, particularly the satisfaction of family members, provides a perspective to evaluate the quality and benefits of a service, improves accountability to families, and serves as an indicator of perceived quality of service (CODMP/AHA, 1998).

A range of questions posed to family members, to coordinators, and to other participants can help assess the success of the conference by providing information about preparations for the conference, the actual conference proceedings, the nature of the family plan, and stakeholders' overall evaluation of the value and effectiveness of the conference. Questions posed to family members could include the following:

○ Before attending the family group conference, did you understand its purpose?

○ In your opinion, was the conference helpful?

○ At the end of the conference, how comfortable were you that the child(ren) would be safe?

○ Did you feel that the FGC coordinator was helpful to your family?

○ In general, did you feel you were respected and your comments valued?

○ Did you feel that the FGC coordinator listened to you?

○ Did you feel that your family listened to you and understood you?

○ Did you feel that the family's private time was helpful?

○ In the end, how satisfied were you with the way that the family plan was reached?

○ Would you recommend FGC to other families like yours?

Questions posed to FGC coordinators could include the following:

○ From your perspective, how comfortable are you that the child(ren) are safe?

○ From your perspective, how comfortable are you that the child(ren) are in an appropriate placement or home?

○ Would you recommend FGC to your colleagues?

○ How satisfied are you with the referring worker's involvement?

○ How satisfied are you with the involvement of other professionals?

○ How satisfied are you with the conference overall?

○ How satisfied are you with the fine-tuning of the family plan?

Questions posed to referring workers could include the following:

○ Prior to the FGC, to what extent did the coordinator share information with you that you needed or wanted to know?

○ Were you satisfied with the pre-meeting contacts made with you by the coordinator?

○ Overall, were you satisfied with the conference?

○ Were you clear about your role in the conference?

○ During the conference, do you believe that the other participants listened to

and understood the comments or information that you offered?

○ At the conference, were you comfortable saying or contributing what you wanted to say or contribute?

○ To what extent were the hopes that you had when referring this family to FGC met?

○ Before the meeting, how interested were you in participating in this particular conference?

○ Since referring this family to FGC, has your original level of interest in FGC increased, remained the same, or decreased?

○ Would you recommend FGC to your colleagues?

Questions to participating professionals could include the following:

○ Were you clear about your role in the conference?

○ At the conference, did you say what you wanted to say or contribute?

○ If you did speak or otherwise contribute to the conference, do you believe that the participants listened to you?

○ To what extent did the conference result in a potentially safe and effective plan for the children?

○ To what extent were your hopes for the family's participation in FGC met?

○ Would you recommend FGC to your colleagues?

○ Overall, were you satisfied with the conference?

○ To what extent has your interest in FGC increased, remained the same, or decreased?

The Casey Outcomes and Decision-Making Project, with the American Humane Association, noted that family satisfaction is not in itself an outcome measure. However, "family satisfaction issues related to quality have a heightened importance in involuntary relationships, where respect and empathy reinforce the basic principles of child welfare service delivery" (CODMP/AHA, 1998, p. 23). Gaining an understanding of participants' satisfaction with FGC and their assessment of their roles and contributions to the successful development of the family plan provides valuable information about the usefulness of FGC. To the extent that different stakeholders provide an assessment of the value of the family plan in ensuring the safety of children and the appropriateness of the child's placement, the satisfaction questions posed begin to address child welfare outcomes of safety, permanency, and well-being.

Intermediate Outcomes

Questions about family participation, the respectfulness and collaborativeness of the process, and the creation of a family plan address issues of importance to FGC, but seem to assume that the ultimate goal of FGC is to have a productive conference. As valuable as a positive conference experience may be, there must also be a focus on a range of other FGC outcomes. The development of a family plan that is acceptable to the family and professionals, and addresses the specific issues related to the safety and well-being of the focus child is a necessary, but not a fully sufficient, outcome. Other important outcome issues relate to the successful implementation of the family plan and a post-conference assessment of child safety, permanency, and well-being.

After the conference, the achievement of intermediate outcomes can be assessed by asking questions such as the following:

○ To what extent is the plan actually carried out?
○ What features of the written family plan were implemented, and what aspects needed to be renegotiated or dropped from the plan?
○ To what extent are the resources necessary to successfully implement the plan available and accessible to family members?
○ To what extent do family members express satisfaction with the plan after the conference, and at later points in time?

There also are post-service outcome questions related to child welfare systems' fundamental outcome measures:

○ Does FGC provide for the *ongoing safety* of children?
○ To what extent are the children who participate in FGC because of reported child abuse or neglect, *re-reported* for abuse or neglect?
○ To what extent does FGC assist in maintaining children *safely in their own homes*?
○ To what extent does FGC reduce the use of *out-of-home* placements?
○ To what extent does the FGC interventions improve children's educational, health, and mental health status?

Cost and benefit issues are also central to the development, implementation, replication, and generalization of new program models:

○ Does FGC result in cost savings for child welfare systems or keep costs neutral while improving outcomes?
○ Is FGC more expensive than other innovations or existing/traditional

service delivery options in the short term, in the long term, or both?

Addressing long-term outcomes is important because FGC is ultimately concerned with the safety and well-being of children and families. These outcomes are reinforced by their link to federal policy.

What are the expected long-term outcomes for FGC?

The detailed process descriptions of FGC programs, the meeting of objectives that are distinct and central to FGC, and the assessment of key stakeholders' perceptions all contribute to the evaluation of FGC. However, a crucial assessment of the success of FGC rests with a demonstration that FGC achieves the highly valued child welfare outcomes. Achieving these outcomes is especially important in commending FGC to child welfare administrators and funders. An approach that is respectful of families, encourages family participation and responsibility, and results in collaboratively developed and implemented plans is important, but even these powerful positive values may not be sufficient for all state leaders and may not compensate for the lack of information about traditional child welfare outcomes. Ultimately, developing a solid foundation of support and moving FGC from pilot programs to a highly valued part of the child welfare continuum will depend on addressing traditional child welfare outcomes.

Safety

A primary goal for FGC is the protection of children. The purpose of the family plan is to craft a set of actions that will, at a minimum, ensure the immediate and long-term safety of children. Depending on the program and location, safety may be a particularly pressing issue particularly if families referred for FGC have been assessed as being at moderate to high risk for child maltreatment, there is an imminent risk of out-of-home placement, or such a placement may already be arranged to protect the child.

The issue of safety is also relevant to evaluating the experience of the child and family during the conference. In fact, when hearing a description of the model and the stages of FGC, some professionals and family advocates wonder if it is safe to bring a wider circle of family members together and then leave them alone. The success of the safety plan developed by the coordinator for the conference is an essential component of measuring safety. The number of incidents of harm and threats to safety at conferences constitutes one measure of safety. In more than 200 FGC cases in Michigan's pilot program, for example, there were sometimes reports of considerable emotion, but no reports of dangerous behavior or harm at the conferences (Anderson, 2003). Other studies have reported no violence (Marsh & Crow, 1998; Pennell & Burford, 1995) or only rare incidents (Paterson & Harvey, 1991).

The primary measure of child safety is whether the child is safe after the conference. Does the plan address the factors that contributed to the risk of maltreatment or the need for an out-of-home placement? Even if the plan addresses the appropriate issues, are sufficient resources available and accessible to the family? Did the family comply with the family plan?

One way to determine the safety of the child is to look for re-referrals to child protective services after the initial conference. It may not be possible to state absolutely that a re-referral constitutes new or additional harm to children, as the re-referral may not be accurate or substantiated. Consequently, it is important to ascertain whether a child protective services report has been substantiated.

The measurement of re-abuse or neglect requires identifying children at risk, tracking those children through a state's data system, and being aware to some extent of the outcome of that child protective service re-referral. If the family is still being monitored or is in a relationship with a coordinator or other child welfare worker, the case record may contain information about potential and actual risks to child safety. However, a case record or worker testimony generally cannot substitute for the official documented report. Documentation ensures some measure of conformity and congruence in calculating ongoing risk to a child's safety. Documentation using administrative data may have a number of limitations. For example, this information may not include an in depth look at what was happening in the family or community, or its meaning for children and families, communities and workers.

How should child protective re-referral rates be interpreted? A point of comparison between the re-referral rates for an FGC program and other programs provides some basis for understanding the meaning of this measure of safety. This point of comparison could be a targeted percentage of cases or existing state date and benchmarks (Titcomb & Lecroy, 2003). For example, in a Washington state study, the re-referral rate for children who had a family group conference was lower than the state's average re-referral rate (Gunderson, Cahn, & Wirth, 2003). What if the number of substantiated re-referrals for children who have had a family group conference exceeds the state average (or some other comparative measure) for recurrence of child abuse or neglect? For example, a Swedish evaluation of FGC found that re-referrals for child abuse were higher than re-referrals for a comparison group of children (Sundell & Vinnerljung, 2004). Does this mean that FGC has a negative outcome and should be judged to be a failure? There are multiple reasons why there may be re-abuse or neglect following FGC. For example:

○ The families served by FGC may present with higher risk (severity of child maltreatment or past history with CPS, for example) than generally found in the child protective services system. Referring workers may be sending very difficult cases to FGC; they may be seeing FGC as a last resort for a family that has failed to benefit from other services. Consequently, with a higher initial rate of risk, a higher rate of recurrence is probable.

○ The monitoring of families who have been involved in FGC may be greater than that of other families, particularly with the sharing of information and the sensitizing of a professional and extended family network through FGC. Consequently, higher referral rates may correlate with a more vigilant environment rather than greater actual rates of re-abuse.

○ Relatedly, the FGC process may result in a partnership between the FGC program and CPS, resulting in a closer working relationship and stronger communication and mutual respect—increasing the likelihood of referrals to CPS.

○ Other variables may distinguish the children who are referred to FGC from children who are not referred to FGC. For example, one study reported that children in FGC cases were more likely to be older children and adolescents whose behavior may more easily come to the attention of school and community officials (Lupton & Stevens, 1997).

○ Expectations with regard to the impact of FGC in affecting the behavior and patterns of family dynamics may be unrealistic. The power of one conference and its resultant plan may not be sufficient to undo long-term family patterns or neutralize the effects of multiple environmental stressors.

○ A referral may result from noncompliance with the plan or the unavailability of needed resources. The plan itself may not have been realistic or deliverable. Implementing a plan that requires consistent family member actions with, perhaps, minimal professional support may not be sufficient to support some families.

○ Sometimes, crises happen, and even well-crafted plans are not sustainable—this is a reason to craft a backup or contingency plan at the conference or to plan a second family group conference to review new circumstances and create a revised plan based on a different landscape.

In some cases, particularly those involving safety issues, FGC may be contraindicated. If children and family members were not consistently safe during the preparation for the conference and at the conference itself, FGC would not be an appropriate model. If it is impossible to construct plans that ensure the safety of children through a shared decision-making process with families, then there should be no conference. If children are consistently left or placed in dangerous situations following FGC, this is not an appropriate model. However, if children and families can be worked with safely before and during conferences, and these conferences can consistently result in acceptable plans that demonstrably ensure the safety of children, FGC warrants consideration.

Permanency

A number of children referred to FGC may already be placed outside of their homes for their protection. A conference may also result in a plan that removes the child from the parents and places the child with a relative or in a traditional foster home. Consequently, the evaluation of FGC also involves an assessment of permanency outcomes for children.

The primary consideration with regard to permanency is, Does FGC promote permanency by maintaining children safely in their own homes or by moving them into the least restrictive out-of-home placements that are best able to meet their needs?

Measurement of permanency requires identification of the child's placement at referral to FGC (that is, before the conference), the provisions or recommendations for placement at the conference, the steps taken for placement after the conference, and a review of living arrangements at various points of time following the conference. For example, how many children are in their own homes before the conference? What placements are determined at the conference? If a move is required (during FGC or after the conference), where does the child go, and how long is this new arrangement in place?

Some children need to be removed from their homes and placed in a safer setting. To interpret placement of children in a setting outside their own home as a failure negates the desired outcome for safety. Sometimes parents request and acknowledge the need for a placement outside the home. Permanency focuses on maintaining children in their homes, enabling a timely and safe reunification with their families (such that a re-referral for placement does not occur in a short time period), or arranging for a timely move to an adoptive home or other permanency outcome (such as guardianship). The family plan may result in sufficient support for a child to remain with the parents. If a child has already been placed outside the home, the family may craft and expedite a reunification plan. Or, the family plan may identify extended family resources so that a child is maintained within the extended family. There is some evidence to suggest that kinship care is a permanency outcome promoted by FGC (Anderson, 2003; Lupton & Stevens, 1997; Merkel-Holguin, 2003). Adoption is a less likely outcome of FGC because most programs use FGC at earlier points in intervention. There is some indication that parental rights may be terminated more quickly through FGC, however, if a judge knows that this has the agreement of all parties (Merkel-Holguin, 2003; Pennell & Burford, 2000a).

Permanency is a significant outcome as it has implications for the attachment and family connections of children. There may also be cost implications associated with permanency outcomes as children are kept in their own homes, placed with extended family, moved out of foster care, or adopted.

Well-Being

Although oftentimes the primary focus is on child safety and permanency, the federal CFSRs do include attention to child well-being outcomes. Specifically, they address a child's educational and physical health needs. The family plan crafted at the conference may include items related to the child's education—enrolling children in special programs, keeping the children in school, ensuring their consistent attendance, gaining other supports for children in school—and the child's physical health—calling for doctor's visits, promoting good nutrition, and making sure that the child gets enough rest. Assessment of parental/family implementation of family plan items and an assessment of the child's educational and health care status would address these well-being standards. One study showed that FGC led to improvements in children's development and in the support networks of mothers, which had implications for improved child well-being (Burford & Pennell, 1998).

What are some of the results and issues raised by outcome studies?

The majority of evaluations of FGC have focused on descriptive and process elements of the model (Merkel-Holguin, 2003). This focus has made some sense, given the new nature of the intervention. Why has FGC been implemented in multiple locations without strong, evidence-based outcome studies demonstrating its effectiveness? First, the values of FGC—respect for families, enhancement of family leadership and responsibility in case planning, and community involvement in responding to abuse and neglect—have resonated with professional values and perspectives. The experiences reported from New Zealand and the observations of professionals in other locales have supported the value of an intervention that is respectful of culture and tailored to families. Anecdotal information has provided some assurances with regard to the benefits of FGC. Satisfaction surveys have consistently reported high rates of positive involvement from family members and professional participants. Also, FGC has fit with system attempts to identify and implement nonadversarial means of conflict resolution (such as mediation) in response to the high cost and continuing challenges associated with traditional child welfare and court practice.

The child welfare system has been searching for means to reform and improve performance, but there are substantial evaluation studies for few models in child welfare. Advocates of FGC have recognized the need for evaluations that focus on program outcomes. A traditional, and generally preferred, means to demonstrate the effectiveness of FGC would be the use of an experimental design with control and experimental groups. This research design has rarely been undertaken for reasons familiar to child welfare researchers and evaluators, including (1) sample sizes are insufficient in size and diversity to support randomized case assignment; (2) there is sufficient support for the model so that withholding the intervention from appropriate families would create some ethical and/or political discomfort; and (3) there are practical barriers to an experimental design, including cost. As FGC has been in the early

stages of acceptance and implementation in the United States, the need, capacity, and support for experimentally designed evaluations may be met in the near future (for example, Thomas, Cohen, & Berrick, 2003).

One relatively early study in England concluded, "In contrast with the evidence on the FGC process, that on the outcomes of the process, particularly in the longer term, and in respect of child protection, is underdeveloped and ambiguous" (Lupton & Stevens, 1997, p. 10). These authors noted that the measurement of outcomes in FGC was problematic because of the "limited part played by the meeting in the lives of the families concerned" (p. 10). In other words, is it possible to attribute either success or failure to FGC when so many variables impinge on the lives of families and when FGC is a relatively brief intervention? Some of their conclusions with regard to outcomes included:

○ There was a high rate of overall agreement on family plans, with more plans rejected by family members than by professionals.

○ Less than half of the identified components in the family plans were delivered. They attributed this in large part to family member failure to do as they had agreed in the plan. They also noted that agencies did not always deliver resources and support as identified and that the reasons for this were unclear as the items identified in the family plan did not seem to be unrealistic.

○ Compared with those served in traditional meetings, the FGC families received less direct work and resources from professionals, perhaps because there were greater expectations that family members would find resources and support from the wider family group.

○ There was no evidence that FGC diverted children from state care; the number of children in residential care was not reduced; and the length of time children spent away from their original caregivers was greater than that of children placed through traditional meetings. Within family accommodations were being used in place of foster care.

A study conducted in Washington state (Gunderson et al., 2003), evaluating the outcomes of 70 family group conferences, noted a number of immediate outcomes:

○ Family member participation was high.

○ Parental involvement in conferences was high.

○ Family plans combined traditional and family-specific strategies.

○ Native Americans were represented in higher proportions in conferences.

Long-term outcomes included:

○ More children were living with their parents after the conference.

○ Fewer children were living with nonrelatives after the conference.

○ There was an increase in tribal jurisdiction over children after the conference.

○ The rate of re-referral for abuse and neglect was low over time.

○ Placements were stable over time.

An evaluation study of a blend of the Oregon and FGC models in San Diego,

California, reporting on more than 700 family meetings, concluded that "more children remain with their families; satisfaction with CPS [child protective services] is increased; public trust and satisfaction with the fairness of the case management decision-making process is enhanced; and certain types of re-referral rates for families and children who participate in FUM [family unity meetings] decrease" (Quinnett, Harrison, & Jones, 2003, p. 102).

In an evaluation study involving 54 families in Toronto, it was found that 58 children were in out-of-home care prior to FGC (Schmid & Goranson, 2003). Only six children remained in care or were taken into care after their conference. Family members reported many positive responses to FGC, including increased support from extended family and a sense that their children's safety and well-being had improved as a result of FGC. Child welfare staff were generally satisfied with FGC family plans. The study also concluded that FGC was cost-effective.

A review of outcome studies demonstrates that in the past decade, as FGC programs have been introduced in the United States and around the world, information about the impact and outcomes of these projects is growing. Relying on agency records, administrative data, interviews, surveys, and observations, evaluators are working to develop a body of knowledge addressing the short-term and long-term outcomes of FGC (Merkel-Holguin, 2003). These studies examine the FGC process and the long-term outcomes commonly associated with the child welfare system—the safety of children, the permanency of their placement, and child and family well-being.

What are some of the challenges in evaluating FGC outcomes?

There are a number of challenges in measuring the achievement of outcomes. For example:

O Critical data are often difficult to locate and compile, as there are shortcomings in data collection systems; the information gathered may be insufficient or inconsistent.

O Some events or factors may be difficult to identify.

O Measurement instruments may not yet be developed, or may be relatively untested.

O Comparisons may be nearly impossible, as data and program elements are not comparable.

O Without controlled trials, other interventions, life circumstances, community and service array factors, and personal factors may cloud the "true" effect of FGC. Even with controlled trials, an array of factors may make it difficult to assert effectiveness, or noneffectiveness, with confidence.

O There may be some confusion between compliance with a plan and genuine, substantial family and personal change.

O As time passes, it is more difficult to separate events that might naturally occur over time from the effect of FGC.

O Even when outcomes are noted, it may not be possible to trace the specific processes that either affected or failed to affect the outcome.

O Agency records, coordinators, or others may not capture the factors that affect the outcomes.

O Some factors may have inverse relationships. For example, maximizing

family responsibility and decision making may minimize the safety of the child.

O There may not be enough cases to clearly identify the significance of program elements.

O Measures may be too broad to be helpful.

O Definitions may be imprecise.

O There may be conflicts between the desired outcomes of family members and those of professionals or other participants.

O Data may be retrospective, so that it is subject to memory or other distortions (Health Care Advisory Board, 1993).

The importance of identifying, describing, and addressing outcomes is certain; the challenges in doing so are many. These issues in studying outcomes can be addressed, but there is another challenge—finding the time and resources to devote to this important aspect of program development and implementation.

Conclusion

Informed and guided by a set of values and building on family and community resources, FGC produces a wide variety of short- and long-term outcomes. The immediate outcomes include convening a conference, conducting the conference, and creating a plan, all of which result in

O improved parental and family knowledge of the child's needs and actions that may endanger children

O increased family knowledge about the resources in the community that are available to support the children and family

○ increased safety for family members during the conference.

Intermediate outcomes, which follow soon after the conference, include

○ increased family ability to work together to address safety and other needs of children
○ improvement in the community's ability to support the parents and children
○ increased community involvement with the family
○ less stress for parents and children
○ clear direction for the family and community partner to ensure longer term outcomes.

Long-term outcomes address the safety, permanency, and well-being of children:

○ Reducing the risk to children after the conference
○ Preventing worsening or recurrence of harmful parental behaviors
○ Removing or reducing the need for involvement with child protective services

○ Keeping children with their parents, when safe to do so
○ Keeping children within the wider family circle, when there are appropriate caregivers
○ Restoring the family when a temporary out-of-home placement is required
○ Implementing a plan that addresses the educational, physical health, and mental health needs of children and family members

The central values and processes of FGC focus on shared decision making within the context of an extended family and those community members and professionals connected to the family. This respectful approach to families supports a plan and process designed to keep children safe and promote their connection to their families. Although the processes and outcomes of FGC match the goals of the child welfare system and provide a model for addressing and achieving these desired goals, gaining and strengthening evidence that demonstrates the effectiveness of FGC is an ongoing challenge.

9

Calculating the Costs and Benefits of Family Group Conferencing

Andy Rowe

In the context of contemporary governance and accountability, programs must recognize that they are accountable for the achievement of desired results. Programs are supposed to be making information-based decisions to adapt and improve their services so that they are as effective as possible, and they are also supposed to have the flexibility that they need to make the changes necessary to enhance that effectiveness. This flexibility can open doors for family group conferencing (FGC), but programs must accept that their funding is contingent on their achieving and reporting the accomplishment of desired results. Potential funders view innovative programs, such as FGC, as "riskier." Successfully addressing these funder perceptions can be an important part of ensuring funders of the viability of FGC.

Effectiveness is a concept that is freely expressed and rarely addressed. Yet, it is at the core of this governance logic. It is integral to useful social programming such as FGC.

Why is effectiveness important?

The effectiveness of a program represents the return that society receives from its investments in addressing the problem. Put simply, effectiveness is a means of comparing the benefits (from a social program) to the resources (costs) that were required to obtain those benefits. Given the deeply entrenched social problems that need to be addressed, it is essential to obtain the greatest net value or benefit from social investments.

Unfortunately, measurement of costs and benefits sometimes misrepresents a program. There are many reasons for this, including the difficulty of the measurement task itself and resistance on the part of the program. Although it is a real barrier, this resistance is understandable when the requests for effectiveness measures usually come from funders who are starting to question the usefulness of their investments. This is particularly applicable to innovative programs such as FGC.

The dysfunctional relationship between funders and programs around program effectiveness has been finely tuned into an intricate dance in which both sides are elegant and skillful partners, as co-dependent as any good dance team. Perhaps the Dysfunctional Effectiveness Dance, or the Social Program Six Step, sounds familiar:

1. The program, running for several years, is required to produce measures of effectiveness by funders who are looking for a concrete and defensible reason for renewing, reducing, or discontinuing funding.

2. The funder is frustrated by and resentful of the apparent unwillingness and disinterest of the program in trying to improve the effectiveness of its investments.

3. The funder defines a measure of effectiveness that is incomprehensible to the program and seemingly bears little resemblance to the program itself. The funder either uses data from the program proposal and annual reports or requires that the program provide the information, to calculate the measure.

4. Those whose job it is to measure effectiveness experience extreme frustration at the systematic lack of planning and record keeping by the program. Because they have only limited data, what they can measure is an unrepresentative snapshot of the program—an overestimation of the more easily accessible costs against the more difficult to measure benefits, leading to systematic underestimation of the effectiveness of the program.

5. The program resents the use of unrepresentative snapshots that systematically underestimate their effectiveness and that are used in decisions to reduce or eliminate funding.

6. Funders resent the resistance of the program, first to measuring effectiveness and then to using the measures to adjudicate among the many valid competing requests that they receive for support. They interpret this as a lack of accountability by the program.

The emergence of results-based accountability has changed the dance card. Government and foundation funders now require programs to be accountable for the results that they are supposed to be achieving and to undertake defensible outcome measurements. In essence, the government, through such acts as the Government Performance and Results (GPRA) Act of 1993 (P.L. 103-62) in the United States and funders, such as the United Way, are after effective social investments.

The logic and rationale for understanding the costs and benefits of programs is unavoidable and undeniable:

o Program effectiveness is the measure of what society gains from the investments it has made in addressing a problem.

o Society has unlimited requirements for social investment and limited investment resources. Making each investment as effective as it can be allows society to have the greatest impact on social problems that resources permit. This leads to measuring cost-effectiveness across programs.

o Programs can use information about their effectiveness to improve their performance, thereby improving the payback from each social investment. This leads to measuring cost-effectiveness within the program.

○ Social investors (for example, government, foundations, program participants) can use information about the effectiveness of programs as a consideration in choosing where they will invest their own scarce resources (cost-effective across programs).

○ The net effects are potentially better performing programs, better informed social investments and, as a result, greater benefits for those who bear the consequences of social problems (cost-effective across social problems).

Although the need for information on a program's costs and benefits is clear, data collection is another matter. Implementation, however, leaves quite a bit to be desired. A core problem is that much of the authority rests with funders, and they do not generally show awareness of the distinction between effectiveness *across* programs and effectiveness *within* programs. In essence, investors need to be patient during the early periods of new program initiatives; during this time, a new program should be obtaining cost and benefit information and using it to improve the effectiveness of the program (effectiveness within programs). Once the program has matured and is functioning with reasonable effectiveness, it is appropriate for funders to use this information to compare programs that address similar social problems (effectiveness across programs). As long as the program uses the effectiveness within-programs information to improve benefits and ensure that costs are reasonable, it is very likely that FGC will prove at least as effective as its alternatives. In

circumstances where this is not the case, FGC is not proving to be as effective as alternative methods and should be discontinued. The goal is to use the most effective approach for the circumstance, and information about program effectiveness is the essential key for this.

Only funders have the political capital and leverage to require programs to gather reasonable cost and benefit information and to wait patiently while the programs use this information, and other evaluation data, to improve to a point at which they are a good representation of the program approach. It is rare, however, to see funders separate within and across program uses of cost and benefit information, and even more rare to see them patiently using their leverage to ensure that the programs understand the value of effectiveness data, and obtain and use cost and benefit information for their own improvement.

What are costs and benefits? What is effectiveness?

At an elementary level, costs and benefits are quite simple concepts: *Costs are the value of everything that goes into providing a service, and benefits are the changes that the service generates.*[1] The two combine into effectiveness measures, of which there are many variations. The most elementary is the amount of benefit received for the resources invested. Economists are familiar with estimation techniques to express this in a variety of ways, thereby facilitating comparison across programs (for example, benefit-to-cost ratios and internal rates of

---

[1]Economics literature on cost-effectiveness is usually very technical. Useful and readable sources include Yates (1996) and Levin (1983).

return). Another measure—net incremental costs—compares the effectiveness of a given program to that of a reasonable alternative. Measures such as this are unrealistic for most social programs because they are used for across program decisions that are the responsibility of funders, not individual programs.

It is fair to expect social programs to articulate their expected costs and benefits and to obtain valid and reliable measures of these. Such measures can be qualitative as well as quantitative. Usually, cost measures are quantitative, often in monetary units, whereas benefit measures are a mix of descriptive information and Likert-like indicators of particular benefits.

Costs include all of the resources that go into providing the service that generates the benefits. In FGC, costs may include the following:

○ Direct program expenditures paid by the FGC program, such as salaries and employment expenses (for example, benefits and employment taxes) of FGC coordinators, other direct service staff, supervisors, and support staff, as well as overhead expenses that are necessary for the program

○ Expenditures on services for the process and paid by the FGC program, such as the costs of holding the conference (for example, child care, interpretation, transportation to the conference site) and the costs stemming from the FGC plan (for example, substance abuse treatment, a day care center)

○ Expenditures paid by participants in the conference, such as the value of the time of participants, any direct expenses paid by them and not reimbursed by the program

○ Expenditures paid by others, such as by the court system child welfare systems

Benefits include the positive results generated by the investments of the program and participants, for example:

○ Measures (not just anecdotes) of the extent to which individual participants are better off.

○ The social savings resulting from improved self-reliance and reduced requirements for social expenditures. Social savings include reduced direct reliance on public funds (for example, welfare, unemployment benefits, medical benefits/insurance) and other public resources (for example, social workers, foster care, court and other legal costs).

○ The social benefits to be gained from citizens who now contribute more to the running of society through increased tax payments, volunteerism, and so on.

Effectiveness is the balance between costs and benefits: what society and individuals receive for the amount that they invest. In the absence of information about other similar programs, those evaluating a program's effectiveness make a judgment about the balance between costs and benefits. Was the program worth it, given what was required from participants and the level of social investment? The answer is rarely unambiguous, but the information can stimulate valuable reflection in a learning organization.

Until relatively recently, the argument that most costs were time-limited while benefits would run forever was sufficient to interest social funders (Figure 9-1).

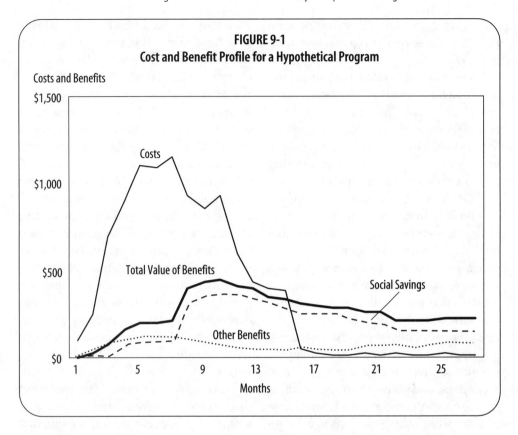

FIGURE 9-1
Cost and Benefit Profile for a Hypothetical Program

However, in the age of results-based accountability, it is necessary to show the causal link to the claimed benefits (social savings) or at a minimum show that FGC is at least as effective as alternatives that may also claim part or all of these same social savings. The demonstration of effectiveness became necessary, in part, because the promised benefits either were not occurring with sufficient intensity or frequency or because they were not being measured so that they could be assessed.

How is cost information obtained?

Information about costs is no more difficult to obtain than information about any other outcomes. The task just appears more difficult because information about costs is usually not accorded the same status as information about client outcomes. *Some of the information already exists for most programs; for example, direct disbursements are usually available from bookkeeping records. Sometimes a very modest (but unpopular) effort is required to obtain the information; for example, it may be necessary to record the time spent on each case. In some cases, it requires more effort to obtain cost information (for example, court costs).*

In the worst case, some of the information (for example, information on salaries) exists, but there are no records of the amount of time spent per family or case; records of direct disbursements (for example, travel support) do not identify the case; and there is no indication of the amount of time that supervisors and managers spend on FGC cases, because FGC is one of several programs operating in the agency.

The accounting system is a primary resource in both worst- and best-case situations. It contains information on direct expenditures that can at least be related to vendors. Thus, by using case files to identify expenditures through purchasing documents such as vouchers, it is possible to obtain the cost, or a reasonable approximation of it, from the accounting system. Thus, the case files are another essential resource for worst-case situations.

Time sheets are a nuisance to keep. Where required, they are usually used for control purposes or billing, rarely for program improvement, stimulating many to resist the use of time sheets. Nevertheless, it is important to have an estimate of the amount of time that staff, supervisors and managers, and family group members spend on conferencing. Sometimes case files report how long sessions take by recording start and end time, but this does not include setup time, recruitment and all the pre-conference discussions, travel time, and so on. The most realistic approach is to obtain estimates for a sample of a representative range of cases (for example, tough, average, easy). It is crucial, however, that the key stakeholders consider the number and distribution of cases used to estimate costs to be appropriate. Figure 9-2 illustrates this approach.

Accurately recalling the amount of time spent on something is challenging, and the task becomes even more difficult when the time has been spent in different-sized segments over weeks or months. For example, recall is not a major challenge in working with a service that is provided intensely over a finite period, such as a two-day training provided once every two months.

Likewise, it is not difficult to calculate the total time spent filing travel claims, even when the travel is sporadic. The number of trips can be determined from the number of claims filed, and multiplying this figure by the estimated length of time that it takes to file a typical claim produces a reasonable estimate of the total time spent filing expense claims.

Interventions such as FGC are more complex. Rarely are there regular time cycles; cases tend to be differentiated and the services provided for each case heterogeneous. There are a number of ways to produce these estimates, but they inevitably require a larger investment compared to the more simple examples given earlier. They may require interviews, focus groups, diaries, and combinations of these (Figure 9-3).

There are several options for estimating time spent per case. After the direct disbursements have been determined, it seems best to directly engage the staff that worked on the case to get their estimates of the number of hours that they spent working on it.

Costs of Direct Service Staff

The three key elements are the time spent on a case, the costs of that time, and overheads. Time sheets that record time by client or case make this information readily accessible. If time sheets are not available, time can also be estimated. Staff turnover is not a problem; the focus is on the time spent, not on the time spent by a particular person. The modest changes in hourly rates usually do not affect the overall measure. Similarly, joint appointments to two or more positions require only simple adjustments; the total time can be multiplied by a suitable factor such as the percentage of time that the person estimates he or she

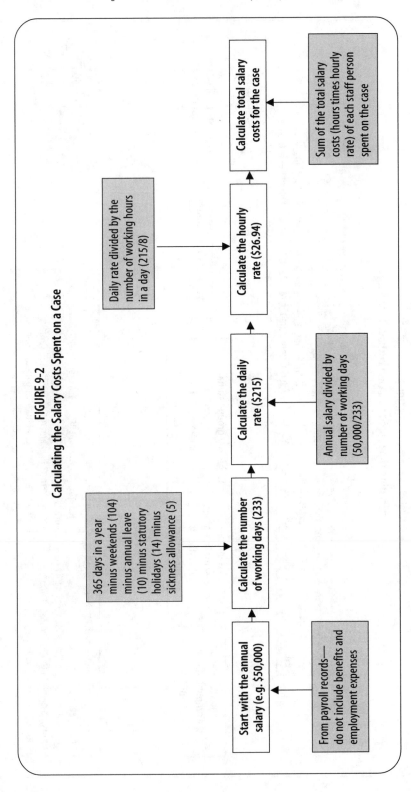

FIGURE 9-2
Calculating the Salary Costs Spent on a Case

Start with the annual salary (e.g. $50,000)

From payroll records—do not include benefits and employment expenses

Calculate the number of working days (233)

365 days in a year minus weekends (104) minus annual leave (10) minus statutory holidays (14) minus sickness allowance (5)

Calculate the daily rate ($215)

Annual salary divided by number of working days (50,000/233)

Calculate the hourly rate ($26.94)

Daily rate divided by the number of working hours in a day (215/8)

Calculate total salary costs for the case

Sum of the total salary costs (hours times hourly rate) of each staff person spent on the case

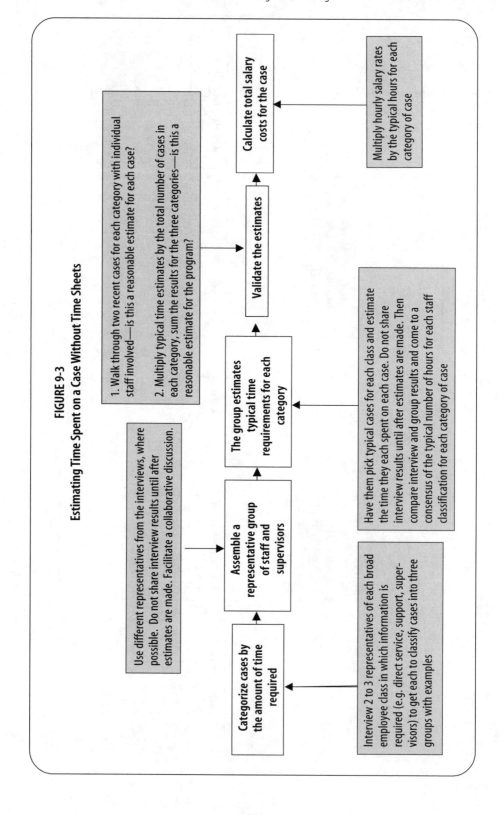

FIGURE 9-3

Estimating Time Spent on a Case Without Time Sheets

Calculate total salary costs for the case

Multiply hourly salary rates by the typical hours for each category of case

1. Walk through two recent cases for each category with individual staff involved—is this a reasonable estimate for each case?

2. Multiply typical time estimates by the total number of cases in each category, sum the results for the three categories—is this a reasonable estimate for the program?

Validate the estimates

The group estimates typical time requirements for each category

Have them pick typical cases for each class and estimate the time they each spent on each case. Do not share interview results until after estimates are made. Then compare interview and group results and come to a consensus of the typical number of hours for each staff classification for each category of case

Use different representatives from the interviews, where possible. Do not share interview results until after estimates are made. Facilitate a collaborative discussion.

Assemble a representative group of staff and supervisors

Interview 2 to 3 representatives of each broad employee class in which information is required (e.g. direct service, support, supervisors) to get each to classify cases into three groups with examples

Categorize cases by the amount of time required

spent on FGC or the contracted percentage of his or her time for FGC. The key is to assess whether such detailed adjustments will make much of a difference in the overall measure.

The other key element is the cost of time: costs of staff and overheads. It is possible to calculate annual salary costs from accounting information. However, some care must be taken to avoid double counting. Some accounting systems record "all in" salary costs, which include salary, employment costs such as insurance and taxes paid to the government, costs of benefits such as annual leave, health care, and so on. It is important to ensure that the costs that are included in salary are not counted again under overheads.

Overheads include all non-salary costs that are necessary for staff to do their job: purchase or rental of facilities; utilities; furnishings; computer hardware, software, and support; disposables, such as pens and paper. A great deal goes into overheads, and program financial people are the best placed to provide an estimate. Often, it is possible to get only an annual total for overheads from financial statements. That is fine; dividing that total by the total number of people working there provides an average annual total cost per staff member. Then an hourly estimate can be calculated by using the same procedures as for wages. If sub-contracts do not include overhead charges, then an estimate of the staff time for this can be produced by using the methods articulated earlier; overhead time becomes one of the categories.

Costs of Support and Supervisory Staff

The same elements are key: the amount of time attributable to a client or case and the hourly wage rate. Obtaining the information is an intrusion that should be strategically planned and executed. Ideally, acquisition of cost and benefit information should model the rationale for considering effectiveness and be effective itself; that is, obtain the maximum benefit (most useful information) for the resources invested in acquiring the information.

Optimally, effectiveness information can be obtained routinely through the operations of the program and in a manner that is minimally intrusive. Program and client information systems can be adapted (1) to record immediate benefits to clients, the staff time, and other resource inputs from staff, and (2) to obtain staff and client predictions of the type and level of longer-term benefits (for example, as part of an agreed-upon plan or contract between the client and the program). If volunteers provide support to the program or its clients, their time should be estimated and valued at a rate appropriate to the services that they provide. Volunteers will sometimes have disbursements they cover themselves, such as child care or taxis.

That effectiveness is often somewhat of an afterthought imposes some limitations on the quality of information, but it is still possible to satisfy most evaluation and review requirements. This is particularly the case if there is a credible and resourced commitment to integrate effectiveness into routine information gathering and reporting in the next funding cycle.

An illustration

A systematic effort to articulate the benefits and costs of FGC does not yet exist, although there are many valuable contributions that provide part of the story (see appendix 9-A at the end of this chapter). However, a fairly similar practice area, alternative dispute resolution (ADR), is helpful in illustrating how cost and benefit information can be obtained and used strategically in funding dialogues.

ADR is a collaborative approach that parties can use to address their differences and reach agreement, or at least reduce the intensity of the disagreement and clarify their positions so that they can focus on the main issues under dispute. Proponents of ADR claim that it is "cheaper, better, and faster" than the alternatives. *Cheaper, better, and faster* means more effective (more/better benefits for the total resources expended). For many years, government and foundation funders of ADR programs were satisfied that, together with the intuitive appeal of ADR, positive anecdotes and some case studies, provided sufficient evidence of effectiveness (much like FGC today). However, with the emergence of results-based accountability, these funders have begun to ask for better evidence of effectiveness and are discontinuing funding to programs that cannot provide such evidence.[2]

In response to the requirements of funders and to gain information to improve programming, the Policy Consensus Institute (PCI), along with the U.S. Institute for Environmental Conflict Resolution (USIECR) and the Oregon Dispute Resolution Commission (ODRC), contracted with the author to develop an evaluation system that would address the results-based accountability requirements of funders, including the need to report

on effectiveness.[3] The focus of this effort was on complex public policy and environmental disputes encompassing some of the most entrenched and expensive types of disputes.

The resulting evaluation system is outcome-based and systematically gains valid and reliable information for all key stakeholders to assess how well the program is faring in terms of process and agreement gains (benefits) and costs. Figure 9-4 provides an overview of the main outcomes that ADR seeks to achieve. Each of the outcomes charted in Figure 9-4 is further deconstructed into additional outcomes that nest under the charted outcome. For example, the outcome "Appropriate mediator[4] leads ADR" in Figure 9-4 is constituted from four *nested* outcomes representing what the mediator must do to be "appropriate": understand the process, understand the issues, manage the process, and be available for the emerging needs of the parties and the case. These four nested outcomes are presented in Figure 9-6.

The technique used to articulate and present these outcome structures is called

---

[2]For example, three leading state programs (Oregon, Massachusetts, and Florida) have been terminated or seriously cut back, the William and Flora Hewlett Foundation will stop funding ADR programs entirely in 2004, and a number of federal agency programs are now under close scrutiny.

[3]See PCI (http://www.policyconsensus.org/), USIECR (http://www.ecr.gov/), ODRC (http://www.odrc.state.or.us/). This evaluation system has subsequently been adopted by the Environmental Protection Agency Conflict Prevention and Resolution Center (http://www.epa.gov/adr/cprc_about.html), the Florida Conflict Resolution Consortium (http://consensus.fsu.edu/), and other federal environmental agencies.

[4]The namings used to identify a third party who facilitates the process include neutral, facilitator, mediator, dispute resolution practitioner. This is sometimes a sensitive issue, and different programs use different terms. For the purposes of this paper the use of the term "mediator" is synonymous to "neutral," and both are used because this section draws on more than one program and so adopts their terms.

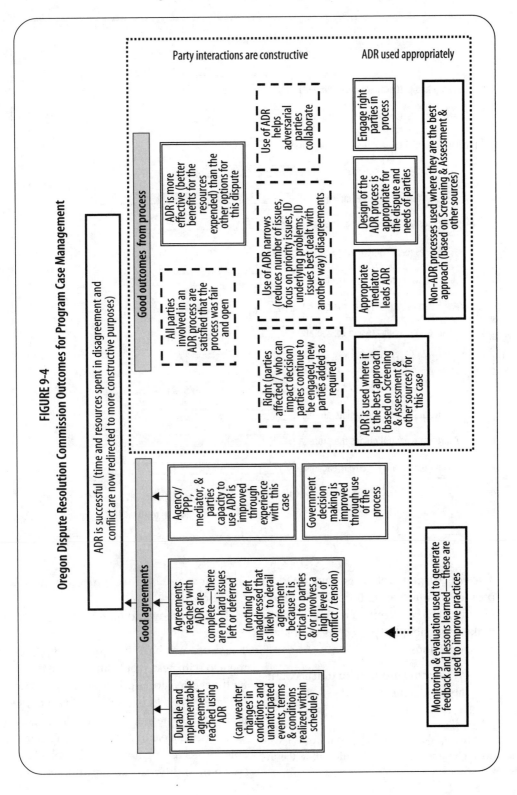

FIGURE 9-4

Oregon Dispute Resolution Commission Outcomes for Program Case Management

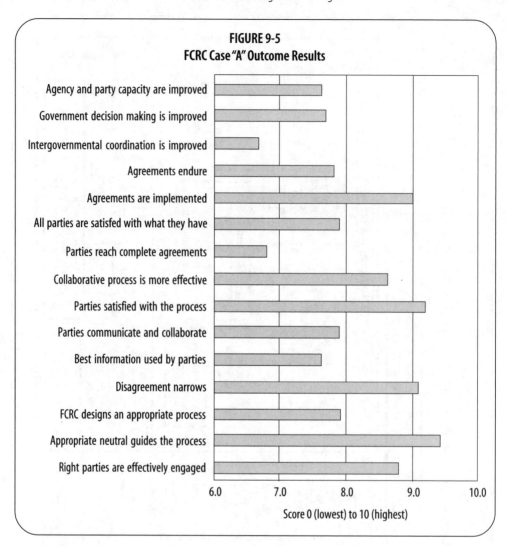

FIGURE 9-5
FCRC Case "A" Outcome Results

Score 0 (lowest) to 10 (highest)

outcome charting, and was developed to provide an alternative to logic modeling (Rowe, 2003). Outcome charting seeks to make it possible for programs to answer three questions:[5]

1. What is my program or unit accountable for achieving?

2. How will we recognize it when it occurs?

3. How are we doing now?

The outcome chart in Figure 9-4, supplemented with nested outcomes as illustrated for the charted appropriate neutral outcome in Figure 9-6, addresses the first two questions. By the time these charts are developed, the agency is clear about what it is accountable for achieving and what it looks like. (Accountability can be represented in a

---

[5]My colleague, John McLaughlin, developed these questions as a way of articulating the intent of GPRA.

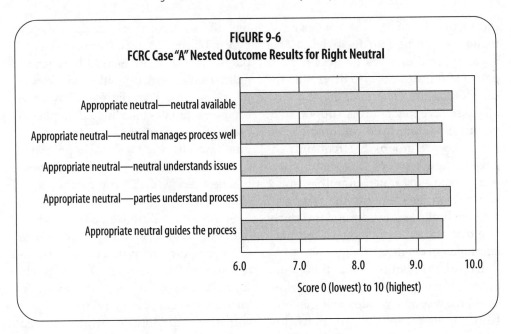

FIGURE 9-6
FCRC Case "A" Nested Outcome Results for Right Neutral

number of ways. In Figure 9-4, the ODRC is accountable for the outcomes outlined in solid black, the neutral for outcomes outlined with a dashed black line and the neutral and the ODRC for outcomes outlined in with a double line). Measurement of performance on these outcomes through an outcome-monitoring system addresses the third question. The particular program presented in Figure 9-4 is ADR as practiced by the ODRC; examples from other ADR programs are used in Figures 9-5 and 9-6 to ensure confidentiality.[6]

Information is gathered on each case from questionnaires administered to the parties involved, the neutral facilitator, and the case project coordinator. Most of the outcomes are measured with numeric scales (see Figure 9-5 as an example). Figures 9-5 and 9-6 illustrate the presentation of the benefit information, first for all of the outcomes, then for the nested outcomes for the charted outcome "appropriate mediator leads ADR." This technique provides the program with systematic information about benefits that can be compared with the information about costs. At the same time, it provides directly to the programs information about their performance, which they can use to identify areas for improvement.

Cost information is obtained from the parties involved and from program files. The primary cost of ADR is the time spent by the parties preparing for ADR, engaging in the ADR process, and implementing the agreement. Other important costs are fees for attorneys and experts, as well as the costs of the process itself, such as the fee for the neutral facilitator(s), meeting

---

[6]Particular care is exercised with confidentiality of ADR evaluation information because of the high stakes of many cases. However, because each program tailored the evaluation system to its own circumstances and approach, there are some disconnects. For example, the charted outcome in Figure 9-4 refers to "appropriate mediator leads ADR," whereas in the following figures presenting results reference is to "an appropriate neutral guiding the process."

rooms, travel, and so on. All of this information, requiring four to six additional questions on the parties' questionnaire, is gathered for each case. To determine the costs of the time required, the lead and other senior representatives, support staff, volunteers (often from community and environmental groups that frequently engage in these types of cases), and others were asked how much time they spent working on the case, and the responses were multiplied by an appropriate hourly rate that includes employment and non-employment overhead charges.

During the pilot phases of this evaluation system, respondents were asked about the response burden and the difficulty of answering the questions. Responses were very positive; respondents stated that providing the information was not a problem, nor was the time required to complete the questionnaires. Response rates are running from 65 percent to 90 percent, depending on the agency.[7] Table 9-1 illustrates the type of cost data obtained. (Note that the costs of these environmental cases are much lower than those for most environmental disputes.)

Continued investments to improve the effectiveness measures of the ADR evaluation system have started to provide (in 2004) much better information about the longer-terms costs and benefits of ADR in complex public policy and environmental settings.[8] A separate research effort is developing methods to gain the information necessary to compare ADR approaches to

their likely alternative; in the case of complex public policy and environmental disputes, likely alternatives include litigation, judicial settlements, legislation, administrative rules, or inaction. The research will also produce estimates for a limited number of types of environmental disputes.[9] At that time, it will be possible for ADR programs to respond to "so what" questions about the effectiveness of ADR compared to likely alternatives.

Some very telling statements can already be made about the effectiveness of ADR compared with that of selected alternatives. For example, for relatively simple Case 1 in Table 9-1, how many attorney hours could have been purchased with the expenditure on a neutral or even the total process costs, assuming $250/hour as a minimum hourly rate? Is approximately four hours of attorney time sufficient to settle the case, considering that each party would require an attorney? In much more complex Case 4, with six parties or about $1,100/party for the costs of a neutral or, alternatively, an attorney, would settlement have been reached with an average of 4.5 hours of attorney time? The story that ADR can now tell is:

○ There is now valid and reliable evidence that ADR is less costly than a reasonable alternative.
○ The benefits that are expected from ADR can be detailed, and measures that show these benefits to be very positive are valid and reliable.

[7]Survey methods followed those described by Dillman (2000).

[8]Funding is provided by the William and Flora Hewlett Foundation and the U.S. Environmental Protection Agency.

[9]Ongoing research (The Economic and Environmental Effects of Alternative Dispute Resolution), funded by the William and Flora Hewlett Foundation and the U.S. Environmental Protection Agency through a grant to the author.

TABLE 9-1
Estimated Costs of Alternative Dispute Resolution Processes

	Costs Borne by Parties					
	Cost of Parties' Time	Total Cost of the Process	Total Costs (Including Settlement Costs)	Cost of Neutral	Total Cost of Process (Not Including Settlement)	Total Costs (Including Settlement)
Case 1	$6,700	$6,700	$46,700	$900	$7,600	$47,600
Case 2	$2,437	$2,437	$2,437	$1,500	$3,937	$3,937
Case 3	$8,750	$8,750	$8,750	$2,550	$11,300	$11,300
Case 4	$7,075	$21,085	$71,085	$6,900	$27,985	$77,985

○ Current efforts to improve cost data will permit more systematic and accurate comparisons within the next one to three years.

○ The benefit (outcome) information is being used to target program improvements whose benefits will become apparent within one year.

○ Quality information demonstrates very positive benefits and relatively lower costs against selected alternatives, provisionally substantiating the claim that ADR is an effective program alternative.

○ Over the next three years, efforts to use this information to improve program benefits and provide additional comparisons to a range of likely alternatives will continue.

ADR is not dissimilar to FGC. There is considerable programmatic emphasis on process; the time required from participants and overheads are some of the major costs of FGC; and although the approach has intuitive appeal, it is relatively new, is under pressure to provide effectiveness information, and does not have a large body of knowledge or established methods to draw upon to obtain such information. The main distinguishing characteristic between FGC and the particular body of ADR practice used in this illustration is that these ADR cases are usually very large and heterogeneous, making it very difficult to identify reasonable alternatives. For example, what would be a reasonable alternative to the collaborative process that addressed the water problems of the Florida Everglades and ultimately led to an $8-billion allocation from Congress to implement the agreement reached? Additional methodological development is required to permit comparisons of ADR to likely alternatives. However, FGC has a ready-at-hand likely alternative, such as traditional case approaches to child welfare.

This example illustrates how modest investments in articulating the costs and the benefits of ADR can provide immediate benefits in terms of systematically measuring costs and benefits. It also shows how this information can be used strategically in the dialogue with funders, relegating the Social Program Six Step to history, improving program effectiveness, and providing quality evidence that the previously intuitive claims about effectiveness are both valid and reliable.

Additional Considerations

Shelf Life

As time goes on, memory becomes less accurate, and this can be an important consideration in estimating time, costs, and similar measures. For example, a significant amount (approximately 40 percent) of expenditures on maintaining a home are less than $50, and the shelf life for reasonably accurate recall of small expenditures is measured in weeks. Many inquiries into the costs of maintaining a home are conducted quarterly or annually, thereby systematically and significantly producing an underestimation of expenditures. In estimating the costs of FGC, shelf life will most directly affect recall of time spent on a case. The best solution is to keep records of time spent per case.

Unit of Measurement

Costs and benefits should be collected at the family or individual level, because both vary widely across cases, and because data collection at this level provides an opportunity to reflect upon and learn from individual cases or aggregations of cases. More pragmatically, if measurement is not disaggregated, benefits and costs will be averaged across all cases, which may overestimate effectiveness for cases that have not worked out that well and underestimate effectiveness for more successful cases. The consequences are serious; the opportunity to systematically learn from exemplary cases is lost, discouraging reflective practice, and the program reports average performance levels always below its potential. In the more challenging and risky program areas such as FGC, reports may present the intervention as dramatically below its potential performance.

Monitoring and Evaluation Services

In response to contemporary governance requirements and practices, many programs have monitoring and evaluation as integral elements. FGC programs are still considered innovative—in other words, risky, by most funders—and these programs need to ensure that they can report on their results and effectiveness with valid, reliable, and credible information. As a general guide, monitoring and evaluation should be allocated at approximately 8 percent of total program costs. However, many of these are internal expenditures—for example, the development and implementation of improved record keeping.

Timing

Making retrospective measurements is always more difficult and less accurate than keeping adequate information records from the outset. Timing is particularly important with a new initiative that needs information to make decisions about how to improve the effectiveness of the program—both to reduce costs and to increase benefits. The primary cost is time, so it is important to keep time information from the outset.

The first use of this information is for improvement within the program. Later, once the program is operating well, it can make a strategic decision to use this information to show how they have improved effectiveness and internal accountability, and how they are continuing to do so.

The Alternative Intervention

Information on effectiveness is often used in a comparison to some other alternative, including inaction. For example, how cost-effective is FGC in child welfare settings compared to normal case management approaches?

It is not the job of an FGC program to obtain information on suitable alternatives (termed counterfactuals), except in settings in which the FGC program is being undertaken on a pilot basis. In such settings, the proponents of the FGC program should request funders to participate in identifying the alternatives and either obtain the effectiveness information for the likely candidates for comparison or provide funding to obtain such information. However, funders will not accept the absence of evaluative information about alternatives, such as case management, as a rationale for not obtaining this information about FGC. Innovative programs usually attract disproportionate attention and evaluation requirements compared with traditional approaches. The best strategy is to accept this as an opportunity to gain useful information about the FGC program and to use this information strategically.

The evidence that currently exists consistently shows that there are no statistically significant differences in the measured costs between FGC and comparison programs. Studies such as these should provide assurances to FGC programs that their costs can be fairly measured and prove useful to the FGC programs and their funders.

Conclusion

Innovative programs such as FGC should recognize the now-widespread emphasis on results-based accountability and increasing requirements for programs to measure and report on effectiveness as an opportunity. The effectiveness and achievements of more established approaches are increasingly under critical scrutiny from contemporary governance requirements, which provides opportunities for alternative approaches that can show themselves as viable alternatives. However, this will require evidence that FGC is an effective alternative; FGC programs must show that the desired benefits are being achieved to a high degree and that they are cost-effective. Some FGC programs have demonstrated that they can be no more costly than traditional approaches and that they achieve a high level of benefits for participants. In other words, there is evidence that FGC is an effective alternative. It is important that planning for FGC adopts a results-based accountability stance and that programs prepare to obtain the necessary measures to enable assessments of effectiveness. Programs are the first beneficiaries of this information, as it aids managers and staff in improving the contributions of the program. Once the program is running well, this effectiveness information is beneficial to funders and other external stakeholders.

Costs of Family Group Conferencing

Joan Pennell

The costs of any human service program need to be assessed in the context of (1) the stage of its implementation and (2) its outcomes for service recipients, communities, and public agencies (Knapp, 1984; Netten, 1996). When a program is initiated, there are usually costs relating to start-up and training; thus, at first, programs tend to cost more. In determining acceptable levels of expenditures, the outcomes of a new program must be compared with those for regular services.

Costs for family group conferencing (FGC) can be divided into conference costs (for example, food) and post-conference costs (for example, placements). The number of studies on FGC costs is limited, but the available studies have produced some information on these two cost categories.

Conference Costs

Costs for holding conferences are minor, except when family group members at a distance require assistance with transportation:

○ A California study found that the conferencing costs averaged $31 per child (Walter R. McDonald & Associates, 2000, p. 4.5). The most common expenditure for the 65 children in the study was for food. Transportation, when required, was the most expensive item, but was needed by relatively few families (Walter R. McDonald & Associates, 1998, p. 3.19).

○ A Fresno County, California, study of 27 conferences reported that the average cost was $355. The largest component was usually for worker time, and averaged $292 per conference; food averaged $18 for each conference. When interpretation costs were incurred, expenditures ranged up to $400 for a conference (Berzin, 2004, p. 12).

○ A Canadian study found that the first-time conferencing costs averaged $304 (Canadian dollars) per child; the bulk of the costs was for transportation to island or northern locations (Pennell & Burford, 1995, pp. 247–251).

Post-Conference Costs

Families are reasonable in what they ask for in their plans:

○ A British study found that three-quarters of the 80 plans examined were considered to be medium or low (or no) cost (Marsh & Crow, 1998, p. 147).

If children enter care, there is no statistically significant difference in placement costs for FGC children and comparison children:

○ A Santa Clara County, California, study reported that although the average cost of placement for FGC children who entered care did not differ in a statistically significant way from those for comparison children (Walter R. McDonald & Associates, 2000, p. 4.5), the 65 FGC children tended to be older than the 599 comparison children. When the researchers controlled for age, they found that the placement costs for the two groups were still not statistically different. It should be noted, however, that the placement costs for the comparison group were on average $400 more than those for the FGC children.

FGC prevents children from entering care and saves money, as long as the children do not require higher cost placements:

○ A British study estimated that FGC reduced the number of children placed in care by one-fifth (Marsh & Crow, 1998, pp. 156-157). Without the conference, the social workers predicted that 19 of the 64 children would have entered or stayed in care.

○ A Canadian study found that fewer FGC children than comparison children were placed in care. However, those FGC children who were in care were in higher cost placements (for example, group homes rather than foster care; Andy Rowe Consultants, 1997, p. 9). However, the 32 FGC families had nearly twice the number of indicators of child risk before conferencing than the 31 comparison families had (Pennell & Burford, 2000a).

Court costs stay the same or are reduced by FGC:

○ A British study showed that for at least seven of the 64 children studied, FGC avoided the costs of court proceedings or further child protection procedures (Marsh & Crow, 1998, p. 157).

○ A Santa Clara County, California, study found that if children entered care, there was no statistically significant difference for the court hearing costs of the 65 FGC children and the 599 comparison children (Walter R. McDonald & Associates, 2000, p. 4.5).

For families receiving in-home services, predictors of higher costs are provision of mental health and substance abuse services:

○ A Fresno County, California, study comparing costs for 38 experimental and 24 control families receiving in-home services reported that the experimental intervention did not predict costs. Instead, receiving at least one mental health or one substance abuse service were strong predictors of costs for both groups (Berzin, 2004, p. 13).

Combined Costs

The largest cost item is for care. Thus, when costs are combined, there is no statistically significant difference for FGC and comparison children:

○ A Santa Clara County, California, study found that even when conferencing costs are added to post- conference costs, there is no statistically significant difference between the costs for FGC and comparison children (Walter R. McDonald & Associates, 2000, p. 4.6).

○ A Fresno County, California, study comparing costs for 38 experimental and 24 control families receiving in-home services reported that the experimental intervention did not significantly affect total costs, even when the costs of the conference are added in, and these total costs might be lower for the experimental group (Berzin, 2004, p. 13).

○ A Canadian study found no statistically significant difference in total costs between the 31 FGC and 32 comparison cases (Andy Rowe Consultants, 1997, p. 2).

IV

Reshaping Child Welfare

Gary R. Anderson and Joan Pennell

From one perspective, family group conferencing (FGC) seems to be a conceptually simple method of intervention for families. It can be succinctly described as bringing together a whole family so that they can plan together for the safety of their children. However, its implementation and the implications for the child welfare system and beyond are more complex. The participants in FGC describe it as different from standard child welfare services in its expanded role for families, its emphasis on family responsibility, and its engagement of the family. The FGC model itself poses complicated tasks in ensuring the physical and cultural safety of family members and in balancing professional responsibility with family empowerment. This fourth, and final, section highlights a number of issues and opportunities associated with FGC.

These issues and opportunities include the contributions of FGC in relation to domestic violence, FGC in relation to other family involvement models, and FGC in relation to juvenile justice. This section concludes with an overview of FGC and child welfare reform, as well as projecting challenges for FGC. The core values and FGC practices are presented and connected to these approaches to work with children, young people, and their families. The examination of these differing approaches will fine-tune an understanding of FGC applications. Although most descriptive of program models in the United States, there are implications for, as well as lessons learned from, FGC in other countries.

How does FGC reshape child welfare systems to ensure the safety of children and their mothers?

In chapter 10, Joan Pennell addresses the central theme of child and family safety. She identifies and explores domestic violence issues in detail. The possibility of providing a safe environment that encourages mothers who have experienced domestic violence to make a confident contribution to the decision-making process is also explored. Reshaped child welfare systems do not need to be blind to families that have experienced domestic violence or to exclude them from this collaborative family planning and decision-making model.

How does FGC reshape child welfare systems through family involvement, and what are some of the other models for involving families?

Through a description of several partnership models, Lisa Merkel-Holguin and Leslie Wilmot demonstrate in chapter 11 the primary importance of family involvement in planning and crafting the steps to be taken to reduce risk and strengthen the family. In recognizing the importance of family involvement in reshaping child welfare systems, FGC is one of a number of approaches that reframe the relationship between the family and the child welfare system. A survey of these approaches helps clarify and, to some extent, contrast these approaches while showing that a continuum of family involvement is possible.

How does FGC contribute to reshaping the integration of the child welfare and juvenile justice systems?

There is a need for the integration of services, as multiple social systems often serve the same families. The values that have shaped FGC have also influenced, and been influenced by, other human services systems and partnership models. In chapter 12, Gale Burford sets forth how the strategic integration of planning and

service delivery would coordinate these services rather than pull families in different directions. With FGC, one of the most promising examples of this integration may take place between the child welfare and juvenile justice systems. The application of FGC in juvenile justice settings and issues in the integration of juvenile justice with child protection conferencing is described in chapter 12.

What child welfare challenges are posed by FGC and for FGC?

Finally, FGC is a promising model for inclusion in child welfare, but it is not a panacea. It highlights and puts into practice a set of ethical principles that are congruent with professional standards of ethical conduct. FGC illustrates the implementation of a strengths- and family-centered perspective without compromising the safety of children. Building on the contention that a child protective service agency cannot solely ensure the safety of children, it reinforces the role of extended family and the community in achieving outcomes of safety, permanency, and the well-being of children and families. Yet, as Gary Anderson explores in chapter 13, challenges remain for FGC and the child welfare system. Issues related to cultural competence, power sharing, the stresses on families, and the infrastructure requirements for FGC are enduring arenas for discussion and improvement. The potential important place for FGC in the child welfare system is affirmed, but securing this place seems at times to be tenuous.

Conclusion

Taken together, these chapters focus on different aspects of reshaping the child welfare system. The concern for safety is not new; the recognition of and the capacity to address domestic violence present newer challenges. Family-centered practice has been around for some time, and the development of a continuum of models of family involvement provides concrete expression and application of family-centered principles in child welfare. The fact that families often receive services from multiple systems and have multiple needs is well recognized. The application of FGC to juvenile justice and child protection issues serves as an example of potential cross-system integration. The ethical and practice approaches advanced by FGC present not only potential strengths for its use as a part of the child welfare system, but also principles that could and should broadly inform a professional response to children and families.

10

Safety for Mothers and Their Children

Joan Pennell

The premise of "widening the circle" is that with support and protections in place, family groups can make and carry out decisions for the good of their members. Families in which the mother is the victim of violence or its survivor present a crucial test of this belief. Questions arise about her batterer assuming control of the conference, colluding with his family, and intimidating or abusing her and her relatives. With child welfare involved, the stakes are even higher. Although increasingly a questioned practice, domestic violence is a common reason for removing children from their homes, even if the battered mother has not abused the children (Edleson, 2004; Lyon, 1999). Batterers use this threat to silence their partners (Bancroft & Silverman, 2002).

Possibly more common than the active cases of domestic violence on the long-term child welfare caseload are the many women who no longer are being abused and are trying to lead their lives and par-

ent their children. Often, these survivors struggle to meet their children's needs as both they and the children deal with the aftereffects of violence. Their social workers and their families may not understand these struggles and may become frustrated and blaming, thus severing important sources of support for the mother and her children. The conference offers a way of educating the family group about the dynamics of domestic violence and helping them plan together for the welfare of their relatives.

Whether or not the parents continue to live together, family group conferencing (FGC) more than most child welfare interventions involves fathers and their families (Gunderson, Cahn, & Wirth, 2003). They are seen as significant ties and resources for the children and potential kinship placements. By its nature, FGC pushes to include all family members, but what if some family members are a danger to their relations? For this reason, some agencies have established policies to exclude domestic violence referrals from FGC, especially if the couple continues to live together. Putting such a policy into practice is problematic, however, because the referring workers often are unaware of the extent of woman abuse on their caseload. Coordinators who are aware of the violence may decide to exclude abusers and their side of the family from the conference. This decision frequently provokes strong resistance from the referred families, including those members who have been victimized. In some situations, exclusion is the only conscionable route, but in others, alternatives can be developed with the family group.

Practitioners acting alone cannot be expected to determine how best to address family violence, that is, situations in which there are both domestic violence and child maltreatment. In general, child protective services overestimate or underestimate the risk that children face, with approximately one-third of cases erroneously assessed (Gambrill & Shlonsky, 2000), and the evaluation literature provides only limited guidance on how to help domestic violence victims and especially their children (Graham-Bermann, 2000). Conferencing offers the opportunity for the worker to give the family group members clear information about the situation and involve them in the decision making.

Before proceeding to a conference with a family that has experienced domestic violence, the FGC coordinator should work with the family group, closely consulting with survivors, to assess whether a conference should take place and, if so, what safety measures must be in place. The conference should be structured in a way that is congruent with the family group's culture and safeguards individual participants. Domestic violence often splits family groups along the lines of her and his side of the family, with the children as intermediaries. To make participants feel safe at a conference, the coordinator must pay attention to who is present, how the conference is carried out, where it is held, and whether sufficient supports and protections are in place. As discussed in chapter 7, all of these are components of cultural safety.

What is domestic violence? And what are its effects on women and children?

At heart, domestic violence is a profound betrayal of trust. Expressed through physical violence, sexual assault, emotional humiliation, economic exploitation, and social isolation, it develops into *a recurring pattern of abuse that controls and traps an intimate partner*. According to the U.S. Department of Justice (2000), domestic violence usually takes place against a woman in the home and is more likely to result in physical injury to a woman than to a man. Severe and prolonged domestic violence is likely to lead to post-traumatic stress disorder (PTSD). Studies show that the percentage of battered women who exhibit PTSD symptoms ranges from 31 to 84 percent; that symptoms include painful memories, irritability, and psychic numbing; and that PTSD for abused women is often accompanied by other mental health issues, such as substance abuse, depression, and suicidal behavior (Hughes & Jones, 2000). All of these affect a woman's capacity to enjoy life, hold a job, and care for her children.

In nearly one-half of cases (43 percent), children under age 12 reside in a household with domestic violence (U.S. Department of Justice, 2000). It is estimated that in approximately 40 percent of cases, the children of an abused parent are physically abused (Edleson, 1999). *Besides being the direct victims, children are seriously affected by exposure to the batterer*, especially if he is their father, stepfather, or a father figure (Sullivan, Juras, Bybee, Nguyen, & Allen, 2000). Approximately half the children exposed exhibit symptoms at the clinical level. These symptoms include depression, anxiety, aggression, and conduct disorders; the likelihood of PTSD increases with the severity of the exposure to domestic violence (Rossman, 2001). Those children who are both physically abused and living in homes with domestic violence have the most severe symptoms.

Typically, *perpetrators of domestic violence are controlling, angry, and punitive toward the children*, manipulate the children in custody evaluations to favor the father, and seek to undermine the mother's parenting even after the couple separates (Bancroft & Silverman, 2002). They often force the children to observe the mother's victimization, punish the mother for the children's behavior, and blame the mother for their own excessive disciplining of the children (Mbilinyi, Edleson, Beeman, & Hagemeister, 2002). In later relationships with other women, perpetrators expose the children to further violence.

Battered mothers may physically abuse their children, but once they are safe, they are less likely to do so (Edleson, Mbilinyi, & Shetty, 2003). Commonly, they try to compensate for the violence and protect their children. *Despite severe stress, abused women are quite similar to other mothers in how they feel toward and nurture their children*. Their decision to leave or stay with the batterer is influenced by what they see as their children's best interests.

How do women get away from domestic violence?

Increasingly, women are reporting intimate partner violence to the police (U.S. Department of Justice, 2000) for good reason because arrests help to prevent them from being killed in the future (Campbell et al., 2003). But stopping domestic violence is difficult. Woman abuse is maintained by the manipulations of the batterer; the well-founded fears of victims that leaving will provoke more and lethal violence against themselves and their children (Fleury, Sullivan, & Bybee, 2000); the reluctance of family and community members to intrude (Kelly, 2003); the limited economic resources and legal recourse available to victims (Ptacek, 1999); and expectations that no matter what the cost, women must keep their family together or, conversely, must separate (Radford & Hester, 2001). All these factors are compounded when the women have children, little income, or face racist/ethnocentric policies and practices (Martin, 1997; McGillivray & Comaskey, 1999). Women are more likely to be battered if they are African American, have lower income, or are young (U.S. Department of Justice, 2000).

Nevertheless, *women use various strategies to survive and eventually disconnect from the battering relationship* (Campbell, Rose, Kub, & Nedd, 1998). Typically, they do not immediately exit a battering relationship because of caring for the batterer and worries about the children's welfare, retaliation, finances, and so forth. Instead, they move fluidly in and out of the battering relationship until they finally make a complete break. The decision to sever all ties frequently turns on the realization that the violence may become deadly or the children are being hurt.

During the process of separating, *the large majority of women seek help from family and friends, whose reactions significantly affect the women* (Goodkind, Gillum, Bybee, & Sullivan, 2003). On the one hand, the seemingly endless revolving door of the relationship frustrates the women's close supports and can provoke negative reactions, especially if the batterer threatens them as well. All this adds to the women's isolation and depression. On the other hand, offers of tangible support, such as housing, and nonjudgmental responses are crucial to the women's sense of well-being. Notably, the more dependent children the woman has, the less criticism she receives from family and friends.

Because many abused women are already turning to family and friends, *FGC is a means for the child welfare system to work with the women's informal networks and encourage supportive responses.* When the battered partners have been too frightened, too ashamed, and too isolated to reach out, the FGC coordinator can ease this process by working with them to develop the invitation list and prepare participants. At a carefully organized session, the family group members are less likely to feel overwhelmed and react negatively. With agency and community resources made available, the family group can offer help without putting themselves at the same level of risk.

Are family group conferences likely to take place if there is a history of domestic violence?

In cases in which domestic violence is an issue, workers more often approve a family for a conference, and families more often agree to hold a conference. A study of conferencing in Kent County, Michigan, examined 593 referrals, of which slightly more than half (322, 54 percent) were approved for a conference; among these approved referrals, 173 (54 percent) families agreed to try a conference (Crampton, 2001). In looking at the family characteristics, it was found that child protection workers and conference coordinators were significantly more likely to approve referrals if the family had a history of domestic violence. Among the 64 families referred for domestic violence, 45 (70 percent) were approved. The same study found that families were also significantly more likely to agree to hold a conference if the case files mentioned domestic violence: Among the 45 approved referrals that cited domestic violence, 35 (78 percent) of the families consented to trying a conference.

For 20 percent (35 of 173) of the consenting families, domestic violence was noted as an issue in the Kent County, Michigan, study (Crampton, 2001). This percentage is somewhat higher than that found in another Michigan study, which included pilot programs in eight counties (Anderson, 2003). The second study reported domestic violence as a reason for the referral in 13.3 percent (25 of 188) of cases. The difference in percentages is probably the result of policy. Unlike the Kent County program, the eight-county pilot programs included only families in which the batterer was out of the home.

Nevertheless, the exact frequency of families that experience domestic violence is difficult to gauge. As discussed in chapter 2, an FGC referral is typically constructed around a goal for the children rather than around violence directed at an adult. In addition, workers may not know that the family has a history of domestic violence until it surfaces during the preparations, at the conference, or later. For instance, the

North Carolina FGC Project found that no family had domestic violence cited in the conference's stated purpose. In the case of the 27 families that took part in all or the majority of the project's evaluation, multiple sources were available to check for the presence of domestic violence. Among these 27 families, at least seven (or 1 of 4) had experienced domestic violence at some time before the conference. This rate is somewhat higher than those found in the Michigan studies and lower than that found in a study conducted in Newfoundland & Labrador (Canada), which reported adult-to-adult abuse in two out of three families (Pennell & Burford, 1995). Unlike the North Carolina study, however, the Canadian study explicitly requested family violence referrals. Its referrals came mostly from the child welfare system, but included referrals from adult or youth correctional services. The North Carolina FGC Project had referrals solely from child welfare.

What is the impact of FGC on domestic violence?

Although the number of outcome studies on FGC and domestic violence is limited, *the findings suggest that FGC increases safety for women and their children*. The Newfoundland & Labrador study is, to date, the most comprehensive in determining the impact of FGC in situations of family violence (Pennell & Burford, 1995). Three diverse sites took part in the federally funded project: (1) a northern Inuit settlement; (2) a rural region inhabited by people of French, English, and Micmac descent; and (3) the provincial capital with residents of largely Irish and British heritage (Pennell & Burford, 1995). During the one-year period of FGC, 32 families took part in 37 conferences, five of which were follow-up sessions. Demonstrating how FGC widens the circle, these 37 conferences had a total of 472 participants; the clear majority of participants were family group members (384) rather than service providers (88).

The Canadian project requested and generally received the most difficult referrals (Pennell & Burford, 1995). In 21 of the 32 families, a history of violence against an adult in the household was documented; almost all incidents of domestic violence were committed by men against women. Participant safety was closely monitored by observing conferences and carrying out individual interviews shortly after the conferences with 129 (34 percent) of the family group participants. No violence occurred at the conference, and no one reported violence as a result of the conference. For the most part, participants from all three sites expressed satisfaction with FGC. In the two sites where participants were primarily of European descent, the decision-making process was viewed as primarily consensual; in the Inuit community, it was seen as primarily guided by a trusted leader.

To measure the impact of FGC, interviews with family group members and reviews of child welfare and police files were carried out (Burford & Pennell, 1998; Pennell & Burford, 2000a). The follow-up interviews took place over a period of one to two years after the conferences and involved 115 individuals from 28 families, representing 30 percent of all family group participants. Reflecting on developments since the conference, two-thirds (76) of the interviewees concluded that the family was "better off" because of the conference, one-fifth (22) said the family was left the "same," and a minority (7) viewed the family as "worse off," (nine said they did not know, and one did not give a rating). The main reasons cited for the family being "worse off" were that parents had been separated from their children and that important parts of the plan had not been carried out by family group members or service providers. In describing how the families had progressed, numerous interviewees noted that the conference had made them feel proud of their family, had helped them speak more openly, had increased supports and resources for their relatives, had improved the care of the children, had reduced drinking problems, and had decreased violence against adults and children. Pre- and post-assessments showed advances in children's development and social support for mothers.

Reviews of the child welfare and police files of the families in the year before their conference and the year after the conference supported the interviewees' statements (Burford & Pennell, 1998; Pennell & Burford, 2000a). The child welfare file review encompassed the 32 families, as well as a comparison group selected under the direction of an independent consulting group. Although the two groups were similar on factors such as ages of the children, the subsequent file review showed that the families referred for FGC were more worrisome to child protection workers. As they later confirmed, child protection workers had sent their most troubling cases to the project and had difficulty developing a comparison group.

A Children's Protection Events checklist of 31 items was used to enumerate the presence of indicators of child maltreatment and woman abuse before and after FGC (Pennell & Burford, 2000a). The FGC families started with close to twice the number of indicators that the comparison

families had (233 vs. 129); in the second year, however, the FGC families had halved their number of indicators (from 233 to 117), whereas the comparison families had increased theirs (from 129 to 165). The last 17 items on the Children's Protection Events checklist were indicators of mother or wife abuse, such as, "mother exhibits fear and anxiety in presence of her partner." On these items, the FGC families showed improvement, with the events falling from 84 to 34, whereas the comparison families held fairly steady, with the events slightly rising from 45 to 52. The police records backed the child welfare findings for the FGC families: They showed a decrease in police involvement regarding family violence matters.

A British study and the North Carolina FGC Project evaluation supported the Canadian findings. The British study reported on the initial stages of the Dove Project's application of FGC to severe family violence situations (Social Services and Research Information Unit, 2003). For the six families that took part in the research, all were free of violence on the day of the conference, and all six mothers afterward showed a decline in indicators of depression. To the question on how their families had developed since the conference, the five responding mothers agreed that their families were "better." The benefits to their families that they identified included bringing difficult issues into the open, finalizing separations in the case of four couples, improving housing and security, and heightening safety for the women and their children.

For the seven families in which there was a history of woman abuse, the North Carolina FGC Project study found no evidence of domestic violence occurring during the conference or in the follow-up period. The feedback on the conferences was generally positive. On the FGC Evaluation form distributed at the end of five of the seven conferences, most of the 26 family group respondents agreed that they liked the way in which the conference was carried out and the resulting plan. When the 399 scores across the 16 items were combined, 68 percent of the responses were "strongly agree," 22 percent were "agree," and 11 percent were "disagree" or "strongly disagree." (The total does not equal 100 percent because of rounding.) (For the items in the FGC Evaluation form, see chapter 2.) A further examination found that the bulk (32, 74 percent) of the dissent was amassed on one conference. At this acrimonious conference, the mother thought that the family's private time would have been better if only the immediate family members (including the father) conferred. Present at the conference were all people on the mother's invitation list, including three of the father's relatives. None of her relatives, though, agreed to come. The resulting plan was highly disciplinary of the two teenagers, who, along with their mother, did not support the group's decisions.

At other North Carolina FGC Project conferences that involved a history of domestic violence, participants were generally satisfied with the proceedings. If they wanted changes, it was for wider participation. In a conference that lasted longer than expected, the mother had to leave during part of the session to take a child to a medical appointment. In a second conference with a different family group, the mother's sister wished that "everyone had participated more and had been more supportive of the child." And in a third conference, the father cancelled at the last moment, and his relatives who were caring for the children were unwilling to allow the family's private time to go ahead without him.

If the family group members voiced a concern about their conference in the Newfoundland & Labrador Project, it usually revolved around the absence of key family members, especially fathers, who were seen as crucial to making and carrying out the plans (Pennell & Burford, 1995). For instance, a former partner was excluded from one conference because of his history of family violence; at the first meeting, the family group (including his former wife) demanded that he be allowed to attend. A second and, later, a third meeting were held, and the father contributed extensively to making and carrying out the plan.

Often the question is raised, Should the batterer and his family attend the conference? A more useful question is, How can the batterer and his family contribute to conferencing? The latter question refocuses attention on the purpose of conferencing—safeguarding child and adult family members—and widens the lens for examining how they can productively take part.

How can the battering partner and his family contribute to the FGC plan?

Sometimes the battering partner takes part directly in the conference and participates in making and carrying out the plans. Even more often, his relatives are present, share their ideas, and serve the very useful function of ensuring that the batterer stays under control if he is in attendance. *The contributions of the father and his relatives are evident in the plans created at the conferences.* The following are examples of their contributions as found in various families' plans from the Canadian, British, and North Carolina studies:

○ Abusive father to provide financial support to the mother and children.
○ Abusive father to take children to sports events.
○ Nonabusive father (of one of the children in the family) to fund playgroup for his daughter and then to assume parental responsibility for her.
○ Paternal relatives to care for the children.
○ Paternal relatives to baby-sit the children.
○ Paternal relatives to take course in first aid to assist with ill child.
○ Paternal relatives (along with the police) to be contacted if the father comes to the mother's home.
○ Paternal relatives to supervise visitation of father with the children.
○ Paternal relatives to provide transportation for father's visits with the children.
○ Paternal relatives to collect funds for the family to alleviate the financial pressures.
○ Paternal relatives to monitor the plan's implementation to ensure that it is working properly.
○ Paternal and maternal relatives to meet on a regular basis to evaluate implementation of the plan.

After the conference, the workers and the relatives have important roles to play in helping the mother, father, and children carry out the plan. An example below is a family in which the father and mother had a history of assaulting each other. In their case, both sides of the family ensured that this young couple had both the support and monitoring to keep them in line.

Family Example 1: Where the Father and His Family Contributed to the Conference and the Plan

"We stayed on Jerome and Tiffany; others checked on them. They didn't want their kids taken from them. They're young, and they had to work on it. With family you can talk, communicate. Tiffany liked having our support because she doesn't have much family. Having someone behind you, pushing, encouraging."

—JEROME'S MOTHER,
SIX MONTHS AFTER THE CONFERENCE

Jerome and Tiffany lived in a rural community and were the parents of three young children—Teena, Tamra, and Randy. All the children were removed from their home after Tiffany attacked Jerome and he went to the hospital emergency department for treatment. The violence, though, went two ways. As Jerome's aunt observed, "Those two can't keep their hands and fingers off of each other." The three children were split up; Teena and Tamra were placed with Tiffany's sister, and Randy was placed with their father's aunt. The case was referred for FGC to determine where the children were to live in the long term.

Both sides of the family were present at the conference: Tiffany had three members of her family, and Jerome had three of his relatives. All the family group members were African American. The service providers included the child welfare worker and her supervisor, Jerome's mental health counselor, a women's advocate, and the FGC coordinator; they were a mix of African American and white people. The conference started with a confrontation between Tiffany's sister and Jerome, but once they vented, both sides were able

to move on. Reflecting on this confrontation, Jerome's mother said, "Well, at first
it didn't start off too good, but then at the
end it got better. There was some conflict
when Tiffany's sister came in, but then we
worked it out."

The fact that the family group had not
anticipated how long their conference
would run proved to be a greater problem. Tiffany and her relatives had to leave
during the family's private time to take
the youngest child, Randy, for a health
checkup. In an interview a month after the
conference, Tiffany's cousin continued to
be concerned about this:

> [The conference] was initially sched-
> uled for three hours and ended up
> being six or seven. And because Tif-
> fany missed a great deal she felt
> alienated. . . . She felt so much had
> been decided while she was not
> there. . . . All people need to be there
> at all times.

Jerome's side of the family shared this concern. His mother commented on the private time, "Only Jerome was there; it was
like a one-sided thing. I think that we
would have been better off if Tiffany was
there to answer the questions that came
up during the planning."

Despite these problems, Tiffany, Jerome,
and their relatives were satisfied with the
results of the conference. A month after the
conference, Jerome expressed his determination to keep his family together and recognized the benefit of having all the family work together to make this happen:

> To me, [the conference] went by
> good. . . . Everybody said that they
> would be there for us if we got into
> a bind. But we aren't going to get into
> a bind; everybody is doing what they

said they would do. . . . Me and Tiffany got the kids back, and we're
doing fine.

In an interview six months after the conference, Tiffany's cousin agreed with
Jerome, and she emphasized that the family was supporting the young couple:

> Tiffany has the support she needs
> from her support system, and from
> me and my husband. Tiffany's
> mother is involved and supportive.
> The relationship with Tiffany's sis-
> ter has strengthened. . . . Jerome and
> Tiffany are engaged. Jerome is still
> in anger management.

Likewise, Jerome's mother identified the
progress that both Tiffany and Jerome
were making. She also noted the importance of the family keeping an eye on them
and their children:

> The conference made a difference. . . .
> Sometimes Tiffany would try to start
> something, but Jerome walks away
> and ignores her. Tiffany is talking
> about going back to school. . . . We
> check some and Tiffany's cousin
> checks, and I see the kids everyday.

A year after the conference, Tiffany concluded that her family was "better off" because of the conference: "I got married. Went
back to work. Everyone's healthy. . . . My
sister helps with Teena until school time, and
my cousin helps with the school transportation. . . . Jerome and I are doing fine.

Why are battering partners and their families not present at the conference? And what can the impact of their absence be?

*In some cases, the battering partner cannot be
located; in other cases, he may be legally prohibited from taking part or excluded after a*

safety assessment; in still other cases, he may simply refuse to participate. At times, his family attends even if he is not in attendance because of their ties to the children. For instance, in the seven North Carolina conferences for families with a history of domestic violence, the abusing fathers were present at only two. One of these fathers (Jerome, in the previous family example) resided with his wife and children, and the other father had recently separated from his family. The five men absent from their family's conference did not attend for various reasons: One chose not to attend, although his relatives who took care of the children attended; by the follow-up conference, a protective order prohibited him from attending. Two were barred by protective orders from the outset. One was incarcerated at the time of the conference, and he and the mother had protective orders against each other; and one was no longer involved with the family.

When the mother has taken out a protective order against the father, the FGC coordinator should ensure that he is excluded from the conference. The same applies when the father has a protective order against the mother. Domestic violence is a crime and should be treated as a crime. There are good reasons for seeking legal protection for the abused parent and the children. If the couple have no children in common and do not plan to continue their relationship, the abusive partner should probably be excluded from the conference. The issue becomes murkier when it involves excluding one side of the family from the invitation list when the couple have children in common. A case in point is the conference in which the father had been incarcerated at the time of the conference. The mother's family and the child protection worker wanted to

ensure that the father and mother remained apart. As described in the family example below, the social worker later had second thoughts about the exclusion, however.

Family Example 2: Where the Father and His Family Did Not Contribute to the Conference and the Plan

"Nothing went as it was supposed to happen. Ashleigh is living with the twins' daddy. . . . and the twins are back with their mom."

—Ashleigh's aunt,
one year after the conference

Reflecting on preparations for the conference, the FGC coordinator wrote about the struggles in dealing with a family with multiple issues—domestic violence, substance abuse, and mental illness:

The main issues we faced were (1) reaching the mother, Ashleigh, and (2) including the father, Brian. Ashleigh was difficult to reach. She was very transient. She was staying with a family member; they had a falling out. Then she was with a friend until they had a falling out. Initially, when we met with the social worker, she tried to discourage us from including Brian who lived in another city. In retrospect, she thought that including him would have been a good idea. . . . Ashleigh's issues included substance abuse, mental health, and domestic violence. Ashleigh and Brian each had a protective order against the other. Sometimes they'd spend time together, and then they'd get upset and report each other. Ashleigh assaulted her husband and went to jail. Their [two-year-old] twin sons, Jonathan and Adam, were temporarily placed with Ashleigh's parents. Jonathan and Adam were with them at the time of the conference. Custody had not been removed; social services did not take custody of the children. The idea was to wait until Ashleigh stabilized so that Jonathan and Adam could return to their mother.

Finally reaching Ashleigh, the FGC coordinator asked her to complete a form called the People in Your Life (adapted from Tracy & Whittaker, 1990), to map out the invitation list: "It was a challenge to do with her. . . . It did clarify in her mind and solidify who she wanted to invite. She did list people she didn't want to invite." Ashleigh's People in Your Life list included 17 individuals, all white with the exception of her employer. Neither Brian nor his relatives were included. Her ratings of the extent to which her family and friends offered her concrete, emotional, and informational support varied considerably. In her view, more than one-half of her network was "hardly ever" emotionally supportive.

At the conference, Ashleigh, four members of her family, and her friend (who was also her support person) created a detailed plan. It covered where the twins, Jonathan and Adam, would live and how Ashleigh would undergo treatment for substance abuse and mental health issues, get housing and transportation assistance, and receive domestic violence counseling. No reference was made to the children's father, Brian, although his influence was intimated during the conference. For instance, the research observer noted:

Ashleigh mentioned driving a car with a grin on her face. Her relatives

reacted because they knew she was driving Brian's car without a driver's license. The child protection worker sprang in and told Ashleigh that it was a bad idea to drive without a license.

Nevertheless, on her evaluation form, Ashleigh wrote, "I think the conference was very helpful; it made me think about a whole lot." Likewise, her family was generally satisfied with the conference and the resulting plan. The five respondents on the FGC Evaluation form almost invariably concurred that they were satisfied with the proceedings.

As specified in the FGC plan, the coordinator worked with the family to hold a follow-up conference 10 weeks later. This second meeting never took place. The coordinator explained:

As the case progressed, Ashleigh was seeing her counselor more, but by the time of the scheduled follow-up . . . she was not seeing her counselor. She spent a couple of nights in jail due to violation of the protective order between the time we received the referral and the time we tried to hold the follow-up conference. We had to cancel the follow-up [conference] . . . because there was a death in the family. We were going to reschedule it, but Ashleigh went into inpatient treatment by the time we tried to reschedule it.

Ashleigh was not staying away from Brian, and her treatment plan had deteriorated.

A year later, the researcher tried to contact Ashleigh for a follow-up interview. These attempts were unsuccessful, but the researcher interviewed the aunt with whom Ashleigh had been staying at the time of the conference. This aunt was disappointed by the developments after the conference—Ashleigh and Brian had reunited, and Jonathan and Adam were living with them. In her view, the family had been left the "same" by the conference:

> Seems like if the social worker and the substance abuse counselor could've been right there, pushing Ashleigh, maybe we could've gotten further. But if you turn your back one second, she's out of there. . . . The meeting . . . succeeded in getting everyone to the table, did a good job, but we, family, had to do more. . . . Ashleigh never had guidance. . . . Jonathan and Adam are OK for now.

The protective orders never kept Ashleigh and Brian permanently apart. The family group's plan never addressed their relationship, which would have been difficult to do at any rate without input from either Brian or his family. It would have been ill-advised to break the protective orders by having Brian at the conference, even if he had received permission to leave the jail to take part. Another possibility, though, would have been to seek out Brian's input or at least that of his family. Perhaps with this fuller perspective, the family group might have reached a more lasting solution. Having only Ashleigh's side of the family present at the conference in all likelihood made for greater participant satisfaction and higher ratings on the FGC Evaluation form. Leaving out Brian's side, however, reduced the likelihood of achieving the objectives of the conference. Such an experience was not unique to this conference.

How does omitting one side of the family affect the achievement of the FGC objectives?

Having only one side of the family present appears to go hand in hand with a greater sense of effectiveness at the time of the conference. After the session, however, difficulties may become apparent in fulfilling the conference's objectives. (The analysis was on families with and without domestic violence.) For the North Carolina FGC Project, a striking pattern was found for families who had or did not have a known history of domestic violence. This pattern was revealed in a comparison of the responses on the FGC Evaluation forms filled out at the end of the conference (see chapter 2), with the responses to the Achievement of FGC Objectives questionnaires administered, on average, a month after the conference, usually in a telephone interview (see chapter 7), revealed a striking pattern. One of these FGC objectives is inviting multiple sides of the family to the conference. Meeting this objective is assumed to help in fulfilling the FGC principle of "foster understanding of the family and creativity in planning" (see chapter 2, family example 2). An analysis found that according to family group members, including different sides of the family was linked to achieving three other FGC objectives, but achieving these four objectives accompanied a lower sense of effectiveness at the conference (Pennell, in press-b).[1]

---

[1]The two instruments were compared by using a canonical correlation analysis of matched responses of 73 family group members (Pennell, in press-b). One significant canonical correlation ($p = .0172$) was found. The nine FGC Evaluation items indicating effective planning had positive correlations ranging from .3573 to .6160. The four Achievement of Objectives items in inclusive

The four FGC objectives form a set relating to decision making that is inclusive and encourages ongoing collaboration (Pennell, in press-b). These four objectives combined point to a possible fourth pathway to safeguarding children and other family members.[2] This potential pathway is termed "inclusive planning" and incorporates the following four objectives:

○ Different sides of the family were invited to the conference (for example, father's and mother's sides of the family).
○ The plan included ways that the family group will help out.
○ The plan included steps to evaluate whether the plan is working and to get the family group back together again, if needed.
○ Social Services approved the plan without unnecessary delays.

The reverse of inclusive planning also happened at conferences. If family group members disagreed that different sides of the family were invited, they also disagreed that the other three objectives were achieved. This makes sense. With only one

_____

planning had negative correlations ranging from −.3210 to −.3972. The canonical correlation between these two sets of variables was .8989.

[2]In chapter 7, three pathways to widening the circle and safeguarding children and their families were set forth: cultural safety, community partnerships, and family leadership. Inclusive planning may be a fourth pathway. Its relationship, though, to the pathway family leadership needs to be explored further. One item, "the plan included ways that the family group will help out," is found in family leadership by the factor analysis and in inclusive planning by the canonical correlation analysis.

side of the family present, there are fewer people offering to help, less tension pushing the participants to include steps for evaluating the impact of the plan and revising it, and lower unanimity on the plan across the family group, impeding approval by the child protection worker.

When the responses on the Achievement of FGC Objectives are compared with those from the FGC Evaluation, a counterintuitive finding stands out (Pennell, in press-b). If the four objectives of inclusive planning were achieved, then the family group members expressed lower satisfaction on nine of the FGC Evaluation items. Likewise, if planning was less inclusive, then satisfaction at the conference was higher. These FGC Evaluation items all relate to the sense that the planning process was effective:

○ Preparation for the conference was adequate.
○ I liked where the conference was held.
○ During the group meeting, I got to participate whenever I wanted to.
○ I felt that I was a genuine member of the group.
○ The group reached the right decision.
○ I support the final group decision.
○ I would be willing to put my best effort into carrying out the group's final decision.
○ I think that the right people were involved in reaching the decision.
○ I am satisfied with the plan that was agreed upon at the conference.

Why is there a divergence between greater satisfaction at the time of the conference and later reservations about achieving some FGC objectives? The more nuanced responses a month afterwards may reflect a more realistic appraisal over time. With the glow of the conference at a distance, people may give lower ratings. If they had a highly satisfying conference, they may feel a greater degree of upset if its promise is not fulfilled. Another reason is the dynamics of conferencing. If one side of the family is in attendance, the process is likely to go more smoothly. Consider the second family example presented earlier: If Brian's side of the family had been present, it is quite likely that Ashleigh's family would have been far tenser at the conference. In the first family example above, both sides of the family attended, and this led to an initial confrontation between Jerome and his wife's sister.

The findings indicate the need for outreach to multiple sides of the family to take part in the conference, and mechanisms to support the family group's involvement over time to enhance the efficacy of FGC. This inclusive planning should help to maintain the positive momentum generated at the conference to resolve the issues of concern. Such inclusion can be problematic, however, when there is a history of domestic violence, unless close attention is paid to safety measures. One way of developing such measures is to seek the guidance and participation of women's advocates.

How can the domestic violence community contribute to safety?

Women's advocates can contribute to safety by helping to develop local protocols for organizing conferences, educating child welfare workers about domestic violence, serving as consultants to FGC coordinators, providing information at conferences, and supporting the plan's implementation. From the start, the domestic violence community should be involved in planning an FGC program, particularly in establishing measures to keep participants safe. The North Carolina FGC Project found that the participation of women's advocates was essential in developing practice guidance. Their participation was encouraged by including them in planning bodies at the state and county levels, inviting them to FGC training sessions, asking them to attend conferences, and soliciting their input through focus groups. The last, in particular, revealed the extent to which women's advocates saw both the promise and the dangers of conferences for families that had experienced domestic violence.

Women's advocates welcomed an approach that gave abused mothers another way of planning for their own and their children's safety, but expressed doubts about women's safety during and after the conference (Francis, 2002). Most of all, they were concerned about child welfare workers' approach to FGC: Would they seek out and listen to the advice of women's advocates? Would they remove the children if the mother refused to attend a conference? Would they blame the mother if the father failed to carry out the plan? Would they approve unsafe plans? To further explore these valid concerns, later focus groups were held separately with abused mothers and shelter staff to consider holding "safety conferences" to address issues of domestic violence (Pennell & Francis, 2005). Both the survivors and staff saw the benefits of safety conferencing: educating family members about domestic violence, building supportive networks, combining the resources of informal and formal networks, and enhancing safety. Notably, the survivors of domestic violence also called for conferences for their children, for whom they recognized the importance of family ties. If safety concerns did not prohibit the father's participation, they wanted him to attend a conference—as long as it focused solely on the children's protection.

Many survivors and their children no longer have a direct connection to the father and his family. The focus then becomes a matter of resolving the aftereffects of the familial disruption on the women and children. Here, too, women's advocates can play a crucial role in educating the family group members and service providers so that they can engage with mothers in a supportive and non-blaming way. A women's advocate would have been helpful at one North Carolina conference for a survivor of domestic violence and her children, all with extensive mental health issues. During the information-sharing part of the conference, the social worker stressed that the mother needed to demonstrate her ability to use what she had learned in parenting class. As noted by the research observer, this comment provoked an angry reaction from the mother: "Mother rebukes social worker's perspective of why she relapsed, Mother says it is because of her relationships with male partners, not because she is overwhelmed."

At another conference, a women's advocate provided crucial information on the effects of domestic violence. As shown in the following family example, this was a pivotal point in the conference and heightened understanding of the mother who suffered from PTSD after years of battering.

Family Example 3: Women's Advocacy and Posttraumatic Stress Disorder

"Everybody communicates better. There's not a lot of anger now. . . . I think about how *I was back then—emotionally stressed. I've made a good change."*

–DEENA, DOMESTIC VIOLENCE SURVIVOR, ONE YEAR AFTER THE CONFERENCE

Before the conference, Deena was a lonely, frightened, and angry mother of six young children. She had been diagnosed with PTSD as a result of years of violence inflicted by the children's father. The parents were separated, but the father continued to show up drunk at her door. In preparing for the conference, the FGC coordinator was keenly cognizant of the effects of PTSD: "Deena's at-risk behaviors included violent rages, which the children had seen. . . . [They] had also been in the house when she made a suicidal threat." The coordinator made sure that in addition to the child protection worker, Deena's mental health counselor was present at the conference to lend support and that a women's advocate was there to address "the confusion of family members" about PTSD.

In planning the conference's invitation list, the coordinator asked Deena to complete two questionnaires regarding her family group relationships: the Index of Family Relations (Hudson, 1992) and the People in Your Life form (adapted from Tracy & Whittaker, 1990). On the Index of Family Relations, Deena characterized her own family as loving, close, and a source of joy and pride. At the same time, she said that "all of the time" she felt "left out" of her family. For the People in Your Life, she charted an extensive and well-established African American network in which members were emotionally close, hardly ever critical, and in frequent contact. With some exceptions, however, Deena saw herself as the person helping others, rather than the person being helped by others. This perception was understandable, given that Deena had recently suffered two significant losses: the death of her grandmother, who had raised her, and the death of her best friend.

The absence from the conference of certain people from both sides of the family emerged as an issue. In planning the conference, the coordinator noted, "The invitation list was limited, largely ... [because of] the lack of involvement with the paternal side of the family." The father was excluded because of Deena's protective order against him. Deena, however, wanted his mother in attendance, and later at the conference the researcher observed, "Deena is very upset about [her mother-in-law] not being present and not giving support." Also absent were half of the adults expected from Deena's side of the family. Four of the invitees never arrived at the meeting for various reasons, including illness and inability to find the church at which the conference was held. A week after the conference, Deena continued to feel their absence: "[The conference] was good. I liked it a lot. ... [But] if everybody could have been there, it would have helped out a lot."

Deena's six children accompanied her to the conference, but they stayed in an adjoining room with a baby-sitter, except during the dinner hour. Deena was joined at the conference by three of her family group: her mother, her cousin, and the children's godmother, Aster. At the outset of the meeting, its purpose was established: "To avoid foster care placement by strengthening family and community supports."

Soon after the conference began, the women's advocate arrived and was asked to make a presentation. Both the coordinator and the research observer were struck by the impact of her words. Characterizing this as a "very moving moment," the research observer recorded:

The information provider talks from the perspective of what happens after one leaves a domestic violence situation and shares a testimony of a survivor and her own experience with PTSD. The godmother Aster says she was a survivor of domestic violence. Deena then says that she was, but says, "I don't know if I am surviving!" Deena's mother also speaks up and says she was a survivor.

Impressed, the coordinator reflected: "The whole tenor of the conference turned at that point."

Later in the conference, the group was able to discuss Deena's PTSD openly and supportively. The research observer recorded one such exchange: "The social worker says that Deena is doing better because of her medication. Deena agrees; others agree. Deena talks openly about her feelings—how she dealt with things like her fits of rage and breaking dishes."

Four months after the conference, Deena's worker changed, and child protection services transferred the children to their godmother's home. In Deena's view, "Taking the kids made my depression worse—they kept me going." A year later, however, the children were to be returned to Deena. Commenting on Deena's progress, Aster noted, "Deena has admitted she has major depression problems. I told her that she's going to be fine now, now that she has recognized that she has a problem."

For her part, Deena was striving to follow through on the family plan. She reached out to her family for support; accompanied her children to the library, movies, and church; met with her therapist; took her medication as prescribed; and attended a support group for abused women. Since the conference, Deena reported that there had been no further violence in her life. Although the conference did not avoid placement for the children, it achieved its aim of "strengthening family and community supports." All of these Deena productively used to bring her children home. First, the women's advocate and then, the abused women's support group, helped to create a climate in which this was possible.

What protocols should be followed when there is a history of domestic violence?

The five decision points for screening referrals outlined in chapter 2 should be followed for any family—especially for those in which there is domestic violence:

1. *Is there a clear reason for referral?* Knowing the purpose of the conference reduces speculation and volatile feelings about the reason for the meeting. Child welfare workers and other involved protection authorities (for example, police, juvenile justice system) need to clearly state the purpose. In this way, victims cannot later be blamed for calling the meeting and setting its agenda.

2. *Can worker use family input?* If the family group members are going to take the risk of attending, they need to know that child welfare workers intend to give serious consideration to what they propose. Frustration in the family builds if their views are ignored.

3. *Is the family interested in learning more about FGC?* With a clear explanation of the conferencing process and purpose, family members can better assess whether they want to attend and what they want to say at the conference. They can think through what they really want to say rather than only reacting at that time.

4. *Does enough family group agree to take part?* Having a conference with only the abuser and abused present is dangerous. The intent of FGC is to widen the circle, and increasing the support for battered individuals is crucial to counter the batterers' intimidation, isolation, and entrapment of their victims.

5. *Can family take part safely?* A conference should not proceed unless the coordinator has determined that participants can take part without further jeopardizing their safety. The coordinator should consult closely with victims/survivors on whether they want the conference to proceed and, if so, what needs to be in place to keep them safe before, during, and after the conference. In preparing for the conference, the FGC coordinator might ask: What are your concerns about holding a conference? What is likely to happen if you and your partner disagree at the conference? What do you and the children need to be safe during and after the conference? What needs to be done in advance of the conference so that both sides of the family can take part in a positive way? Are there some issues that you want someone else to raise at the conference, and who would be a good person to do this? Are there some people who should

not be invited to the conference? Are there some people that you really want at the conference?

For families with a history of domestic violence, recommendations have come from the Newfoundland & Labrador Project (Burford, Pennell, & MacLeod, 1995; Pennell & Burford, 2000b), the North Carolina FGC Project (2002), the Michigan pilot programs (Anderson, 2003), the Oregon Department of Human Resources (1999), and the Family Violence Prevention Fund (Carter, 2003). FGC coordinators should consider a variety of safety measures, such as the following:

○ Taking any actions immediately necessary for safeguarding family members (such as a protective order, move to a shelter).
○ Not using FGC as a way to divert family violence from the legal system. Any needed legal safeguards should be used.
○ Consulting with domestic violence programs on how to design the FGC program and organize conferences when there is a history of family violence.
○ Consulting with victims/survivors and domestic violence programs on whether to hold the conference and, if so, whether the abuser and his family should be invited to attend. The coordinator should take public responsibility for canceling or holding the conference rather than putting the decision on the shoulders of the victim/survivor.
○ Protecting the confidentiality of survivors who have had to seek sanctuary and change their identity to escape the batterer. In these cases,

anyone who might possibly reveal, knowingly or unknowingly, the woman's location to her batterer must be excluded.
○ Excluding perpetrators who pose a danger to the safety of the survivors, other participants, or themselves at the conference.
○ Excluding perpetrators who have a restraining or protective order against them or those whose participation would violate a court order.
○ Encouraging and preparing all sides of the family to attend, with the victims'/survivors' agreement.
○ Arranging for, if needed, security at the conference or having the police on call for a quick response; having a telephone available to call for help.
○ Planning with the family group where, when, and how to hold the conference to establish a sense of cultural safety.
○ Making sure that victims/survivors have a safe way to get to and from the conference.
○ Assessing whether the conference is likely to put anyone in jeopardy; checking on whether the victim/survivor is intimidated and has had prior injuries, whether the batterer is threatening violence or suicide, and whether the batterer or survivor has a weapon.
○ Encouraging victims/survivors to select a support person to stay by them during the conference; requiring that abused minors have an adult support person with them at the conference.
○ Encouraging batterers to select a support person who can help keep them under control.

○ Preparing support people for their role.

○ Encouraging victims and victimizers to think through in advance what they want to say at the conference.

○ Developing a strategy with victims on how sensitive issues can be raised at a conference (such as having another family member or counselor bring up the issue).

○ Having the involved service providers lay out the history of domestic violence and areas of concern so that the victims/survivors do not have to disclose their abuse at the conference.

○ Inviting staff from women's centers and batterer intervention groups to provide information at the conference on domestic violence and available programs.

○ Asking involved protective authorities such as police, parole officers, and juvenile justice workers to attend so that they can provide some legal leverage over the batterers.

○ Having the coordinator always on the premises and available to assist during the family private time.

○ Taking a break or closing the meeting, if necessary; working out signals in advance with the victim/survivor on when the coordinator should intervene.

○ Ensuring that the involved protective authorities take responsibility for reviewing and approving the plans and remaining vigilant about the safety of child and adult family members.

○ Ensuring that the plans include mechanisms for monitoring and evaluating the plan's implementation and for reconvening as needed.

○ Hosting joint FGC training for child welfare, domestic violence, substance abuse, mental health, juvenile justice, courts, police, public health, and other involved agencies.

○ Remembering that the purpose of the conference is to safeguard all family members. The family group, with support from community organizations and public agencies, usually knows what action steps must be taken to protect their relatives.

11

Analyzing Family Involvement Approaches

Lisa Merkel-Holguin and Leslie Wilmot[1]

"We have begun to recognize that the best and often the only way to save children is through their families."

(NELSON & LANDSMAN 1992, P. 3)

Family involvement models in child welfare are proliferating, often leaving systems and workers uncertain about the similarities and differences of various approaches, and raising several questions.

[1]Although the perspectives herein reflect those of the authors, the perspectives, challenges, and questions posed by many individuals enriched this chapter. The authors thank Paul Vincent and Linda Bayless from the Child Welfare Practice and Policy Group; John Mattingly and Pat Rideout from the Annie E. Casey Foundation; Nancy McDaniel, American Humane; Paul Sivak, CSU Stanislaus; Teresa Turner, North Carolina Family Centered Meetings Project; and coeditors Gary R. Anderson and Joan Pennell. In addition, the authors thank representatives of six communities experimenting with model integration for sharing their experiences.

Why involve families?

Are families who are involved in the child welfare system seen as subjects of an intervention, or are they partners in determining an intervention? Historically, the child welfare literature routinely has not described families as partners or collaborators in goal setting, assessments, and interventions. According to Thoburn (1995), parental participation was absent from the literature on efforts to resolve the problem of child abuse until the mid-1980s. Since that time, the notions of parental participation and family involvement have emerged as themes in the ever-shifting practice of social work. The resultant discourse has placed the concept of family involvement front and center, which has helped the child welfare system begin to conceptualize the differences between a worker-driven system and a family-driven system, in which family members and informal supports are considered active experts on family processes, problems, and solutions (Garbarino, 1976; Goodman, Wandersman, Chinman, Imm, & Morrissey, 1996; Mannes, 2001). There has been a systematic thrust toward partnership-based practice, which views consumers as contributors to the solution, integral in aligning services with needs.

A number of phenomena have converged, propelling the child welfare field toward family involvement and away from an isolationist approach dominated by professionals. First, experience and research show that the success of an intervention correlates to the quality of the relationship between the worker and the family (DePanfilis, 2000). Second, there is a growing recognition that paternalistic practices and policies have harmed minority communities and have underemphasized the importance of family and culture (Roberts, 2002; Turnell & Edwards, 1999). Ample research has demonstrated the presence of natural and informal supports, as well as their influence on families when creating solutions to a wide range of complex family challenges (Anderson, 2001; Hegar, 1999). Third, child welfare systems continue to be resource-constrained and challenged to deliver positive outcomes for children and their families. Fourth, federal and state policy frameworks and audits (for example, the Child and Family Service Reviews conducted in every state, beginning in 2001), as well as foundation-sponsored initiatives, are providing additional support to embrace families and their support networks as valuable partners in decision making. And, fifth, concepts of democracy and self-regulation are inching their way into the child welfare literature, adding a

new and refreshing theoretical dimension to child welfare constructs (Braithwaite, 2002; Merkel-Holguin, 2004).

These factors are spurring a redefinition of values that, in turn, are shaping child welfare practice. *There is a growing recognition that families have inherent knowledge, expertise, and wisdom that is unavailable to service providers and that when leveraged, these family strengths can result in safer, stronger plans.* Parents are no longer defined as clients but, rather, as partners. A strengths-based perspective has replaced the deficit or pathological analysis of families (Saleeby, 1997).

What is meant by the term "family involvement models"?

Connolly and McKenzie (1999) suggested that the concept of involving the family in child protection is generally embraced; what remains a point of debate is the appropriate level of family involvement and authority. Individual social worker values; cultural respect and awareness; wider family interest, willingness, and capacity to participate; the views of families espoused by formal child welfare systems and society at large; social work education; and statutory and policy frameworks are all likely to influence the degree of family involvement.

The child welfare system is simultaneously criticized for unnecessarily removing children from their homes and for not sufficiently protecting children in their homes. The historical, inherent tension between parental civil liberties and the government's role in protecting children rages on (Connolly & McKenzie, 1999). Corby and colleagues (1996) surmised that involving families as decision makers in child protection will lessen this tension. *Family involvement models invite a wider circle of individuals connected to the family to meaningfully participate in a decision-making process to promote child safety, permanency, and well-being.* How is "involvement" defined? Undoubtedly, family involvement has broad and diverse connotations and perhaps is best described on a continuum.

Based solely on a philosophy of family involvement, this continuum clearly demonstrates the variability in family voice, partnership, responsibility, self-determination, and legitimized authority as decision makers in determining goals and outlining the necessary steps and responsibilities to achieve them.

What are the predominant family involvement models currently being implemented in child welfare?

Although there are a myriad of family involvement strategies used in child welfare, three models took hold in the United States in the 1990s and are committed to involving families in a decision-making or planning process. *These are family group conferencing (FGC), family team conferencing (FTC), and team decision making (TDM).*

Origins of the Various Family Involvement Approaches

FAMILY GROUP CONFERENCING. In 1989, FGC was federally legislated in New Zealand through the Children, Young

Family Involvement Continuum

Family Voice in Decision Making ← → System Voice in Decision Making

Families, along with their support network, are the primary decision makers. As a group, families craft initial plans that are subsequently shared with the professionals who work collaboratively with the family to ensure they are attainable and meet the highest standards for achieving the goals of safety, permanency, and well-being.	Families are part of the decision-making team. In these instances, families partner with professionals to create consensual decisions acceptable to all parties.	Families have a genuine voice at the meetings. Their ideas, needs, perspectives, and other inputs are sought at the meetings, but the decision making rests with professionals.	Families are present at meetings where decisions will be made about their children.	Families are not included in meetings or other forums where decisions are made about their children.

Persons and Their Families Act. Maori indigenous practices, in particular the family meeting, or *Whanua Hui*, informed the development of the formalized process that became family group conferencing. *Whanau Hui* is a broad term that can refer to any type of family gathering (Atkin, 1988–1989). Before this legislation, the 1986 *Report of the Ministerial Advisory Committee on a Maori Perspective for the Department of Social Welfare*, known as Pau-te-Ata-tu (Rangihau, 1986) outlined the impact of racism and the effects of Westernized laws and policies on New Zealand's child welfare and justice systems. It provided a Maori perspective that helped in the development of an alternate, culturally compatible model of family and tribal involvement in decision making regarding issues related to the safety, permanency, and well-being of children and families (Love, 2000).

In the United States, interest in FGC was closely tied to one of the earliest and most substantive paradigm shifts in social work practice; a transition from a prescriptive medical model of intervention to a family-centered and strengths-based model. A new partnership mentality unfolded that was inculcated with the concept of shared responsibility for child safety between the child welfare system, the community at large, and the family. In addition, the simultaneous development of state and federal child welfare policies and mandates that heightened the emphasis on kinship placements when children were removed from a parental home spurred communities to consider other family partnership efforts that would achieve better permanency solutions (Merkel-Holguin, 2000b). In the United States, these factors contributed to the expansion of family group decision making (FGDM) implementation from

five communities in the mid-1990s to hundreds of communities in approximately 34 states by 2003; furthermore, communities in 22 countries were using this approach by 2003 (Burford & Nixon, 2003; Nixon, Merkel-Holguin, Sivak, & Gunderson, 2000).

FAMILY TEAM CONFERENCING. In the early 1990s, a lawsuit was initiated in Alabama to address and correct child welfare system failures, much like those grappled with throughout the United States. The lawsuit focused on such issues as excessive and lengthy foster care placements, a backlog of investigations into child abuse and neglect reports, and limited or unavailable treatment options for children and their families (Kaplan, 2003). Instead of going to trial, the State of Alabama entered into what is now known as the R. C. class action child welfare settlement, the result of which was a statewide system change that incorporated a strengths-based perspective and family involvement into everyday child welfare practice. This transformation of frontline practice became an impetus for the development of FTC, which evolved from various approaches used to engage families and children in service planning and decision making.

Family team conferencing was part of a more expansive framework of practice in which family involvement in decision making, team building and coordination, strengths- and needs-based assessment and interventions, and highly individualized planning were core expectations. The developers leveraged best-practice knowledge from various systems, including child welfare, children's mental health (particularly wraparound practice—a case-planning process used predominantly in mental health systems and child and family teams), special education (with its emphasis on individualized education plans), and developmental disabilities (related to client and family participation in case planning). With experimentation, the concept of family teams as a decision-making forum was born and instituted as a practice framework in Alabama (Child Welfare Practice and Policy Group [CWPPG], 2001). Initially called individual service planning (ISP), this approach was universally implemented throughout Alabama's system, from intake through case closure for all families.

The individuals who were the principal leaders of the Alabama reform later formed the nonprofit Child Welfare Practice and Policy Group (CWPPG) to promote the experience of the Alabama reform to other systems. When the CWPPG became involved in the (then) Edna McConnell Clark Foundation's new initiative, Community Partnerships for the Protection of Children, the initiative planners relied substantively on Alabama's experiences with family involvement and needs-based practice in creating its own practice framework, called the Individual Course of Action. This new approach recognized the significance of using informal and community supports, and the preventive potential of meetings. Ultimately, the meetings were defined as family team conferences, a term that conveys the idea of a family team converging to create plans and make decisions (CWPPG, 2001). In 2003, FTC was being implemented statewide in Utah, Iowa, Maine, Tennessee, and Alabama and in 25 communities in five other states (CWPPG, 2003).

TEAM DECISION-MAKING MEETINGS. One of the four core strategies of the Annie E. Casey Foundation's Family to Family Initiative, TDM was first implemented in 1992 in five states (DeMuro & Rideout, 2002). However, the origins of TDM precede the foundation's larger initiative. According to Saunders (2002), the roots of TDM can be traced back to Lucas County Children Services, in Ohio, in the early 1980s. There, an administrator recognized a phenomenon occurring in the county's child welfare agency. One child protection unit was removing children and placing them in foster care at a rate 300 percent greater than that of another unit. On further exploration, it became clear that child welfare decision making around placement determinations was often not reflective or congruent with system policies (J. Mattingly, personal communication, January 27, 2004).

According to John Mattingly (personal communication, January 20, 2004, the TDM approach was initiated as a structural change in the child welfare system to ensure that decisions made at critical child placement junctures involved more individuals than a single social worker and his or her supervisor. This structural change supports the goals of TDM, which are to

> improve the agency's decision-making process; encourage the support and "buy-in" of the family, extended family and the community for the agency's decisions; and develop specific, individualized, and appropriate interventions for children and families. (DeMuro & Rideout, 2002, p. 8)

Hamilton County Ohio (Cincinnati) and Cuyahoga County Ohio (Cleveland) were the next locales to implement the TDM case-staffing process (Saunders, 2002). Their experiences have been instrumental as TDM expands throughout the United States. In 2003, there were more than 30 communities in 16 states instituting this practice (DeMuro & Rideout, 2002; J. Mattingly, personal communication, January 20, 2004).

Unique elements of the models

FAMILY GROUP CONFERENCING. Structured to promote family leadership in decision making, maximize family responsibility, widen the circle of caring individuals, embrace family culture, and harness the community's involvement in protecting children and strengthening families, FGC practice has a variety of distinguishing elements. First, comprehensively seeking and preparing maternal and paternal family members and their support networks to participate in a family group conference is paramount to this process. Not only does extensive preparation provide families with the opportunity to emerge as leaders, but also it creates a far-reaching network of caring participants converging to develop and resource plans. During this phase, great attention and care are given to developing a growing understanding of family culture and its rightful place in the meeting and the decision-making processes. Along with FGC's solution or decision-making orientation, the identification of what the family members view as their important cultural attributes and rituals, and the integration of these attributes across the process and during the meeting itself distinguish FGC from a number of other family involvement models and traditional case practice. The preparation phase is also an important opportunity for identifying and planning for any participant safety issues that may surface.

Second, during a family group conference, the process for sharing information differs from FTC and TDM. In a conference, the referring worker shares the information that brought the family to the attention of the public agency with the gathered participants so that they can consider them in their deliberations; after the information sharing, the family has an opportunity to question and/or clarify the information presented and then moves directly into private family time. Although both FTC and TDM processes include a facilitated discussion of family strengths, the information shared in a family group conference focuses squarely on the critical concerns and the case history related to child safety, permanency, and well-being. One important premise of FGC is that when families are provided all of the critical case information and are comprehensively prepared, they can craft solutions that maximize the opportunity for family leadership, participation, and self-determination.

The third, unique element—private family time—FGC recognizes that families have the knowledge, wisdom, and expertise necessary to serve as primary decision makers. The concept is as simple as it sounds; family members meet alone in private to review information and strategize solutions to the previously identified concerns. Private family time is not an abdication of the child welfare system's statutory responsibility for the protection of children. Rather, it recognizes the capacity of families to self-regulate and uniquely craft and resource a plan to address the issues that led to the family's involvement with the public child welfare system. At the conclusion of private family time, the referring worker and service providers join with the family to detail and finalize the plan, illustrating the partnership framework of this approach. The referring worker ultimately decides whether the plan achieves the standards of safety, permanency, and well-being. International research shows that FGC plans are accepted approximately 90 to 95 percent of the time (Merkel-Holguin, Nixon, & Burford, 2003).

Finally, central to the FGC process is an independent coordinator responsible for the preparation of, and facilitation at, the conference. The coordinator is never the case-carrying social worker to ensure the neutrality of the process, heighten the "buy-in" and willingness of the family to try something new, eliminate the family's view of the worker as "expert" or "sole" problem solver, and reduce the inherent disparity of genuine authority (power imbalance) between the child welfare system and the individual family.

This approach, with its corresponding distinctive elements, raises some interesting questions:

○ How do professional and system mandates, responsibility, and professional or personal power manifest during the FGC process?

○ Without the opportunity to discuss family strengths and concerns, does the wider family network have sufficient and comprehensive information to construct a plan during private family time?

○ As hypothesized, does adequate preparation correlate to emotional and physical safety and more comprehensive and better informed decisions during private family time?

○ Given the time involved in preparation, how do systems, particularly those that are strained because of inadequate staff resources, reach significant numbers of families who can benefit from this process?

○ Do systems engage in FGC to maximize informal familial supports or to minimize the use of government resources? If the latter, does that undermine the philosophy and intent of FGC?

FAMILY TEAM CONFERENCING. According to the CWPPG (2001), FTC is structured to strengthen families, increase their likelihood of achieving independence, coalesce a broad team of individuals to protect children and support families, and build individual courses of action based on team strengths and family needs. In its process, FTC has some unique strategies to follow these principles.

Like FGC, family team conferencing espouses wide-ranging preparative activities that occur pre-conference. This essential part of the process underscores the family's significant role in designing the conference to include a cross-representation of individuals from their family, from their informal social support network, and from their community. It also enhances their understanding of FTC and their roles at the meeting. It is believed that preparation increases the likelihood that families will harness their strengths and expertise during the conference and that preparation will also demystify the FTC process. Educating the family about the FTC process and preparing them for their active role in that process aid in the transformation of the conference process from one that is professionally controlled and dominated to one that is centered on the family.

As described by the CWPPG (2002), the FTC process promotes the team as the decision maker and gives family members a genuine voice as team members. The process contains a number of distinguishing elements. First, early in the conference, the facilitator asks the family to tell its story and to describe what prompted the conference. This strategy uniquely maximizes the family's perspective at the conference and provides an opportunity to embed and flavor the meeting with a sharing of important family cultural values, history, and perspective. Second, the facilitator uses a very systematic structure in organizing the decision-making process by asking the team to focus on the family strengths and needs that correlate to the risk factors; develop specific goals for the identified needs and the behavioral measures that will demonstrate the attainment of defined goals; brainstorm strategies that will meet the goals; and select the steps and services, matched to needs, that achieve the goals. Although the process is thoroughly delineated, FTC developers also recognize that the approach must have flexibility and individuality to respond to family uniqueness, culture, and situations. This facilitated structure purposefully leads to the achievement of individual courses of action.

It has been suggested that because case-carrying social workers serve as the facilitators of FTCs, FTC encourages social workers to form an alternate relationship with families that may lead to a more comprehensive partnership and support a transformation of social work practice. Proponents of FTC believe that assigning this role to social workers—rather than concentrating such critical skills and values in the role of an independent coordinator/facilitator as is done in the FGC model—will result in a systemwide expectation that all workers will develop solid engagement skills and treat families respectfully.

The primary responsibilities of the facilitator are to neutrally build a team, direct the process, and resolve differences. According to the CWPPG (2002), "often the best facilitator may be the helping team member with the most trusting relationship with the family" (p. 20). However, if conflict exists between the worker and the family, the FTC process suggests that another professional (for example, supervisor, case manager, provider, family support staff) should become the facilitator.

Given the workforce crisis in child welfare, including shortages in staff and burdensome workloads, and the public's often negative perception of social workers in child welfare, the FTC approach raises some interesting questions:

○ Is there an unavoidable power imbalance between the caseworker and the family that discourages the family's self-determination and the emergence of natural family leaders?

○ How wide and inclusive is the involvement of extended family and informal supports?

○ As with FGC, how does the need for adequate preparation influence the availability and reach of FTC to families in large public child welfare systems?

○ How is family culture more fully integrated into this process if FTC is structured so specifically at defining and achieving behavioral objectives?

Both FGC and FTC can be used at most critical junctures in the life of the case, when plans need to be reviewed or revised or a decision needs to be made. They both encourage any participant to request a conference any time that he or she believes it is warranted. These flexible structures support families and teams by ensuring that conferences are need-driven rather than bureaucracy- or event-driven.

TEAM DECISION-MAKING MEETINGS. According to Mattingly (personal communication, January 20, 2004), "the key strength of TDM is that it brings families to the table in situations where they are almost always excluded." Historically, significant emergency (and other) case placement decisions that have long-term impacts on children, families, and the broader community rested in the hands of individual social workers and their supervisors. TDM is organized to provide family and community providers with an opportunity to participate in some of the most critical decisions that staff in public child welfare agencies make. It increases the opportunity for families to participate in decision making under exigent circumstances, whereas the time and resource constraints of organizing a meeting based on immediate, urgent need may challenge other models of family involvement (including FGC and FTC).

> Team decision making meetings are structured to "revolve around issues of child placement, and are held prior to the removal of a child from home, or in an emergency, prior to the initial court hearing, prior to any change in placement, and prior to a recommendation for reunification or other permanency plan. TDMs [team decision-making meetings] are always held before the agency petitions the Court regarding a placement-related decision." (DeMuro & Rideout, 2002, p. 11)

For communities implementing TDM, meetings are mandatory any time a child-placement change occurs. They are designed to ensure the involvement of some family members, at the minimum, the birth parents, before any changes in living environment or circumstance for the child. These criteria, therefore, require communities to hold a significant number of meetings, some of which become necessary on an emergency basis.

The impetus for TDM was to create a change in public child welfare agency decision-making policies at emergent and critical junctures; it was not created through a family involvement lens. This historical evolution provides a rationale and context for understanding the differences in the TDM process when compared with other family involvement approaches.

One unique characteristic of this model is that trained senior child welfare agency staff members (not case-carrying social workers) facilitate TDM meetings. Developers believed the clinical expertise, knowledge of public systems, and family engagement capacities of these individuals would not only improve the quality of facilitation of TDMs, but also would also infuse expert knowledge and transfer best practice skills to external participants and inexperienced workers. In addition to their primary responsibility of managing the group process through facilitation, TDM facilitators actively participate in decision making at the meeting. They serve as quality control agents for the decision and have the responsibility to seek a higher level review of any decision that they do not believe attains safety, permanency, or well-being for children.

Also unique is the fact that TDM meetings are time-limited, lasting approximately 1.5 to 2 hours (DeMuro & Rideout, 2002). Although this is typically a shorter allotment of time compared with other family involvement approaches, it reflects the pragmatic issues of volume and timeliness of TDM meetings. Systems implementing a structural change, like TDM, must be able to respond, often on an emergency basis, to the unanticipated safety needs of a child or family.

After a discussion of risk and safety concerns, strengths, and the perspective of family attendees about the current situation, "the caseworker recommends a plan of action (including placement plan) based on the discussion up to that point." (DeMuro & Rideout, 2002, p. 14) Next, the facilitator leads a discussion about the caseworker's preliminary recommendation and encourages the group to identify other solutions, with the purpose of avoiding unnecessary removals or excessive intrusion (P. Rideout, personal communication, February 2, 2004). The facilitator then assesses the group's movement to consensus, stating the agreed-upon decision, if it is obvious (DeMuro & Rideout, 2002).

This structure raises a number of questions related to family involvement:

○ Because of the implementation structure of TDM meetings and the critical nature of the decisions made at TDM meetings, should the decisions made at TDM meetings be considered temporary until a more comprehensive family involvement approach can be used?

○ Can TDM be implemented to maximize the presence and participation of extended family and social support networks and, therefore, to affect the balance between informal and system solutions and resources in plans?

○ Although the social worker shares investigative observations with the family, and although there is opportunity through dialogue for participants to reach a consensual decision, how might the worker's initially rec-

ommended plan of action curtail the emergence of family leadership, creativity, and responsibility?

○ How does TDM contribute to the development and integration of family-centered values and practices of the staff who will be implementing the plan—or in other words—how do the espoused values of this approach translate into a transformation of everyday practice for agency workers?

Can the family involvement models work together?

Given the foothold that multiple family involvement approaches are gaining in child welfare, there is a growing sense of optimism that, with thoughtful and careful collaboration, these processes may be able to work together to the benefit of children and families. To date, however, little work has occurred to help facilitate such a process on a systemwide or community basis. This, too, will necessitate a commitment of additional resources, time, and, most important, a philosophical and pragmatic openness to creating such a shift. Theoretically, a continuum of family involvement approaches may provide families and communities, in partnership with public agencies, with rich and diverse opportunities to participate in the making of critical decisions, but a number of communities working to implement multiple family involvement approaches currently report barriers to operationalizing the approaches simultaneously.

Simultaneous implementation has created confusion about the characteristics of various models within the child welfare agency, other systems, and broader community (Pennell, 2002a). Although many of the family involvement models described herein espouse some of the same values, the corresponding practices and processes differ significantly. The infusion of multiple models can result in workers' confusion about model selection for specific cases and the uniqueness of the approaches, and it can increase the difficulty for administrators and supervisors who must devise policies and procedures that differentiate each model.

In addition, communities concurrently implementing multiple family involvement approaches report that it has created a competition for shrinking financial and staffing resources, especially with social service budgets decreasing and states experiencing significant deficits (Pennell, 2002a). It is difficult for administrators and policymakers to support approaches that require more upfront, intensive resources—both time and money—independent of research results. As summarized by Pennell (2002a, p. 12), "the selection of models is often driven by funding availability rather than family needs." Simultaneous implementation also requires additional education and retraining for professionals and community members about the various models and the articulation of a rationale for implementing multiple approaches. Last, a toolbox approach challenges the congruence of values and philosophical underpinnings of practice.

Perhaps, the first question that must be answered is whether the use of multiple family involvement approaches, implemented either simultaneously or through an integrated approach, is in the best interest of families, communities, and public systems. Before family involvement models can be dovetailed or implemented simultaneously, communities would likely

benefit from bringing together a large group of stakeholders to analyze each model's key principles or values and their associated practices. For example, how do each of the three family involvement approaches addressed herein put into practice the following commonly espoused values: (1) families can make well-informed decisions about keeping their children safe when supported; (2) families are experts on themselves; and (3) all families have strengths.

The North Carolina FGC Project provides a solid example for measuring the congruence of practices with FGC principles, supplying a mechanism for matching value or belief statements with actual practices (Pennell, 1999). As an illustration, the FGC principle, "Help the conference participants take part safely and effectively," lists three corresponding FGC practices: "by preparing family group and service providers; by building in supports and protections; and by arranging transportation, child care, interpretation, etc., as needed" (Pennell, 1999). This type of delineation across family involvement processes is a useful approach to ensure congruence between a model's espoused values and its actual practice, as well as to improve model fidelity (see chapter 7).

Defining the operating principles for each approach, determining the core elements of each, and reviewing implementation and practice guidelines can provide insights. Communities could then find areas of commonality and difference from a philosophical, practice, and implementation perspective; determine the elements of each approach that cannot be compromised; and examine the existent research findings. A willingness to reflect critically on a community's values as an ideological reflection of its esteem, trust, and belief in families and their capacities to fully partner with the system and care for their children is critical. Lastly, the broader community of stakeholders can analyze the feasibility and value of integrating various approaches, tying principles and goals to actual practices.

A number of communities are currently experimenting with simultaneous implementation of family involvement models. For example, some communities are using TDM as an initial forum to plan for a more extensive family group conference or family team conference where extended family members have a greater opportunity for decision making. In others, after a temporary decision is crafted at a TDM, FGC or FTC is used to reconvene the wider family and support network to make a more permanent decision. In these instances, all previously constructed decisions are put aside to allow for the FGC and FTC participants to make a new decision, which may or may not be consistent with the initial decision. FGC is a decision making process, not a case planning process. Others, on a limited scale, are determining on a case-by-case basis which process to offer to families. This last strategy, however, positions professionals as the ultimate decision makers about appropriateness of fit and disallows families access to a process that they believe is most beneficial for them. Given the state of large, public child welfare systems, the availability and viability of TDM meetings at urgent child removal/placement junctures can provide a useful platform for initial decision making. The authors believe that a follow-up family group conference or family team conference is necessary to achieve a more comprehensive, culturally sensitive, and family-responsive decision/solution over the long term—one in which

widening the circle presumably increases family responsibility, accountability, and independence, and enhances informal resources.

If models are implemented simultaneously, the remaining question is, How does this translate to families' experiences with child welfare? The structure of TDM, in which limited preparation, particularly for emergency events, is likely to result in a smaller family network and the caseworker, rather than the family, develops the initial plan, sends a different message to the family about their authority and role in decision making than FGC or FTC sends. If given an opportunity to participate in a family group conference or family team conference, will they subsequently embrace or trust those processes in which they are either the primary decision maker or equal member of a decision-making team? How does family involvement in TDM during the crisis of child removal influence their openness and ability to trust other processes? After decades of mistrust between families and child welfare systems, families may find it difficult to believe that their voices and perspectives are respected, supported, and critical to the future of their children and family unit. It will likely require a transformation of practice that is actively and consistently demonstrated over time to begin to heal the wounds of decades of paternalistic and isolationist practice.

Nationwide, the simultaneous existence and rapid expansion of these family involvement models may build a stronger, more coherent, and more rational policy framework for involving families as meaningful partners in decision-making processes. However, there are many questions that require careful deliberation:

○ If a family meets criteria for involvement in a certain process, will that negate their future involvement in a different process?

○ Who decides what process a family is offered?

○ What messages are being sent to families and the community regarding the reasonable or rightful place of family in creating safety plans and solutions for their children?

○ Can a reasonable or fair argument regarding differing degrees of family involvement be articulated, and will it be embraced?

○ What are the intended or unintended messages inherent within such a differentiation of the levels of involvement, and how will families and children interpret those differing opportunities for involvement?

○ Does the promulgation of a continuum of family involvement models give permission to social workers and the system to remain within their comfort zones instead of moving toward better engagement and partnership efforts with families?

As is common when innovations outpace research, there are more questions than answers.

What are the trends in FGDM?

When FGC reached U.S. shores in the mid-1990s, another family involvement model, the family unity model, was simultaneously gaining recognition. Introduced in 1989 within the State of Oregon's Children's Services Division, the family unity model espouses some similar values and contains some distinctive process char-

acteristics. In particular, the information-sharing stage of the family unity model, devised as a facilitated discussion of strengths and concerns involving all participants—family members, representatives of community support systems, and the case social worker—distinguished this approach.

With multiple sources of information and various models, individuals in communities embarked on a process to determine an approach to family decision making that they believed resonated best with their community's culture, resource capacities, system structures, and values about families. *Although many communities elected to pursue the implementation of the FGC and family unity models as originally devised, others blended elements and characteristics of both approaches; in the process, they coined new terms such as "family conferencing," "family group decision making conferences," and "family decision meetings."* Typically, when communities merged these models, the process incorporated the family unity model's discussion of strengths and concerns during the information stage with the private family time feature of the FGC model. In some communities, this model blending may have resulted in a diminished preparation effort and more heavily facilitated FGDM process.

The implementation and adaptation of the FGC and the family unity models in multiple communities encouraged the American Humane Association to elect an inclusive overarching term—family group decision making—terminology that was also used in the Newfoundland & Labrador, Canada, project. Embraced for its adaptability and versatility, communities implement FGDM at various points of family involvement with the child welfare system, including prevention of a child's removal from the home, early intervention, reunification, and post-termination of parental rights. If a case decision is required, FGDM is a viable alternative to traditional decision making.

The practice of FGDM has benefited from the infusion of other family involvement models and critical child welfare advancements. Partnerships with community stakeholders from conceptualization through implementation to sustainability are essential components of any major new initiative. Kinship care practice and policy provides a theoretical emphasis that reconfirms the significance of family connections. Restorative justice practices offer complementary philosophies, such as healing and accountability, as possible byproducts of FGC in child welfare. There is a collective vision to developing more open and collaborative partnerships with families.

As FGDM gains popularity in the United States, there are many initiatives with practices that truly emulate core FGDM values and principles; others struggle to attain them. A significant concern—and the one that has the greatest potential to impede the advancement of FGC—is the trend toward powerful professional and organizational agendas colonizing the model for institutional and systematic gain and stripping the inherent democratic principles away from the practice (Lupton, 1998; Lupton & Nixon, 1999; Lupton & Stevens, 1997).

Toolbox mentality

FGC is a right in New Zealand Children, Young Persons and Their Families Act of 1989 and is considered good practice in the United Kingdom (Nixon et al., 2000). In the United States, however, it is fre-quently described as a tool or technique. Is this a semantic nuance, or does this definition impact the advancement of FGC?

In the United States, systems often organize a tiered approach to working with families. A ladder of access, inclusion, and resources unfolds that often aligns with the degree of concern or perceived intervention needs. Because FGC is still relatively new in the United States, communities often include it in an array of services offered according to a continuum of need and intervention. Although the FGC experience can be exceedingly powerful and meaningful to families and others who have an opportunity to take advantage of this option, what happens to those who do not have this option? How is the evolution of practice and relationships with families supported or undermined?

Nixon (1998) described FGC as primarily family-based rather than organization-based. He wrote, "The key to the development of this work is to build consensus on the principles of FGC and to strive to realize those principles in practice, rather than approaching the work from a mechanistic and procedural base" (p. 17). Individual workers and systems will need a new willingness to critically reflect on the depth of their belief in families; challenge centuries of well-intended, yet paternalistic practices; and harness the motivations, elemental behaviors, and resources that will assist them in transforming their approach to building a relationship with families to achieve child safety. An approach to practice from this perspective far exceeds the toolbox mentality, so prevalent today, in offerings of support and services. Therefore, if FGC remains defined as a tool that can be used at worker or system discretion, its ability to transform social work practice and build community-based child protection practice will not be actualized. It will, instead, lie on the margins as systems advance.

Case targeting and predetermined outcomes

As noted earlier, the Children, Young Persons and Their Families Act of 1989 provided legislative authority for FGC in New Zealand. The act included specific subsections detailing guiding principles, enabling authorities, definitions of children in need of protection or care, and operational protocols. Within this formative act are ample examples of both the intent and direction of FGC processes and procedures. The act noted a wide range of opportunities for families and the system to convene a family group conference in order to consider "such matters relating to the care or protection of that child or young person as the conference thinks fit" and to "make such decisions or recommendations, and to formulate such plans, in relation to that child or young person as the conference considers necessary or desirable, having regard to the principles" that are set out in the act. Key to this declaration is its relationship to the guiding principles of the act and the unique terminology, "as the conference thinks fit." Within the construct of this act are the suppositions that all families have the right to involvement in, and with, the FGC process; that children have the right to live in association with, or be connected to, their family, and that intervention into family life should be as minimal as possible. These suppositions appreciably alter the motivational and prescriptive dominance of the child welfare system in driving case-plan development or predetermining outcomes.

In the United States, many communities strive to uphold the philosophical intent and underpinnings of FGC in their own implementation efforts. However, whether by resource limitations or with other intent, access to FGC in some communities has become increasingly constrained. Many communities have begun to develop referral criteria that have created a pattern of exclusion from the process for some families. Often these are families in which child welfare concerns are considered generational and egregious. Some communities cite "a concern that the attendees, particularly the victim, will be revictimized or disempowered by the process" (Merkel-Holguin, 2000b, p. 186). Yet, in New Zealand, these are exactly the same families and child welfare concerns that the Children, Young Persons and Their Families Act, 1989, was designed to support and address. What are the messages that are being sent to excluded children and families about their capacities and worth?

Fortunately, many communities throughout the United States and abroad have increasingly encouraged the use of FGC to facilitate planning, healing, and responsibility. Burford and Nixon (2003) gleaned evidence from the international Web-based survey on FGC showing that with experience, many programs are expanding the use of FGC to include cases that involve domestic violence and sexual abuse.

Another troubling trend in the United States is the organization of FGC implementation efforts with the intention of prescribing outcomes or predetermining solutions. Often these "family group conferences" are framed with the intention of having families identify a specific family placement solution or detail their involvement in a treatment process. Families must agree to this conference construct in order for the conference to be convened at all or for it to be deemed a success at completion. Whose needs is such a conference process organized to meet? How is this compatible with the intent of the guiding principles?

New Zealand's legislation creates opportunities for family involvement and authority in decision making, but provides great latitude for "fit," which is one of the most remarkable contributions to cultural responsiveness and compatibility in child welfare today. It reduces both the over-involvement of the system and its pre-scriptive influence—a goal that has been one of the key articulations and thrusts of strengths-based practice and family involvement approaches. Family conferences that are organized in the United States for the purposes of developing or supporting a plan with a predetermined path or outcome are not family group conferences.

The preparation dilemma

There is no question that preparation is a cornerstone element of FGC. The dilemma is how to convince community- and state-based decision makers that even though preparation requires additional staff resources, it is one of the non-negotiable components of FGC that transforms child welfare practice from a professional-driven to a family-driven practice. Without comprehensive preparation, the principles of promoting family members as leaders and decision makers, increasing their level of commitment and responsibility, and widening the social support network are unattainable. Preparation requires a commitment of personnel resources, but without this investment, families will not necessarily perceive FGC to be any different than other professionally dominated processes. At its core, preparation is about engaging the family in the building of a trusting, respectful relationship.

Preparation provides an unequaled opportunity to explore family culture, communication, and ritual. Intrinsic to this is the development of a conference experience that is unique to each family. Additionally, trusting and respectful interactions with the breadth of family members make it possible to explore and plan ways to support the safety needs of all participants. Not supporting full preparation before convening a family group conference risks the breadth of family inclusion, leadership development, cultural integration, and safety. In fact, it may seriously compromise those values that are inherently precious in the origin and philosophical underpinning of the FGC process.

Roles of the coordinator and the facilitator

In New Zealand, a coordinator role was established as a core structure in the implementation of FGC. The coordinator is responsible for conducting all preparatory activities, as well as for facilitating the actual family group conference. Therefore, the coordinator likely has built a trusting relationship with the family; has partnered with them to glean their capacities and social support system; has developed an enhanced understanding of the family's culture, communication patterns, and structure; and is keenly aware of any safety concerns that may arise during the actual conference.

In some U.S. communities, predominantly on the West Coast, a debate emerged as to whether the coordinator (defined as the professional engaging in the preparation) and the facilitator (defined as the person facilitating the conference) should, in fact, be the same person.

At first, the discussion centered around the coordinator's ability to remain neutral during the conference, with a number of professionals suggesting that the coordinator's intimate knowledge of the family gained during the preparation stage diminished his or her impartiality during the conference. Using a separate individual to facilitate meetings likely gained popularity because such a narrowed purpose increased the facilitator's availability for conferences by eliminating the responsibility for organizing and convening the conferences.

Although a number of communities still maintain separate coordinator and facilitator roles, it is a practice that warrants challenge. First, the issue is not really whether the person facilitating the conference can remain neutral, but whether the participants perceive this person as fair. Second, safety during and after the conference is paramount, and one coordinator fulfilling both functions can leverage information gained during preparation to create a safer environment. Third, does introducing a person unknown to the family as the facilitator affect their willingness to participate fully? Fourth, does this structure, perhaps unintended, result in a minimization of preparation and an overemphasis on facilitation?

The facilitator role—
Meaningful minimalist

In many communities around the United States, there has been an appreciable move toward developing the skills and capacities of FGC facilitators to support the likelihood of a more productive, respectful, and safe meeting experience. The primary characteristics of an effective FGC facilitator include fairness, perceived neutrality, an ability to organize participant understanding/agreement about the conference's purpose and process, hosting skills, and attention to participant safety. Although communities have supported the acquisition of solid facilitation skills, there has been a trend toward simultaneously breeding a "new professionalism" and deepening the involvement of facilitators within the meeting process. The increased involvement of facilitators creates barriers to the emergence of family leadership and natural family communication style. Positively implemented, facilitation should become less directed by the coordinator as the conference proceeds. Perhaps a better way to regard strong FGC facilitators is as meaningful minimalists and reluctant interveners.

Private family time

As multiple family involvement strategies converged in the mid-1990s, the importance of private family time was robustly debated. Questions were asked. Does professional facilitation of the decision making influence the outcome? Is it essential in order to transform the inherent power imbalance that exists in child welfare practice? What if families ask professionals to stay? Ultimately, the answer to these questions is a philosophical one. Do systems believe in families' capacity and decision-making authority, support families' taking responsibility, and embrace FGDM as a way to promote concepts of democracy and self-regulation? In a meta-analysis of 25 FGDM evaluative studies, Merkel-Holguin, Nixon, and Burford (2003) reported that private family time has been embraced as an essential element and that families indeed develop plans that are seen to be safe. To ardently support private family time reaffirms family involvement and counters the tendency to view and treat families as simply objects of interventions.

Follow-up—The missing link

The FGC process does not end after a plan is finalized. The coordinator has multiple responsibilities, such as recording, transcribing, and distributing the plan. In addition, conference participants discuss a plan for monitoring and reviewing the decisions and a process for reconvening, if necessary. The follow-up phase is also the part of the process in which both informal supports and formal resources are garnered. Anecdotal evidence suggests, however, that the follow-up phase of the family group conference lacks standard conceptualization and application (Merkel-Holguin, 2002). This U.S. trend is consistent with a New Zealand research report that the FGC plan monitoring and follow-up are often deficient (Paterson & Harvey, 1991).

With minimal supporting literature and insufficient attention, it is not surprising that follow-up practices span a continuum from non-existent to overly systematic and intrusive. For example, reconvening a conference may be important to affirm decisions, more fully address issues, and review new information, resulting in the creation of a new plan. Should reconvening be a standard practice at a certain time interval post-conference for every family, or should it be based on the individual needs within a specific case? Adherence to a strict schedule for follow-up conferences would meet a system need, not necessarily a family need.

Are families receiving the services and supports that they need to achieve safety, permanency, and well-being for their members? Who is working with the fam-

ily to ensure that the plan is progressing as conceptualized, minimizing barriers, and facilitating access to services? In New Zealand, the coordinator plays an integral role in reviewing the care and protection plan; In the United States, it is typically the responsibility of the ongoing worker to partner with the family to advance the plan. There is a risk with even the most detailed and comprehensive plan that components will need revision. The larger concern is whether existing formal services are sufficient to meet the needs identified by families through FGC processes.

What is the role of the family in implementing the plan? In many U.S. communities, a family leader is identified as a family plan monitor and given the responsibility of contacting the ongoing worker and/or coordinator to discuss strategies to address implementation concerns. For ongoing workers, follow-up is a delicate, philosophical balancing act. Although FGC espouses values of family empowerment, follow-up must also embrace a partnership framework, whereby formal system representatives and families are working together to advance the agreed-upon plan. Because families have a long-standing concern for their members, it is not surprising that family members provide significant informal supports and resources (Merkel-Holguin et al., 2003), and they follow through on their responsibilities detailed in the plan at a higher rate than do professionals (Lupton & Stevens, 1997).

Conclusion

As the implementation of family involvement approaches gains momentum nationally, there is a sense of hope that families will have the opportunity to become meaningful decision makers in child welfare. Model integration and simultaneous model implementation is a challenging proposition, one that will require discussion, potential coordination, and resources. Finally, increasingly evident through an expanding body of research and anecdotal evidence is the unequivocal importance of widened family presence, involvement, and authority in developing creative, safe, and responsive plans.

Family Group Conferences in the Youth Justice and the Child Welfare Systems

Gale Burford

All too frequently, families are pulled in various directions by plans from different services. Such is often the case when young people are within both the juvenile justice and the child welfare systems. The integration of planning from these two systems through the application of family group conferencing (FGC) can give young people and their families significant roles in the coordination of services from the youth justice[1] and child welfare systems. By achieving their participation in the timely creation, implementation, and monitoring of their individualized plans through FGC, the multiple aims of justice can complement one another for

individuals, families, and communities. These aims include victim involvement, crime prevention, and the young person's protection and well-being. By leaving out the important leadership of these consumers, retribution (punishment), rehabilitation (treatment), and restoration (repair) constantly vie for political and policy dominance over one another.

Why coordinate and integrate child welfare and youth justice?

Coordination and integration are seen as the antidote to families being pulled in multiple directions. Efforts to achieve integration and coordination of services for young people and families involved in child welfare and youth justice processes benefited from the establishment of the Juvenile Justice Division in the Child Welfare League of America (CWLA) in 2000. The goals of reducing juvenile delinquency nationally and reducing reliance on incarceration for

---

[1]The terms "youth" or "young person" and "youth justice" are used throughout the chapter instead of the terms "juvenile" and "juvenile justice," except in citing other sources, particularly legislation. The intent is to emphasize the efficacy of young people and their accountability in contributing to the resolution of issues.

both accused and adjudicated youth were to be accomplished largely through system integration and reform "involving a comprehensive, strategic process that values the inclusion of youth, families and youth-serving agencies and organizations, which uses the best available information, research and practices to guide the process" (Tuell, 2003, p. 2).

The impetus for these efforts comes from the view that families and young people involved in child welfare and youth justice systems frequently have multiple and overlapping challenges, including disability, educational handicaps, mental and physical illness, financial and housing problems, justice and legal problems, and substance abuse (Bilchik, 1995; CWLA, 2000, 2003; Greenwood, Model, Rydell, & Chiesa, 1998; Mears & Aron, 2003; Mendel, 2000; Travis, Cincotta, & Solomon, 2003; Tuell, 2003; Waldfogel, 2000), that go well beyond the mandate or reach of any single agency or provider (Freedman, 2003; Rivard, Johnsen, Morrissey, & Starrett, 1999; Wiebush, Freitag, & Baird, 2001; Wiig & Widom, 2003). Instead of a coordinated continuum of services, families are confronted with an array of agencies and services, each often perplexing in its own right, with varying eligibility criteria, assessment and intake procedures, ideological imperatives and goals, categorically funded pre-set programs, and geographic locations. Collectively, the systems themselves appear designed to favor some groups and to discriminate against others (Cohen, 2000; Roberts, 2003). Many families evidently experience the services as unresponsive, inflexible, and dominated by legal and administrative procedures. This perception increases the unique challenges for families involved with both the youth justice and the child welfare systems.

At the intersection of child welfare and youth justice, the reactivity of the young person and the marginalization of the family can quickly outrun opportunities for reversing the course of events. So established is the link between child abuse and youthful offending that workers from a number of systems, including child welfare, law enforcement, and education, will likely meet one another on a regular basis. Add to that the known links between mental health problems and incarcerated parents and a young person's behavior may have been the cause for introductions among a considerable number of agencies and people. There are long-standing tensions, even at the practitioner level, between the youth justice and the child welfare systems. It is often seen as a failure of the child welfare intervention if a young person is charged with an offense, and the reverse is true if a young person being supervised for an offense is found to be abused. The fact of a charge often means a complete shift away from the behavior of the parents to the behavior of the young person.

Ashby (2003) confirmed the long-standing suspicion that many children end up in the child protection and youth justice systems mainly to get needed services. In other words, some families cannot get the help that they need until either one of their young members is in trouble with the law or matters in the home have escalated to the point at which child protection has a substantiated risk of harm, actual abuse, or both.

Beginning in 1998, the Office of Juvenile Justice and Delinquency Prevention (OJJDP), a component of the Office of Justice Programs of the U.S. Department of

Justice, provided funding to states to use accountability-based sanctions through its Juvenile Justice Incentive Block Grant. The Appropriations Act of 1998 (Public Law 105-119, Title III of H.R. 3) required that 75 percent of the funds available to states be used for developing collaborations among schools, courts, law enforcement agencies, child protection agencies, mental health agencies, welfare services, health care agencies, and private non-profit agencies to offer youth services, share information, and establish policies and guarantees of protection to youthful offenders.

The extent of coordination and integration varies considerably across states according to how each state defines the purpose of its juvenile courts, whether services for young offenders are centralized at the state level (National Center for Juvenile Justice [NCJJ], 2004), whether the state child welfare agency is also responsible for youth justice offenders, and whether data are maintained in mutually accessible systems—let alone whether anyone is keeping track of which young people are involved in both systems (CWLA, 2000). In 2004, 24 states reported that either their state child welfare agency was responsible for youth justice ($n = 7$), or both child welfare and youth justice were administered under a central social or human services agency ($n = 17$). Twenty-seven states reported that youth justice was administered separately from child welfare either by a juvenile corrections agency ($n = 15$), an adult corrections agency ($n = 11$), or some other separate arrangement ($n = 1$).

From the perspective of the consumers, even being under the same administrative umbrella tells little about how coordinated and integrated the services are, whether they work together to harmonize services around the needs of the young people and families, or the extent to which service providers regard the family, or the young person, as an important partner and have found ways to include them. Inclusion has a wide variety of meanings, ranging from families and young people being polled for their views to organizing meetings around their leadership. As is the case in the child welfare system, the youth justice system has been slow to institutionalize the values associated with consumer leadership and empowerment.

Are families capable of participating in "family-focused" work?

The importance of involving young people and their families in identifying their own needs, establishing goals, building on informal support networks, and participating in monitoring their own plans is recognized in a wide variety of endeavors, including child protection, prevention of youthful offenses, and substance abuse treatment (Bureau of Justice Assistance, 2003; CWLA, 2003; Wiig & Widom, 2003). Moreover, family involvement is associated with positive outcomes in child welfare in the 2001 and 2002 Child and Family Service Reviews and Outcome Indicators (Milner, 2003), as a best practice by the OJJDP (Beyer, 2003), and in the CWLA (2003) Framework for Community Action.

The philosophies and practice principles of the child welfare and the youth justice systems converge in an emphasis on the desirability of strengthening family and community capacities to promote health and well-being in children and young people, finding solutions early on when problems are detected, and refining the role of judicial oversight in providing safeguards to informal dispute and conflict resolution processes and avoiding criminal proceedings whenever possible. An example of one approach is the family group conference.

What is a youth justice family group conference?

When used in the youth justice system, a family group conference is a meeting of family members who, along with their extended relations, friends, and other close supporters, come together with formal authorities and other professionals to make a plan for dealing with the young person's offending behavior and matters directly related to the circumstances of that offending.

FGC in the Youth Justice System: A Brief Background.

As first developed in New Zealand and implemented in its 1989 Children, Young Persons and Their Families Act, there were two streams that could result in FGC: one for dealing with care and protection matters, a term roughly comparable to child protection in the United States, and the other for dealing with youthful offending. The addition of the term "young persons" to the New Zealand law (first introduced in its 1974 act) was itself significant, as it made visible the distinctions in needs and developmental issues between children and young people, especially as they relate to young people taking responsibility for their behavior and the use of accountability-based sanctions. This distinction sidesteps the unhelpful classification of a problem as being mainly with the parent until the young person reaches adolescence and then shifting the focus to the young person's behavior. The New Zealand legislation provided for the separation of discussions of the young person's

care and protection needs as a child from discussions of the young person's offending behavior, but kept the family—extended family in this case—and their culture as the constant. The purpose of the separation was to prevent the contamination of each of the two purposes by the other, that is, using care or rehabilitation remedies as sanctions for criminal behavior or, conversely, diminishing accountability for offending by overemphasizing the welfare needs of the child or young person. The practice has undergone considerable evolution since its development in New Zealand.

Youth Justice FGC and Restorative Justice

FGC was introduced in New Zealand as a decision-making method for determining appropriate responses to offending by young people. The law entitles victims to attend a conference and, if they are present, requires their agreement before a plan can be accepted as an alternative to prosecution or submitted to court as a sentencing recommendation if the conference was held after a finding of guilt. This element of the model holds considerable appeal for those proponents of restorative justice who argue that restoration to the victim needs to be an essential consideration in the conference. For instance, Braithwaite and Strang (2002) defined restorative justice broadly in the following way: "Stakeholders affected by an injustice have an opportunity to communicate about the consequences of the injustice and what is to be done to right the wrong" (p. 4).

Essentially a method of empowering the family, including the extended family, and strengthening their influence with the young person, FGC puts the child or young person and the family at the center of the decision process. The job of the professionals, Doolan (2002) argued, is to support the creation of conditions in which the family can exert leadership and be "power-full" in the face of dominant professional, legal, and administrative practices and procedures that may well reflect a range of institutional biases toward families in their decision-making and resource-allocation processes. The FGC approach makes a deliberate attempt to widen the circle to include absent members and others, especially extended family members, who have the potential to exert long-term influence on the child or young person.

The appeal of restorative justice originates in what Crawford (1996) called the criminal justice system's "negative attraction," which emerges from declining confidence in the capacity of the state to control crime, and its "positive attraction," which grows out of a communitarian analysis of the role of wider social values and the importance of civic engagement in a democratic society. Both attractions are evidenced in FGC in youth justice. As is the case with their use in child protection matters, the use of family group conferences to deal with a young person's offending behavior offers families an opportunity to influence decisions. Although there is considerable jurisdictional variation in practice and in philosophical and theoretical orientation, the primary goal is to create an environment in which the family can find the most effective response for them and to engage the professionals in support of that plan.

A major difference in practice is found in the extent to which some restorative justice proponents have limited the involvement of extended family members, or reduced the practice to mediation between the offender and the victim. As developed in New Zealand, FGC aims to serve as a pre-charge mechanism to determine whether prosecution can be avoided, and as a post-charge mechanism to determine how best to deal with cases admitted or proved in the youth court. Hence, youth justice FGCs are used only for more serious or persistent offenders, and are not intended to substitute for police cautions or diversion strategies. Criminal proceedings should not be used if there is an alternative strategy for satisfactorily dealing with an offense, and criminal proceedings should not be used to coerce rehabilitative or therapeutic ends. Additionally, approaches should aim to strengthen the capacity of the family and the community to deal with the behavior of the young person.

Maxwell and colleagues (2002) reported that in New Zealand, 44 percent of children and young people were being dealt with by police cautions; 31 percent, by police-based diversion; 8 percent, by direct referral to FGC; and 17 percent, by charges in the youth court, followed by FGC. They reported that plans made at the conferences were being carried out at a high rate and that young people were being held accountable for their offenses. Even allowing that some measures result in dubious gestures of restoration (for example, insincere apologies), the researchers reported that the accountability measure taken is more likely to be restorative (for example, young person pays victim for damages to car), as opposed to restrictive (for example, young person is restricted with the imposition of a 7 P.M. curfew), when a victim is involved. According to the researchers, accountability objectives are achieved in their most appropriate form with approximately two-thirds of the young offenders.

In the youth justice system in New Zealand, disillusionment with the dominance of the therapeutic-rehabilitative philosophy and the marginalization of victims fostered support for the separation of child protection and youth justice issues, with the emphasis on the protection of children's and young people's rights, on the one hand, but the equally strong emphasis on accountability and responsibility, as well as the endorsement of certain principles of "just desserts" (that is, proportionality, determinacy, and equity of outcomes), on the other hand. The legislation extended a preference for diversion from formal procedures, including the administration of sanctions and penalties in the community instead of residential placement, whenever possible.

Doolan (2003) argued that restorative justice is an umbrella term that covers a wide range of practices, and that although it is useful, especially as a vehicle for exploring common values, there are important distinctions to be made when extended to the use of those protected by legal status from the full force of adult obligations. In Doolan's view, the extent to which face-to-face meetings are harm-focused, that is, organized around repairing harm to the victim, differs when the effort is mainly aimed at empowering the family in partnership with authorities to manage their young person's behavior, and to turn the young person away from future offending. FGC is a whole-child, whole-family approach. The victim may achieve justice, including restoration, in the process, and the opportunity for this should always be sought; however, this aspect of FGC should support and complement its other aims, and should not become its primary purpose. If repair became the paramount aim, in Doolan's

view, it would be unnecessary to have a designation of "youth" or "child" in the eyes of the law. The laws that protect the status of the child uphold the stance that it is possible to prevent further offending rather than only to sanction the young person or to repair the harm to the victim. Thus, it is possible to attend to the child's welfare needs even while dealing with accountability for offending behavior through coordination and integration of the youth justice and child welfare processes, as long as this includes keeping the family and the young person's voices in the forefront of both processes. As long as the family can remain central to both discussions, cooperation between the two processes should be expected while coordinating the result.

What is the role of the court?

The court is one point in a continuum of interventions, from formal to informal, that makes the others possible. In New Zealand, the courts are involved in oversight of the FGC process only when they order a conference to occur. In all other cases, the law designates that a coordinator is to be responsible for the functioning and management of the process. In using the FGC approach as a "best practice" in the absence of legislation such as New Zealand's statute, the role of the court in restorative processes is to provide judicial oversight and to safeguard the informal processes that proceed from, or provide an alternative to, the court. As with efforts in other countries where FGC and other forms of conferencing are being used, the thrust in the United States is based on the recognition that most offending is a one-time event, or part of a developmental phase that will pass. Formal police cautioning (Hoyle,

Young, & Hill, 2002) and pre-charge diversion programs are used to divert young people away from court proceedings whenever possible (for example, in Australia, New Zealand, or England). Seymour (1997, as cited in Daly, 1999) argued for a court role as an important link in the continuum when conferencing is used:

○ Fact finding when the young person is entering a plea of not guilty

○ Safeguarding the processes of informal justice

○ Imposing coercive sanctions such as detention when they are required

○ Enforcing agreements when compliance is not forthcoming from diversion and conferencing. (p. 4)

The court is seen, then, not as a separate, formal mechanism apart from the informal, preventive interventions, but as a point on the continuum of interventions that range from the informal to the formal. The higher penalties, or graduated sanctions, are used to encourage compliance and self-regulation at the lower stages. The theory is that the very existence of these possibilities, in which the court represents the ultimate determination, can have a positive effect (Braithwaite, 2002). The New Zealand philosophy and legislation are clear that it is best to avoid the court system whenever possible (New Zealand Department of Social Welfare, 1999; Rangihau, 1986).

Seymour (1997, as cited in Daly, 1999) noted that the formal system underwrites the capacity of informal processes to safely provide that

○ Parties have opportunities for frank and direct discussion unencumbered by legal procedures and constraints.

○ Victims are given the opportunity to ask questions directly of the offender and their family members, unmediated by legal representatives.

○ Everyone present gets an opportunity to have a say, unconstrained by legal procedures and rules. (p. 5)

This creates opportunities for the expression of emotion and the possibility of apology, which may provide a context that allows people to move from positions of anger, fear, and humiliation to understanding and acceptance (Braithwaite, 2002; Moore, 1997; Moore & McDonald, 2000; Retzinger & Scheff, 1996). It creates space for sanction (retribution/punishment) that is proportionate, permits the development of a plan to help or reform the offender (rehabilitation/prevention), and offers an avenue to help the victim (repair/restoration). The judge makes the final decision, but that decision, or ratification of a plan, is informed through the informal process of relationships and, presumably, is done more quickly.

How can retribution, rehabilitation, and restoration be integrated?

The mobilization of the formal system and informal helpers around the family's plan fosters coordination and integration. The use of FGC to bridge the coordination gap between the youth justice and the child welfare systems acknowledges the important role of reconciling two needs: (1) the need to sanction the young person for wrongful behavior, that is, to set limits and stand up to the young person, to open up an opportunity for the young person to take responsibility and to repair the damage that he or she has caused, or at least to offer amends; and (2) the need to address, or treat, the underlying causes of the problem. If any of these responses diminish or exclude the others, the long-range outcomes will be lopsided. Punishment that is ill-timed, too heavy-handed or too weak, or administered outside the context in which a bad behavior is to be extinguished provokes reactivity, especially from young people; perhaps worse, it fails to provide clear boundaries and to be firm about them. Furthermore, treatments or interventions cannot be expected to have universal or uniform effects on all young people under all the varying conditions under which they are administered (Dowden & Andrews, 1999; Henggeler, Schoenwald, Borduin, Rowland, & Cunningham, 1998; Palmer, 2002).

In the pendulum swings back and forth from treatment to punishment, or from welfare to justice, as discussions outside the United States have tended to frame them (Maxwell, Kingi, Robertson, Morris, & Cunningham, 2003), crime victims and other persons affected in the community have tended to be left out altogether. The importance of setting things right with crime victims, that is, of restoring the rupture in relations in the community, has come into view—or back into view, as some restorative justice advocates would argue (Zehr & Mika, 1998)—as part of a renaissance of interest in rebuilding civil society (Braithwaite & Strang; 2001; Schorr, 1997). Proponents of restorative justice have raised concerns about the viability of restorative justice as a policy unless new ways to promote accountability in informal justice processes are discovered (Braithwaite, 2002; Mika, Achilles, Halbert, Amstutz, & Zehr, 2003; Roche, 2003a). As has been the case with retribution and rehabilitation when implemented as across-the-board policy, there is no reason

to think that restorative justice processes will not be subject to domination by particular interests without adequate safeguards (Moore & McDonald, 2000).

The significant involvement of the family in the processing of cases for youth justice at the crucial juncture between pre-charge diversion and court creates an opportunity to handle a large percentage of situations without going to court and fosters cooperative alignments among young people, families, victims, and professions, even for many situations that do have to go to court. On a case-by-case basis, it can be expected that fewer cases will require formal court proceedings and that more families and young people will be connected to services that they need. More victims of crime will feel that justice has been served.

Justice proceedings for a young offender can complement child welfare proceedings and treatment. On a larger scale, it should be expected that the young person's respect for the formal process and the court will increase, along with the realization that the authorities are taking his or her family seriously. Perhaps fear of crime at the community level would decrease, to be replaced by increased feelings of security, but this would depend on how well the voices of those who are satisfied with their involvement in such processes are heard (Best, 1999, 2001; Leyton, O'Grady, & Overton, 1992).

How do child welfare FGC and youth justice FGC relate to each other?

As in the child welfare system, approaches to the use of FGC and other conferencing models in the youth justice system vary. In particular, the extent to which the family is invited and given support to take leadership before, during, and after the conference varies. Bazemore and Umbreit (2001) use the term "restorative conferencing" to encompass a wide range of "strategies for bringing together victims, offenders, and community members in non-adversarial community-based processes aimed at responding to crime by holding offenders accountable and repairing the harm caused to victims and communities" (p. 1).

In his discussion of what he called primary restorative justice practices, McCold (2001) noted the differences in approaches to conferencing. To build a definition of conferencing, he drew on the work of Warner-Roberts and Masters (1999), who defined a conference as a process in which a group of individuals who are connected by a past action come together to discuss important issues that have resulted from those actions. McCold added that because the offender's behavior has affected their own and the victim's family group, as is the case in a relational view of crime, these family members are a significant part of the affected community who are brought together.

As mentioned earlier, the New Zealand orientation to FGC is somewhat unique in its legislated inclusion of extended family members, including grandparents, aunts/uncles, and adult siblings, etc. as participants in family group conferences. The law entitles them to be present unless there is good reason for them to be excluded. This notion that the problem of the young person is a relational problem, especially for the extended kin network, is quite different from the assumption that the inclusion of extended family members is a matter of choice for the professionals. The New Zealand law does not allow proceedings to be instituted against a young person, however, unless a coordinator has consulted with the family group and held a conference to get their decisions and recommendations. The importance of this requirement cannot be overestimated, as legislation obliges professionals to give the opportunity to families to exert leadership over the process.

How does a youth justice conference work?

The Youth Justice Conference works much like the child welfare conference except deciding what to do about the young person's offense, how to keep it from happening again, and setting things right for the victim and the community are the foremost consiserations.

The Youth Justice Conference Coordinator

Like the coordinators of family group conferences, coordinators of youth justice conferences need help from people who are knowledgeable about local resources and people with whom they can speak openly about the work that they are doing with a family. A coordinator should be perceived by the family and the victim as someone who may express disapproval of the behavior of the young person—usually by not doing or saying anything that would minimize or trivialize the behavior—and who is fair and respectful of all participants.

A skilled coordinator may organize and facilitate both the child welfare and the youth justice conferences, or separate portions of the same conference, but there are good reasons to create a separation even if it amounts to only a break in the meeting. For example, no non-family victim would ordinarily be included in a conference at which child welfare and protection issues related to the young person were being discussed. In one youth justice conference, however, the victim of the crime was the young person's teacher and coach, and the family and the young person asked the victim to come to the child welfare conference as an important member of their "like family" support network. Clearly, it is risky to try to create across-the-board rules and procedures.

Time Frames

A coordinator must pay careful attention to legal and psychological time frames in setting up a conference. The goal is generally to have a conference as quickly as is feasible after an offense has occurred so that whatever "openness" has been created by the crisis of the events has not soured to cynicism or drifted to indifference. Other conferences may be held much later, especially when they involve serious crimes, if the victim and the offender have expressed interest in meeting for reasons that would not affect the disposition of the case (for example, a victim wants to have a meeting as part of his or her own healing). Conferences of this kind are becoming more common as jurisdictions gain in experience with restorative practices, and it is to be hoped that youth justice and child welfare systems will cooperate and provide supports and safeguards for these initiatives. Given how far-reaching the implications of a conference's outcome can be for the young person, it is all the more crucial that efforts of child welfare and youth justice are coordinated.

Referrals and First Contacts

The youth justice conference coordinator negotiates with the police to set up a conference. In New Zealand, part of this negotiation involves trying to find a less formal way of dealing with the matter than taking it to FGC. This effort is to ensure that only matters that are relatively serious go to FGC or to court. When possible, less formal means are used to resolve matters. In any event, the coordinator's introduction to the young offender and the family is through the police and, if the case also involves a child protection issue, through the child welfare coordinator. It is essential for the coordinator to talk with the police and the child welfare worker if the conference is to coordinate and integrate services for young people involved in both these systems. The decisions regarding who will be contacted first about the conference, who will be invited, and what arrangements must be made are important, particularly in the case of a young person in foster or group care. The coordinator's early actions should include speaking with the young person about the status of his or her relationships with the family, and the coordinator should respect positive alliances with parents and/or substitute caregivers. By working with the police and the child welfare personnel, the coordinator can precisely identify the offending behavior that will be the focus of the youth justice conference.

First contacts require sensitivity to and knowledge about multiple family dynamics and their implications in situations related to child protection, youthful offenses, and victim impact. Especially because the situation may be at a crisis stage, the responses of families and substitute caregivers may vary considerably. Some may be caught genuinely and completely off guard by the involvement of the police, as often occurs in cases associated with drug use and bullying; others may feel that there have been signs of trouble over a considerable period of time.

Family members may be known to agencies—some because they were previously service recipients themselves, some because they have been trying to get help for their definition of the situation for some time. The efforts of family members may have gone unrecognized or may even have been framed as part of the problem, leaving them feeling guilty or angry and giving them a sense that they have no influence over what happens next. The coordinator's job at this stage is to present the conference option to the family members in such a way as to engage or rekindle their optimism.

Invitations and Preparations

In preparing for a conference, the coordinator consults with the young person; the family, including the extended family; and the victim to inform them of the process and to engage them in making plans for convening and facilitating the conference within statutory time frames. The inclusion of extended family members is an important consideration in the use of the FGC approach. However, it is probably not an appropriate intervention to use in cases of youth offenses that are very low-level crimes (for example, shoplifting or truancy) unless there is also substantiated abuse or a need for a child welfare referral. In these cases, behaviors may well be more worrying and suggest the need for treatment to prevent any further developments in a budding career of crime and antisocial behavior.

Again, it is an advantage to have a legislative or procedural mandate that specifies the criteria for a referral. Such a mandate protects against both the tendency to drift toward the inclusion of cases in formal processes that should be steered away from court, and in the silencing of young

people and families when lawyers take over in highly complex formal processes. In any event, FGC should not substitute for less intrusive options, such as police cautioning and other restorative court diversion schemes. There is no reason that the family cannot involve a lawyer in any stage of the process, and certainly the family should have one if the matter is going to court. When the court may be providing oversight of the entire matter, including over the agreements that come out of a conference, legal counsel should be available.

Participants at a youth justice family group conference include the young person; extended family members; the victim and, importantly, the victim's supporters, who may also have been affected by the crime; the police, ideally including the arresting officer; the young person's advocate; and others agreed upon by the young person, the family, or the victim. This is likely to include the foster parents or a worker from a group-care setting if the young person is in out-of-home care. The question of whether the child welfare worker should attend the youth justice portion of the conference should also be determined through discussion with the family, the young person, and the social worker. In New Zealand, the social worker is entitled to attend. In some states, the social worker is already carrying, or will soon carry, the young person in his or her youth justice caseload. The important consideration is to ensure that the youth justice conference, or the portion of the conference devoted to the offense, stays focused primarily on the participation of the young person, the family, and the victim in coming to agreement on the sanction, future behavior, and repair. The achievement of this aim will bring together the roles of service providers and family members.

Conduct of the Conference

Details that are determined during the preparation stage include who should run the conference, how the meeting will be opened, when the breaks should take place, and whether food will be served. The coordinator generally facilitates the conference, although others may be included in the coordination role to enhance cultural appropriateness or neutrality. It is not the role of the coordinator to organize the conference as a confrontation with the offender. The very situation is already rife with underlying feelings of shame.

After the opening, a youth justice family group conference typically proceeds to a description of the offense from the police; then the young person is asked if he or she committed the offense as described. Once the young person has admitted committing the offense, the victim and the others present also have an opportunity to tell what happened, what the impact on them has been, and what they would like to see happen. Practices vary in the extent to which these statements are scripted, that is, follow a pre-set plan of the order of speaking and what the coordinator is to say. Nevertheless, there is growing consensus that this part of the conference should not be hurried, nor should it be designed to amplify confrontation or negative chastisement of the offender.

Typically, statements are filled with emotions and the language and behavior of emotions. Uninitiated professionals who are present often recall this part of the conference as a turning point in their understanding of a key difference between informal approaches to justice, which open up space for dialogue and the expression of emotions, and formal approaches, which aim to regulate exchanges and harden the differences between people through rational argument and the establishment of blame. The opportunities for later translating the emotional experience into healing, including for the young person who committed the offense, are usually apparent to anyone attending the conference and contribute to making the meeting memorable.

In the same way that young offenders should never be at a conference without someone there who cares about them, victims should not, in most instances, come alone. Others who have seen the effect of the crime on the victim, and possibly even experienced its fallout in their own relations with the victim, should be present. If the victim or the victim's supporters are unable to speak at all about their own experience and instead can only express outrage, the effect on the teenaged offender, and possibly the family, is likely to be reactivity. Victims may need help during the conference preparations to think through what they want the young person to hear and what they would like to see come out of the conference for themselves. Conversely, if victims are too benevolent, for example, if they forgive the young person immediately, the effect may be to make the young person feel too comfortable before accounting for the offense. The result may be a reduced incentive to honestly face and discuss the behavior.

The conference then turns to sharing views on how to set things right, after which, in the approach developed in New Zealand, the family members are given time on their own, without the professionals and non-family members present, to develop a plan. (Increasingly, those who practice under the banner of restorative justice are dropping this aspect of the conference, even in New Zealand, if they are dispensing with the involvement of the extended family [Doolan, personal communication, February 24, 2004].). When the family has finished, the meeting reconvenes with the professionals, the victim, and the victim's supporters. After hearing the plan presented, participants can agree, disagree, or recommend amendments or changes. The family is not obliged to accept recommendations or amendments from non-family members, but in practice they generally do. The plans are meant to provide reparative sanctions, such as apologies, restitution to the victim if that is wanted, or community service. The coordinator records the outcomes and ensures that everyone is informed.

Different approaches to conferencing have incorporated variations on practice and philosophical emphasis (McCold, 2001). The greatest divergence appears to be around the involvement of extended family members and in the emphasis given to family empowerment (Daly, 2001; Fercello & Umbreit, 1998; Hoyle, Young & Hill, 2002; McCold, 2001; Moore & O'Connell, 1994) and to the inclusion of some mediation processes in the definition (Bazemore & Umbreit, 2001). The underlying design is relatively consistent, however, given the expectation of face-to-face meetings that bring offenders and victims and members of both their important social support networks together with mandated authorities in a decision-making forum that is characterized by respect, mutuality, reciprocity, and procedural fairness and is safeguarded by the backup of the formal court process (Braithwaite, 2002).

What is expected of the offender?

The young offender is expected to acknowledge guilt or to have been adjudicated, after which the court sent the matter to FGC. In the lat-

ter instance, the conference can proceed on the basis of the facts established by the court, as long as those present are willing to form a plan on that basis. FGC is particularly useful in obtaining the family and victim's input for sentencing, or in formulating a plan when the young offender is being released into the community after a period of incarceration.

The young person is expected to come prepared (1) to describe the crime and the reasons for his or her involvement and (2) to listen to the victim and other persons in attendance as they describe the effect that the crime has had on them personally and what they think the young person's obligations should be in the matter. The impact of the process, it is hoped, will increase the young person's awareness of the harm and suffering caused by the behavior, and thereby foster a climate in which the young person will be moved to express remorse.

The process invites young offenders to participate in creating a plan that contains important mechanisms for regulating their own behavior in the future and to set tasks aimed at restoring in concrete and/or symbolic terms the harm that they have caused. It also places young offenders in a position in which they have the opportunity to hear others' expressions of support, both for them and for the victim, and participation means being willing to listen to both of those expressions. Of course, not all young people are able, or ready, to accept support in a meeting or to offer sincere gestures of apology. This becomes a problem if advocates think a conference, or even "the model," is unsuccessful if the young person does not apologize or if the victim does not forgive the offender. In many instances, however, the apology from the young offender's family to the victims and their families establishes emotional connections between the adults that foster repair. Again, the main purposes of the conference are the creation of a plan and the empowerment of the family, or other caregivers, to take active roles with the young person.

What about the victim?

As in all restorative processes, the involvement of the victim in a youth justice family group conference must be voluntary. Early experience in the use of FGC in New Zealand showed that considerable effort is necessary to engage victims and prepare them for their roles, thereby making a conference inviting and safe for them to attend (Maxwell & Morris, 1993b). This is especially true when the crimes have involved violence or when the victims have concerns about reprisal. Participants need to understand what information about the offense, the young offender, and the offender's family and social situation will be made known to them and to the others present. Especially in the case of more serious and violent crimes, victims need to have a chance to reflect on how they are likely to feel hearing the offender's story and being in the company of the offender's family who, while disapproving of their relative's behavior, will be searching for ways to express their caring for the offender as well. Victims must understand the purpose of the meeting, or meetings if there are to be follow-up meetings to which the victim may be invited, and have an opportunity to think about the outcomes that they may like to see. They must understand that the meeting is likely to be an emotional exchange and anticipate the effect of their own behavior on the others.

Studies of a wide variety of informal justice practices show that victims want to have the option of attending and, like offenders and their families, report high levels of satisfaction with the procedural fairness of these processes (Braithwaite, 2002; Latimer, Dowden, & Muise, 2001). They must perceive that their attendance is voluntary, but whether they choose to come is intimately related to how they are informed and engaged about the process.

What are the challenges to FGC practice in the child welfare/youth justice interface?

As a coordinating and integrating element between the child welfare and youth justice systems, FGC faces some of the same challenges faced by other services that promote the empowerment of the client and cooperation between professionals. Coordinated and integrated services are no easier to implement and sustain in quality and focus over time than those that are top-down, expert, or procedure-driven (Halpern, 1999). Their implementation requires considerable clarity about the reasons for undertaking coordination and integration in the first place, the mission and goals, and monitoring to ensure adherence to the mission, and careful measurement to determine actual outcomes.

It is essential to strike a balance in the use of FGC. The public's confidence in the approach will eventually erode if victims, voluntarily or not, are hauled off to conferences unprepared for what is to happen to them, or if victims must face prescribed apologies or pre-set reparations from young people, especially if they perceive the young person to be insincere or to have little motivation for participating, except possibly to avoid a more severe sanction from the court. More complicated is the situation in which the victim discovers that the young offender has serious personal and environmental deficits and realizes that the conference may represent only an open doorway for the offender and his or her family to get much needed services. If the justice response becomes a vehicle for getting "welfare" services, even if the need for them is obvious to everyone present (including the crime victim), the approach will crumble under the weight of the wasteful expense of such an elaborate pretense. Such practices would also probably violate due process considerations and the established legal rights of persons accused of offenses. Finally, if conferences are to be used to humiliate or scare the young person into "going straight," hostile reactivity or temporary overcompliance can be the expected result.

The challenges or grey areas that require local agreements include such issues as whether a young person's admission of guilt can be used in a civil suit and what happens when a young person admits to a new or previously undetected offense during the FGC proceedings. Under the New Zealand legislation, anything said in a family group conference is privileged and cannot be used in any other court of law. Various jurisdictions handle these matters in various ways, but it is essential to establish policies regarding these issues in advance.

There are multiple tensions in jurisdictions that use cautioning, diversion, and conferencing, especially when these strategies are all elective or add-on rather than part of a formally conceptualized and legislated system of services. The tendency has been to refer young people who have committed only minor crimes to these informal processes. This heightens the danger of net widening, that is, bringing young people into the system of justice in situations where doing nothing had pre-

viously been a satisfactory response, or in the case of conferencing, not referring at all and instead going straight to court. Evidence suggests that conferencing may, in fact, work best for more serious crime (Maxwell et al., 2003).

Questions have been raised about whether FGC should be used for victimless crimes, such as substance abuse, through the Reintegrative Shaming Experiments (RISE) experiments (Strang, Barnes, Braithwaite, & Sherman, 1999); results are promising in this area, too. The question is whether the best results will come from FGC if the victimless crimes committed by young defenders are treated as child protection issues, youth justice issues, or both. Evaluation research will lead ultimately to an understanding of who benefits from FGC, who does not, and under what conditions.

Unless there is a Termination of Parental Rights (TPR) petition in the works, efforts to empower the family in managing the behavior of their young child should not be abandoned. Even if there is a TPR in the works, the significant "like family" who will continue to work with the young person either during the transition or who are vying for adoption can be involved in the conference to take up family roles with the young person. So the process should not undermine the family's potential to exert lasting, positive influence.

FGC appears well suited to achieve the goals of the youth justice system, can serve a vital role in supporting the coordination and integration of services, and appeals to a wide range of political and ideological interests. Nonetheless, concerns have been raised about potential dangers. These dangers include the inducement to admit guilt if the process is used without protective legislation, the potential for tyranny of the young person by their family members, the trampling on the rights of young people and victims of crime, and the potential for false assumptions about mutual aid and self-help processes in communities and families.

Admission of Guilt

Concerns have been raised that in the absence of legislation such as the New Zealand law, young people may admit guilt at the adjudication stage to avoid what they perceive as a potentially harsher sentence if they are found guilty by the court (Daly, 1999). Similar concerns have been raised that young people are faced with double jeopardy if a family cannot reach agreement on a sanction or if the young person is not in agreement with the sanction that the group determines. Research on the use of conferences suggests that young offenders feel in large measure that their rights have been respected in the conferencing process (Sherman et al., 1998). However, young offenders should have the right to appeal to the court if they believe that an informal agreement is disproportionate to their crime and to receive competent legal advice throughout the process. Their submission to an informal process should be voluntary, and the process should be subordinate either to the oversight of the court or to adequate procedural requirements that will safeguard the young offenders' rights.

Tyranny of Families

There is some fear that the FGC process may submit the young person to the tyranny of family members. Critics argue that the process assumes that the interests of the parents and the interests of the young person are the same. Especially when the parents are using substances, these critics

argue, the parents cannot render or follow through on decisions, and their inability to comply with a family plan prolongs permanency when alternative custody is needed. This concern is especially important when the approach to involving the family does not bring in the extended family and other key individuals in the child or young person's life.

A referring worker should look past the name FGC and see what exactly the youth justice conference coordinator has in mind. A number of approaches that call themselves FGC either involve only the nuclear family members or make little effort to widen the circle outside the immediate family and the facilitator. In addition, some facilitators exert so much control through facilitation that the family members simply follow the professional's bidding. The goal of preparation is to invite people to the conference who can add multiple perspectives. In this way, the group meeting is less likely to fall prey to domination by special interests and is less likely to suffer if the facilitation is poor (Braithwaite, 2002).

Accountability in Collaboratively Developed Plans

FGC and other restorative practices in situations of youthful offending raise the question of who is to be held accountable if the family members or, for that matter, the professionals fail to do their part in an agreed-on plan (Braithwaite, 2002; Roche, 2003a, 2003b). It is necessary to delineate clear lines of responsibility in protocols developed and in the individual plans themselves. Although FGC can play an important role in promoting service coordination and integration, it is not the only catalyst. Written agreements and protocols need to complement ongoing conversations at the agency and community levels. Under the legislation in New Zealand, the coordinator monitors plan completion.

Net Widening

Concerns have also been raised that conferencing extends the net of the youth justice system further into situations that do not warrant making the young person's wrongdoing so visible. One argument suggests that this is inevitable, given the extent to which FGC and other restorative practices are marginalized and have tended to receive few referrals, except in New Zealand where they are guided by legislation. By extending the prevention philosophy further into the lives of young people who have not yet offended, This concern is heightened in the case of the youth justice system unless FGC is developed as part of a range of services that are informed by common values.

Unless other clear and specific options, like formal cautioning and diversion programming, are set in place with an overriding value that guides them all, the result could be similar to the experience of diversion programs. These programs found themselves unable to take on more serious cases, so they extended into areas where it would have been better either to do nothing or to support the authority of police, teachers, or parents with lesser sanctions.

Community Involvement

Although local knowledge is valuable, the use of local governance assumes that the community members genuinely speak for the community in some important way and that family and community members' care and concern can rise to the level of taking and sustaining action. There are many practical challenges to ensuring fair and balanced representation over time (Braithwaite, 2002; Roche, 2003a, 2003b) and to safeguarding and supporting the involvement of community (Pavlich, 2001) and family members, especially in communities that may themselves have been overrun with social problems (Halpern, 1999). The need for legislation or clear communication, with the court in a role of providing oversight and safeguarding the informal process, cannot be overstated. Problems in coordination arise when there are multiple or blended sentences. Focusing the young person's attention in one place is no less challenging than getting all the family members and others, including professionals, involved to face in the same direction.

What are the outcomes of practice?

A growing body of evidence from a number of countries supports the use of conferencing and related practices in youth offending (Braithwaite, 2002; Crawford, 1996; Dignan & Marsh, 2001; Hoyle, Young & Hill, 2002; Latimer et al., 2001; Maxwell & Morris, 2001; Maxwell et al., 2003; Maxwell et al., 2002; McCold & Wachtel, 1998; Strang, 2002). In the youth justice system, FGC yields higher levels of perceived satisfaction on the part of offenders, victims, and family members than going to court, and preliminary results point to a reduction in re-offending and costs. Maxwell and colleagues (2003) reported that conferences associated with a reduction in re-offending are those in which the young person both agrees with and completes the plan made at the conference.

Maxwell and associates (2003) argued that the values and practices learned by participants in their conferences ripple into preventive activities, such as court diversion and police cautioning; as a result, the number of families requiring a conference decreases over time. The very availability of the conferences on a continued basis and the presence of the court in the background appear to safeguard and lend authority to the agreements made, and thereby bolster early intervention and prevention activities.

Many other issues and concerns are also related to outcomes. Maxwell and associates (2003) pointed out that when and where the meetings take place, how much sensitivity is shown in matters of preparation, and who they can bring along with them for their own support are important issues for victims. Other issues of importance for preparation relate to how the meeting will be run, who will be in attendance, what information has already been shared and will be shared about the offense in the presence of the victim, what will be talked about, and what the victim's role at the meeting is, particularly as this extends to opportunities for the victim to speakAll this suggests that a commitment to involving victims is resource-intensive. Conference organizers need training in ways to communicate with and involve victims, as well as access to resources to support them. Research in New Zealand (Maxwell et al., 2003) showed that the presence of a victim at a family group conference is one of the main determinants of whether the plan will be restrictive or reparative.

By having FGC available for both child welfare and youth justice situations, the experience of professionals and family members with its values and practices widens exponentially. If mainstreamed and delivered as part of a state/community partnership, FGC can be expected both to provide a safeguard against prescription and domination from administrative, professional, legal, and informal sources and to promote the exercise of rights.

Conclusion

Perhaps the most enduring impact of FGC on the young people will derive from seeing the adult members of their own families taking care of family business on the young people's behalf and seeing those outside the family, including the courts, take these family efforts seriously. This kind of success would add considerably to their sense of belonging to a kinship group that is esteemed in the community and provide a measurable indicator of health and well-being. As for the coordination and integration of services, the professionals can be expected to discover not only that their roles are unthreatened, but also that they can align their efforts in ways that were not thought to be possible. Of course, there will be barriers and obstacles to overcome, but as the research evidence from New Zealand has suggested, the conferences serve a considerable educational function and, ultimately, inform discussions of professionals in other venues with the views of families.

13

Family Group Conferencing and Child Welfare: Contributions and Challenges

Gary R. Anderson

Child welfare policy and practice have come under increasing scrutiny in recent years. With regard to child welfare policy, the legal landscape in the United States has grown with the passage of federal laws such as the Adoption and Safe Families Act of 1997 (P.L. 105-89), the Multi-Ethnic Placement Act of 1994 (P.L. 103-296), and the Foster Care Independence Act of 1999 (P.L. 106-169). For child welfare practice, in the context of dramatic shortcomings in the child welfare system across the United States, the federal Child and Family Service Reviews audit the performance of state child welfare systems and their contract agencies with regard to multiple process and outcome measures. The need and desire to identify the best practices for interventions and programs, ideally supported by some manner of evidence and evaluation, is heightened as child welfare systems respond to public scrutiny and professional standards to achieve these desired positive outcomes

for children and families. In the midst of this legislative change and call for system reform, family group conferencing (FGC) has been introduced and developed.

In less than a decade, FGC has grown from a practice innovation to an accepted, often heralded, service approach in child welfare. In testimony submitted to the U.S. House Subcommittee on Human Resources on the implementation of the Adoption and Safe Families Act, the executive director of the Child Welfare League of America (Bilchik, 2003a) testified, "There is an increased use of family-based approaches and interventions including family group conferencing. . . . These approaches stress nonadversarial, collaborative efforts to achieve permanency for children." The executive director, in a July 14, 2003 speech, noted the "more widespread use of . . . approaches that build on the strengths of families, like family group conferencing" (Bilchik, 2003b). Identifying the increased use of

FGC and highlighting it underscores the compatibility and promise of FGC for child welfare. Embedded in this opportunity for FGC are a number of challenges, however.

What are the guiding ethical and philosophical themes for child welfare and FGC?

FGC practice builds upon ethical principles and values that derive from those principles, but with no specific code of ethics addressing FGC, guiding ethical principles and themes are derived from a variety of sources. In the absence of a professional code of ethics distinctively tailored for child welfare, professionals are advised to follow their own professional organization's code of ethics. These codes embody prescriptions and values designed to protect and enhance the well-being of people served by the organization's members. Common to many human service codes of ethics are a number of underlying principles:

○ autonomy and client self-determination
○ nonmaleficence, defined as one's professional responsibility to avoid or minimize harm
○ beneficence, defined as one's professional commitment to maximize the client's best interests and well-being
○ a commitment to justice (Beauchamp & Childress, 1983; Wenston, 1987)

Each of these principles is valued within the child welfare system. Although child welfare intervention often has an authoritative approach, such as in the removal of children from an unsafe environment, agencies must follow legal policies designed to ensure due process for parents, to respect family privacy to the extent possible, and to engage family members in decision making and planning. Rules designed to promote decisions and actions that reduce harm, or "do the least harm," and are consistent with the "best interests of the child," are translated into agency policy and supervisory direction. Laws, policies, and court processes have been established with the aim to treat people fairly.

In practice, these values prove to be ideals that are not always achieved, and are full of contradictions and complexities. These ethical principles may be more notable in their breach than in their consistent practice. Child welfare intervention can be very paternalistic, with dictates coming almost exclusively from child welfare workers and the courts. Family participation in decision making and planning may be non-existent, merely token, or formally or informally marginalized. Information may be withheld from families. The capacity of family members to participate may be compromised; their resources may be overwhelmed. Harm reduction is not easily determined. The choices, when there are choices, may be limited to determining how much harm and who is harmed, rather than evading a direction that has harmful consequences. Likewise, a child's best interests may not be clear, and alternatives may be elusive. Community resources may be beyond the reach of a family, and protection may be all that practically matters or all that can be addressed. The justice system may not ensure justice. Because agency policies may not eliminate bias in decision making, people in poverty or in minority populations may not be assured of fair treatment and access to the resources and opportunities that their families need to succeed.

These expectations for professional behavior and service provision are not extraordinary—respect my privacy and right to have some measure of self-determination, intervene in a manner that will consider and minimize my pain and suffering to the extent possible, be guided by a concern and commitment for what is best for me and my family, and treat me fairly. However, the ethical principles that underpin the guiding codes of ethics for professionals working in the child welfare system may be difficult to identify or implement in a practice environment full of risk and limited in resources.

The identification of models of practice that incorporate and operationalize the ethical principles endorsed by child welfare and required for professional ethical behavior can at least partially address this quandary. FGC presents this possibility.

Autonomy

Respect for the family, and corresponding family responsibility, is evidenced in the joint preparation for the family group conference. Providing information to family group members so that they can base decisions on knowledge about the children and their circumstances reinforces this respect and builds the capacity for successful decision making and planning. Building in private family time and drafting a family plan for negotiation with the coordinator and child welfare staff strongly counters the tendency to give more weight to professional knowledge and planning than to family initiative. Preservation of family responsibility is meant to extend until well after the conference.

Harm Reduction

Introduced in New Zealand in response to the Maori concerns that traditional child welfare models were harmful to their families, FGC was designed to reduce the harm that comes from a lack of autonomy, a lack of participation, and a lack of respect in decision making—and the results of that system-dominated process. Identifying harm and planning to reduce harm in the child welfare intervention process and its outcomes requires information and perspectives from family members. Physical harm to children may be reduced by enlisting a wider circle of informed extended family protectors, gaining parental engagement in planning, and consequently, heightening compliance with this plan.

The "harm" identified in New Zealand resulted from cultural insensitivity in the way that intervention was structured and in its application. The structure of FGC is such that it incorporates family and community members, including people from the family's culture. Also, FGC coordinators learn to assess the cultural values, traditions, and needs of the family in planning and conducting the conference, and to respond in a manner that reinforces cultural safety.

Best Interests

The ability to advance a family's best interest depends, in part, on having accurate information about the family's strengths, needs, and resources. FGC gains a wider range of information about the identified family from the extended family and close friends; furthermore, bringing the community and professional service providers to the meeting provides additional information. The extended family, friends, and community potentially provide a wider range of resources for the family. For example, the FGC coordinator's work with the parents to identify family and friends may increase the involvement of paternal relatives and identify other community members who can be a resource to the family.

Justice

FGC promotes fairness by encouraging the family to include all relevant parties in the conference. The structure of FGC provides for the family's active participation and leadership. The family has the opportunity to tell its story and shape its plan to ensure the safety and well-being of the children.

What are significant guiding practice approaches for FGC and child welfare?

The affirmation of practice approaches, such as a family system perspective and a strengths-based approach to practice, are central to the use and value of FGC. Congruence between FGC and the practice of child welfare extends to common approaches that derive from a shared set of values. There is at least the inference that adherence to these approaches will be effective in work with children and families. These approaches to working with families served by the child welfare system include a family systems perspective, a strengths perspective, and a community-based perspective.

Family Systems Perspective

Viewing individuals outside the context of their families provides an incomplete picture of their functioning and a narrow and underinformed range of interventions. The connectedness within a family and the family's role in shaping, if not determining, behavior require an assessment that incorporates that family. The importance of a family's full participation in goal setting, planning for services, and

implementation of that plan seems indisputable in child welfare practice, and recognizes the family's powerful role in human behavior (Kelly & Blythe, 2000). Operationalizing this perspective is a greater challenge.

FGC provides a set of strategies that translate a family perspective into model components and actions to promote the welfare of the child. The nuclear and extended family are engaged as a group to plan for the safety and well-being of the child and the family:

- ○ The FGC coordinator approaches the parents to present the concerns about the child and gain the parent's perspective.
- ○ The FGC coordinator works with the parents to identify and approach family members and those people who, because of the quality of their relationships to the family, function as family members.
- ○ The conference is conducted in a manner congruent with the culture of the family, and learning about this culture has been an explicit responsibility of the FGC coordinator.
- ○ The professionals in attendance at the conference have been invited because of their direct interest in and work with the family; their primary role is to provide information so that the family can make informed decisions.
- ○ The family has the opportunity to ask the professionals for additional information or to clarify issues and concerns.
- ○ The structure of the conference provides private time for the family to discuss the information learned and to craft the initial plan for the care of the children.

- ○ The family plan becomes the starting point for negotiations between the coordinator and child protection service representatives—the intention is to honor the family's perspective and plan to the extent possible, while ensuring the safety of the children.
- ○ The family receives a copy of the plan with provisions for follow-up.
- ○ The responsibility for the implementation of the plan remains with the family; professionals do not take over for the family after the conference.
- ○ The post-conference goals include the facilitation of family involvement in the plan's implementation and any plan revisions that may be required.

With the central goal of addressing the safety of the child through a process that meaningfully involves the extended family, FGC works to balance family preservation and well-being with the priority of child safety.

Strengths Perspective

As described in chapter 11, the recognition of and building on family strengths is an important part of family involvement models. In some models, such as the family unity model pioneered in Oregon, there is an explicit point in the conference at which the coordinator, professionals, and family members focus on the identification and affirmation of family strengths (Keys, 1996). In FGC, there is less likely to be a time dedicated to this strengths discussion, but the recognition of family strengths is inherent in FGC strategies. For example, the goal of including a wide range of family members at the conference is, in part, to identify the strengths in the larger family and to mobilize them on behalf of the nuclear family. The convening of private family time and respect for the family plan build on the belief that a family can take responsibility for the safety and well-being of the children.

In some programs, such as in Michigan's, the coordinator assesses family strengths and assets in the pre-conference planning and notes them in the formal case record. This affirmation of strengths is essential, as many family members have been discouraged by the multiple problems that they have faced and the traditional response of social service systems. A strengths perspective informs the assessment, underpins the strategies, and communicates to families a sense of respect and hopefulness that is crucial for successful family engagement and planning.

Community Perspective

A number of child welfare approaches have emphasized the importance of a community response to child abuse and neglect (Seita, 2000; Waldfogel, 2000). It is not possible, however, for a public child protection system to provide all of the needed services for a full and complete response to child maltreatment. Even with full and generous funding, a child welfare agency is only one of the elements required to ensure a safe environment and sufficient support for children and families. In a resource-depleted environment, the need for a full community commitment to child protection and well-being is even more essential. In addition, informal and community supports are not time-limited and provide sustainable relationships and resources for a family.

FGC is a model of family involvement that by its very structure reinforces the role of formal and informal supports to protect children. The preparation for the family conference encourages the coordinator to cast a wide net to include a range of people who are supportive of the family. The respect for the family's culture opens the possibility of inclusion for leaders and support persons from the family's faith or ethnic community. The bringing in of community professionals who have knowledge of the family results in a range of interested parties connected and committed to the family. These parties include mental health therapists, teachers and a variety of school personnel, probation and law enforcement officers, child care providers, foster parents, substance abuse counselors, and others. The family plan may include employers, neighbors, and family friends, in addition to family members and professionals, in the scope of its actions. FGC recognizes and operationalizes the child welfare imperative of community involvement as well as family involvement.

In a call to reform the child protection system, three basic elements were identified: "(1) the provision of a customized response to families, (2) the development of community-based systems of child protection, and (3) the involvement of informal and natural helpers" (Waldfogel, 1998, pp. 46–47; see also Waldfogel, 2000). FGC affirms and expresses these three elements of system reform.

How does FGC address child welfare outcomes?

The processes associated with FGC are designed to promote significant child welfare outcomes of child safety and the well-being of children and families. Although chapter 8 addresses short- and long-term FGC outcomes, some additional observa-

tions on child welfare and FGC outcomes should be highlighted.

Safety

With regard to safety, the Adoption and Safe Families Act of 1997 explicitly affirmed that the central goal of the U.S. child welfare system is the safety of children. Generally, this safety is defined as the child's physical safety—freedom from physical abuse, physical neglect, medical neglect, failure to provide protection and supervision, and, in some cases, educational neglect. The child's psychological safety, less likely to be explicitly identified, is at least partially encompassed in the goal of permanency for children in that permanency addresses the child's needs in relation to attachment and bonding, stability, and a lifelong connection with a family.

As applied in the child welfare system, the goal of FGC is to construct and successfully implement a family plan with the ultimate goal of ensuring the safety of children. In this construction process, the role of the FGC coordinator is crucial. If there are any conditions that, in the assessment of the FGC coordinator or child protection service representative, are essential to the safety of the children, the family must build these conditions into the family plan. Also, if these professionals do not believe that the family plan protects the children's safety, they can renegotiate the plan with the family. The FGC coordinator and the child protection service representative must sign off on a plan. Their central "litmus test" for acceptability is child safety. This is particularly true for the child protection service worker who has the primary responsibility to determine safety.

FGC enhances the child welfare outcome of safety in at least three ways. First, the identification and mobilization of the extended family make additional resources available to assist in the protection of the family's children. These relatives and friends with a connection to the family and the children support the family and lessen the risk of child abuse or neglect. This assistance is evident in many family plans; extended family members have agreed to provide respite care for parents, to transport children and parents to community resources, and to provide kinship care. These relatives and friends are also able to observe vulnerable children and offer assistance at times and in places where it is more difficult to extend professional case management. Although they are not mandated reporters, attentive extended family members can and often do raise concerns about the child's safety when necessary.

Second, FGC identifies and brings together the community resources that are involved with a particular family. The convening of a family group conference with professional and community members present to share their information with the family, and with each other reinforces a network of community resources. The family plan may identify additional resources that the family needs and may outline steps that the family can take to obtain those resources. So, in addition to an identified, informed, and mobilized family network, FGC provides an identified, informed, and connected set of community resources.

Third, through the process of family involvement, FGC heightens the potential for parental engagement, participation in, and accomplishment of the family's service and treatment plan. If the goal is child safety and the risk to the child's safety is the behavior of the parent, then strategies that are more likely to engage and involve parents in behavior that promotes child safety have considerable merit.

Permanency

In the United States, FGC is most frequently offered early in the continuum of child welfare services—at the time of referral to child protective services or soon after. The timing of this intervention provides a special opportunity to support the first permanency option identified in the Adoption Assistance and Child Welfare Act of 1980—the safe preservation of the child's family. The provision regarding "reasonable efforts" to preserve the family unit was never intended to sacrifice the child's safety for family preservation. In FGC, multiple parties—typically, the parents, the coordinator, and the child protective services agency—must approve a family plan. If the child protective service agent does not determine that the family plan ensures the child's safety, that plan is not acceptable and must be revised until it addresses safety concerns.

The timely use of FGC early in the child welfare process has the potential to identify and mobilize family, community, and professional resources sufficient to keep families together. If the family and professionals together determine that a child cannot safely remain with the parent(s), the conference has already identified and brought to the meeting those relatives who can serve as a resource. Placing children in out-of-home care with relatives is an outcome of FGC that can ensure the child's safety and maintain a connection to the child's family and cultural community. These relatives may also serve as resource families if other permanency options, such as guardianship or adoption, are required.

As it can with family preservation, FGC can identify and mobilize family and community resources that will facilitate a timely family restoration and return the children safely to their parents. For example, relatives may assist in transportation and child care so that parents can maintain regular visitation with their children in an out-of-home placement. The child welfare goal of permanency requires that a child welfare worker make reasonable efforts to safely keep a family together, give priority to a relative caregiver if out-of-home placement is necessary, make reasonable efforts to reunify the family, or plan for other permanency options. In a service delivery system in which time counts, FGC processes support and expedite these efforts.

Well-Being

Limited resources, demands on the child welfare system, and its priority on physical safety sometimes make it difficult to fully consider the child's overall well-being in planning and intervention. However, consideration of child well-being is central to FGC. The planning for the conference, information shared, family discussions, and the resultant plan encompass not only any problems with the child's physical health, but also concerns related to the child's emotional and mental health, educational needs, and issues such as recreation and socialization. Widening the number and type of participants in a conference results in a broader scope of attention and planning.

What are the challenges for FGC and child welfare?

As a relatively recent innovation in child welfare service provision, FGC faces challenges that are characteristic of the child welfare system as well as some particular challenges related to the distinctive features of FGC. For good reason, the federal audit of state child welfare systems inquires about the role of families in case planning and decision making. FGC provides a set of strategies built on the value of family involvement, but there are a number of challenges and complications that face FGC and the child welfare system, and their relationship to each other.

Two of the most significant challenges for FGC have been identified in chapter 11: (1) the toolbox approach to child welfare practice and (2) the genuineness and extent of family involvement. If FGC is viewed as only a "technique," something fundamental to the conceptualization and power of conferencing is deeply undermined. FGC is based on values that include respect for families, respect for extended families, incorporation of community resources, power families, and respect for culture. FGC builds on and develops strategies that put these values into practice. Devoid of respect for families and empowering the family's role in decision making, FGC is reduced to a technique without the values and relationships that are linked to FGC's effectiveness. Consequently, there is some concern about using FGC as a tool, without inculcating a set of values, and a commitment to genuine engagement and decision making with families.

There are additional challenges to FGC, however, in particular with regard to FGC's distinctive features and child welfare practice: (1) the role of culture; (2) the multiple problems facing families and communities; and (3) the sharing of power.

Role of Culture

As noted earlier in this book, FGC traces its beginnings to the New Zealand experience in which the Maori community protested that traditional child welfare practices and policies were insensitive to, and disrespectful of, their community, and resulted in culturally harmful actions. This critique focused on the decision-making and case-planning processes; the ignoring of family and community traditions, language, and cultural mores; and the approach to and exclusion of family members and community resources throughout the child welfare intervention. Consequently, FGC was built on a respect for the values of the Maori community, and incorporated the value of respect for the family's culture as a central tenet of conferencing (Walker, 1996).

This respect for, and ability to work with, families from diverse cultures illustrates the principles of cultural competence for social work practice: (1) developing "specialized knowledge and understanding of the history, traditions, values, family systems and artistic expressions of major client groups served"; (2) using "appropriate methodological approaches, skills and techniques that reflect an understanding of culture in the helping process"; and (3) being aware of the "effect of social policies and programs on diverse client populations" (National Association of Social Workers [NASW], 2001, pp. 4–5).

Respect for culture was intended to translate into the demeanor, behavior, decisions, strategies, and actions of the coordinator. As a result, the conduct of the conference would reflect the cultural traditions relevant to the family. The coordinator was expected to learn the outline of the family's cultural heritage, discuss with the family the cultural features that had meaning for them, make preparations for the conference to include valued cultural features, and incorporate aspects into the conference that would reinforce respect for the family. The actual structure of the con-

ference—including and valuing extended family, recognizing the role of fictive kin, and approaching the family from a community perspective—would reflect responsiveness to cultural definitions of family (Walker, 1996). The coordinator's respect for the family's traditions could, in subtle ways, shift the power balance in the conference, as the conference would become more comfortable for, and responsive to, the family.

In the importation of FGC to the United States, the value of cultural respect is affirmed, but there may be a gap between this value and its expression. In most FGC cases, the membership at the conference reflects a wider circle, the stages of the conference include private family time, and the coordinator has prepared for and facilitated an interactive group meeting. However, there may be little evidence of cultural inquiry or tailoring in the conduct of the meetings. Chapters 2 and 3 offer examples of cultural expressions at family group conferences, but in general, a review of descriptions of FGC programs in the United States reveals only limited evidence of intentional attentiveness to family culture.

Why is cultural expression not more evident in U.S. family group conferences, or why would the role of culture be an ongoing challenge? There may be a number of reasons that U.S. conferences appear to be culturally "neutral." For example, a broader American culture that at times emphasizes commonalties, rather than diversity, shapes the implementation of FGC, resulting in ignoring, undervaluing, or misinterpreting the role of culture and diversity. Also, many people in the United States view certain aspects of their culture, such as spirituality, as a private matter; professionals may be unpracticed or uncomfortable with inquiry about a family's cultural practices, perceiving such an inquiry as a further invasion of a family's privacy. Cultural traditions may play a reduced or underdeveloped role in a family; for example, the isolation that may have contributed to the family's abusive or neglectful behavior may also have ramifications for the family's connectedness to their heritage and traditions.

Thus, the absence of cultural expressions at family group conferences may be a result of the coordinator's failing to explore this dimension of the family's life and experience; the coordinator's exploring the role of culture with the family, but receiving little, if any, information or guidance from the family; or the coordinator's gaining information from the family, but being uncertain as to how to be responsive to the family's culture.

In the Michigan study, there were two notable exceptions to the relative absence of cultural considerations. The first exception was related to food. The coordinators received a modest budget to purchase items for the conference, which they used most frequently to buy food. This purchase had a very practical dimension, as the conferences averaged two hours in length, with some extending to six or seven hours. It also had a social dimension, as eating together contributed to an atmosphere of cooperation and congeniality. The incorporation of food into conferences also provided a concrete way for a coordinator to inquire about at least one aspect of a family's traditions, culture, or style: "We would like to provide some food for the conference meeting. What type of food would your family enjoy? Are there specific foods that would be special, or important, or enjoyed by your family?" The resulting menu had the potential to reflect an ethnic or cultural flavor, and

sometimes did, although pizza seemed to be ubiquitous.

The second exception to the absence of cultural considerations was in family group conferences conducted with Native American families. In these conferences, the role of culture was evident in a number of ways. Perhaps most obvious, these conferences were among the largest and longest of all the conferences. The number of family members in attendance reflected a family view that encompassed extended family and friends, and the pace reflected the inclusion of more ceremony, conversation, and silence. For example, one conference could not begin until a blessing had been said, and the blessing could not take place until an eagle feather and a veteran were present.

These conferences with Native American families posed a number of challenges for the professionals. The coordinator had to have the capacity to develop a good relationship with the family and to assess cultural meaning to the family. The coordinator needed to have knowledge of Native American cultures, particularly those of northern Michigan nations. For example, a number of conferences incorporated smudging, and the coordinator needed to appreciate the role of tobacco and other symbols in a family gathering. Knowledge of, and sensitivity to, styles of communication were also important.

The cultural sensitivity of the family group conference often seemed to be a reflection of the cultural competence of the coordinator. In Michigan, the thoughtful and respectful behavior of the coordinators elicited cultural information from the Native American families. The coordinators were involved in the community, exposed to and around Native American people outside of the conferences and their professional work. The coordinators took responsibility for their own education and also listened to elders, family members, and other community members to expand their own cultural competence.

Clearly, cultural competence and culturally responsive conferencing require time and work. The coordinators demonstrated that intention and valuing culture alone were insufficient; study, dialogue, and community interactions were also necessary. Exploring cultural meaning in preparation for a conference required building a relationship with a family that was sufficient to learn about the family's traditions, or absence of traditions. Relationship building can be particularly challenging within the context of child protection allegations or actions, and the constrictions of policy-directed time limits. Having gained information from the family, new time demands can arise. For example, identifying and inviting a community elder or spiritual leader, finding specific foods, arranging a comfortable location for the meeting, or other responses require coordinator time and effort. In one case, a coordinator assembled a family-identified menu for 25 conference participants. Cultural catering is not always anticipated in a social worker's job description.

The conference itself might be prolonged or less comfortable for professionals, for example, when other languages or spiritual practices are evident in the meeting. The coordinator needs a sincere commitment to cultural sensitivity and responsiveness. In Michigan, in some ways, the use of an advocate, who worked with the family after the conference (see chapter 4), helped to make FGC culturally responsive. Although not a feature of the model, there were times when the advocate helped the coordinator in conference preparations before and during the conference, which also served as a way of introducing and orienting the advocate to the family. Cultural sensitivity and responsiveness requires time—to acquire knowledge and to act on this knowledge—and this may pose a challenge for the U.S. child welfare system.

Is this cultural sensitivity necessary? The federal legislation that established a child protective system and the legislation enacted after that date explicitly identify cultural sensitivity and competency as requirements for the delivery of child welfare services. This imperative is based on the recognition that responsiveness to family culture builds a relationship, guides planning, and strengthens family engagement for the safety and well-being of the child. The failure to appreciate a family's cultural heritage is to miss crucial elements of the family's identity, values, and decision-making processes, and can lead to harmful neglect or abuse by the child welfare system.

In New Zealand, it was recognized that cultural insensitivity on a systemic level disadvantaged groups of people and resulted in additional harm to children and families. In general, with cultural insensitivity, resources for safety and permanency can be overlooked in a systemic failure to structure interventions and services in a culturally informed manner. The harm associated with cultural insensitivity can be extended to the individual level in failed relationship building, sterile planning, and family disengagement from professional helpers and their plans. The involvement of the family and sensitivity to their culture were crucial considerations to achieve the desired outcomes of the safety and well-being of the children.

In the United States, FGC has faced, and will continue to face, a number of opportunities and pressures to adapt to different locations and practices. These adaptations may contribute to model drift, including failure to appreciate the importance of cultural competence in FGC practice. Understanding culture is already a challenge for the U.S. child welfare system. The overrepresentation of children of color in the U.S. child welfare system is dramatic and persistent. There may be multiple explanations for this phenomenon, but it may be appropriate to ask if there are structural and systemic ways that the child welfare system is unresponsive to or harmful to specific groups of people, particularly ethnic minority populations. The directive to organize and deliver services in a culturally responsive manner, respectful of diverse families, is a charge to the child welfare system and the individual professionals within that system.

Multiple Problems

Families that are involved with the child welfare system often face multiple, serious challenges:

○ Substance abuse incidence is extraordinarily high, with many locales reporting that the majority of the families that they work with have some form of substance abuse problem. The abuse of alcohol and drugs contributes to the neglect of children, diminished parenting skill, and abusive behavior. Substance abuse can extend to the children and youths in the family as well.

○ Mental health challenges facing these families are numerous and serious. With high incidences of depression and other disorders, parents and children face behavioral and social difficulties. Learning and behavioral difficulties in children and youths further complicate these situations.

○ Other forms of family violence are often identified, such as domestic violence or child sexual abuse.

○ Youth violence and delinquent behavior is evidenced by defiant, disruptive, and destructive behavior in the home, school, and broader community.

○ Involvement with the adult criminal justice system has an impact on family intactness and functioning. One or both parents may have criminal records that affect their employability. One or both parents may be in prison.

○ Overall, there is often a pervasive poverty with multiple implications for family well-being. Concretely, this poverty has powerful implications with regard to housing for families, reliable transportation, health care, educational opportunities for children, and financial credit.

What do these factors mean for families and FGC? Families may experience isolation because of geographic dislocation from extended family members, frequent moves, or forms of stigma; they may experience estrangement from their relatives, friends, and neighbors. This social isolation and relationship conflict may result from stresses on the family system due to substance abuse, mental illness, or the poverty of family members. Connections to family members or friends may not significantly increase the assets and resources available to a family, as these other people may be experiencing similar stressors. The family may be functioning with internal or external threats of violence.

There may be few resources in the immediate community available to the family, and those resources that are available may be severely strained by high demand. Some needed resources, such as drug treatment facilities for women with children, may not exist, particularly in rural or small town locales. Even when such resources do exist in a community, they may have little practical value to a family that cannot get to a required location. There may be limited hours of operation, low capacity levels, or strict eligibility criteria. There may be eligibility and practical ramifications for inclusion in FGC if there is domestic violence or intrafamily child sexual abuse.

Consequently, when working with families to construct an invitation list to a family group conference, the coordinator may find that few people are identified or that those identified may not want to attend. Some people may not be able to attend because of distance or other circumstances. One or both parents may be in jail. Extra accommodations may be needed at the conference to include foster families.

Circumstances may dictate the inclusion of a broad range of professionals, for example, the parents' and their adolescent's probation officers. The conference itself may blend child protection and juvenile justice features (see chapter 12). Professional resources may take on greater importance in the absence of family resources. The need to support the family after the conference may be magnified by the resource challenges identified before and during the conference. The families that are served by FGC are the families served by the child welfare system. The stressors on these families are multiple, severe, and oftentimes interconnected. Addressing the safety of children may be embedded in addressing a range of family difficulties. Although these difficulties cannot be overlooked, identifying family and community strengths and building a sense of hope and optimism are critical aspects of this process.

Sharing of Power

Although there are a variety of models of family involvement and adaptations of FGC (see chapters 7 and 11), central to FGC is private family time—that portion of the family conference when the professionals leave the room and the family members together use the information that has been provided to construct a family plan for the child and family at risk. This is perhaps the most overt step in recognizing and incorporating family power in decision making. There are other FGC processes that also reinforce family power—the coordinator's planning with the parents before the conference; determining with the family the attendees, location, and other aspects of the conference (such as food); enlisting extended family members; fully informing the family at the early stages of the conference; limiting the early professional contribution to the conference to providing information rather than venturing a plan of action; accepting a family plan as the beginning point for case planning and negotiating; and even negotiating the plan with the family. But private family time is the clearest and, for some people, most troubling, affirmation of family power.

Why does the inclusion of private family time produce at least professional uneasiness? In general, this uneasiness may originate in the relationship between families in the child welfare system and the beliefs and perceptions of the professionals who serve them. Are the family members criminals who have hurt their children and need to be punished and restricted? Are they clients in need of service? Are they customers whose satisfaction matters to the agency? Are they consumers of service? Are they partners with professionals, and if so, what is the nature of this partnership? The nature of the relationship between professionals and parents can be complicated and may be shaped by many factors.

There may be a number of specific reasons that private family time has generated some professional uneasiness. There may be concerns for the physical safety of family members if left alone; there may be concerns for the psychological safety of family members if left alone—due to a family bully or forms of scapegoating. There may be concerns that the family will not have the capacity to plan (1) because of a disruptive, potentially mentally ill, or negative family member; (2) because of the organizational and intellectual challenge of sorting through complicated information; or (3) because of ignorance or lack of experience with the system and related issues. The professionals may want to be helpful through note taking or other supports, or the family may request that a professional facilitate the meeting.

There have been few instances of family violence during private family time. In the Michigan study of more than 200 conferences, there were no examples of violence at conferences in general or in private family time. Careful pre-conference planning and explicit attention to safety plans supported this safety. Strong emotions may be expressed at conferences, and the availability of the coordinator to the family is a helpful support; however, the coordinator need not be present in private family time to provide this support. Some family members may make decision making and planning difficult—this will not be a surprise to the family. Family members have been coping with each other before FGC and will continue to do so after FGC. The troublesome family members in the room will also be in the community, so at least the FGC process provides an opportunity to enlist, modify, mollify, or reframe the attitudes and behaviors of negativistic family members.

With regard to the family's decision-making capacity, it is the responsibility of the coordinator, with the professionals in the early stage of the family group conference, to provide the information that family members need for planning. In addition, family members will know things about each other that the professionals do not know, and this information can be factored into their planning as a family. The impulse to be helpful to the family may be powerful, but families have repeatedly demonstrated their ability to talk together and plan together without professional assistance. Reasons for a family asking to have a professional in attendance should be assessed, but again, in most cases, the family has been, and should be, encouraged to attempt to plan together. Respecting private family time is not abdication of professional responsibility.

Sharing power with families as structured by FGC can be difficult for child welfare workers, as child protection service work requires a considerable measure of control and authority on the part of the caseworker. The child protection worker may view the parental right to make decisions and plans as compromised or abdicated in the case of child maltreatment, but eliminating parental involvement will not achieve the desired outcomes. Family planning reinforces family responsibility. Self-reflection and professional consultation may help child protection workers differentiate between their concerns and a natural tendency toward a caring paternalism or control.

Family members exercise considerable, often negative, power in child welfare proceedings. Through their attendance or nonattendance at meetings, through their providing or withholding information, through their conformity or genuine investment in actions, through their positive (even if inconsistent) or obstructionist efforts, family members shape the outcome of their involvement with the child welfare system. FGC attempts to respect the role of the family and extended family and to share power in the service of the child's well-being so that a realistic, safe, helpful plan is crafted and brought to life through the support and actions of the family.

Infrastructure

On a different dimension, FGC faces a number of challenges related to the infrastructure and resources required for the program. Although there may be some cost savings associated with FGC (see chapter 9), there are costs associated with a high-quality program. For example, the implementation of this model requires a caseload size that allows intensive work with families in preparation for the conference with relatively little lead time. Calibrating the most effective caseload sizes, case mixes, and related tasks and duties is still a relatively new and imprecise calculation. As FGC is a relatively new model, documentation and ongoing evaluation—which require the allocation of additional resources—are crucial to pro-

mote quality improvement and to provide validation to external audiences. Ongoing work with community and agency stakeholders is essential to promote community responsiveness and encourage referrals.

Despite high coordinator satisfaction with the model, FGC programs may not be immune to the turnover that characterizes much of child welfare services. The role of supportive supervision and an agency climate that promotes family involvement are important to retain talented professionals. Turnover in the child welfare system also increases the need for ongoing community and stakeholder education with regard to FGC values and strategies. Also, there may be resource needs related to working with families after the conference.

Conclusion

In a relatively short period of time, FGC has been introduced and, in many locales, an accepted practice in the child welfare system in the United States. The values and strategies of FGC resonate with professional values and codes of ethics, as well as with practice approaches in child welfare and in human and social services in general. The outcomes of the child welfare system are supported and advanced by FGC. These multiple strengths commend the practice of FGC.

In addition to the challenges facing both the child welfare system and FGC—such as commitment to cultural competence, multiple family stressors, and power sharing—a number of questions related to FGC are still waiting for answers. For example, in an era of restricted budgets, how does a child welfare system move beyond a tight triage that provides little time or resources for family involvement models? In what ways can FGC be applied to other decision-making points in the child welfare service continuum? How will the child welfare system develop an integrated set of strategies for work with families? To what extent does FGC represent a program model for child welfare or contribute to system reform through its values and strategies? How can this method be sustained in the future? How will it grow and evolve with further knowledge and experience?

FGC is not a panacea for all that troubles the child welfare system. However, its respect for families and extended families, enlistment of community resources and networks, and affirmation of culture reinforce and advance knowledge that has the potential to transform the lives of families and the practice of professionals.

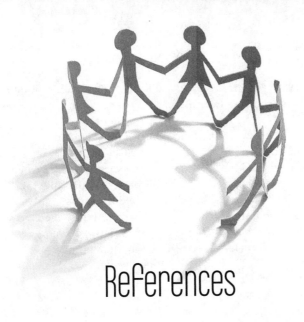

References

Adams, P., & Nelson, K. (Eds.). (1995). *Reinventing human services: Community- and family-centered practice.* New York: Aldine de Gruyter.

Adoption and Foster Care Analysis and Reporting System (AFCARS). (2001). *Trends in foster care and adoption.* Children's Bureau, Administration for Children and Families, Health and Human Servies. Retrieved August 2004 from http://www.acf.hhs.gov/programs/cb/dis/afcars/publications/afcars_stats.htm

Adoption and Safe Families Act of 1997, P.L. 105-89, 111 Stat. 2115.

Adoption Assistance and Child Welfare Act of 1980, P.L. 96-272, 94 Stat. 500.

Alter, C., & Egan, M. (1997). Logic modeling: A tool for teaching critical thinking in social work practice. *Journal of Social Work Education, 33,* 85–102.

American Humane Association. (1997). *Innovations for children's services for the 21st century: Family group decision making and Patch.* Englewood, CO: Author.

Anderson, G. (2001). Formal and informal kinship care: Supporting the whole family. In E. Walton, P. Sandau-Beckler, & M. Mannes (Eds.), *Balancing family-centered services and child well-being* (pp. 179–196). New York: Columbia University Press.

Anderson, G. (with Whalen, P.). (2003). *Best practices: Preliminary lessons learned from the Michigan FGDM evaluation.* Lansing: Report for the Michigan Department of Human Services.

Anderson, G., Hodge-Morgan, D., Snyder, C., & Whalen, P. (2001, May). *Michigan's advocate: A FGC strategy for after the conference.* Paper presented at the American Humane Association's Family Group Decision Making National Conference, Chapel Hill, NC.

Andy Rowe Consultants, Inc. (1997, November). *Comparative costs and cost-effectiveness of Family Group Decision Making Project: Technical report.* St. John's, Newfoundland: Author.

Ashby, C. M. (2003, July). *Child welfare and juvenile justice: Several factors influence the placement of children solely to obtain mental health services.* Retrieved May 15, 2004, from http://www.senate.gov/~govt-aff/_files/071703ashby.pdf

Atkin, W. R. (1988–1989). Children versus families—Is there any conflict? *Journal of Family Law, 7*(I), 231–242.

Baker, G. (2002). *Civil society and democratic theory.* London: Routledge.

Bancroft, L., & Silverman, J. G. (2002). *The batterer as parent: Addressing the impact of domestic violence on family dynamics.* Thousand Oaks, CA: Sage Publications.

Barber, B. (1984). *Strong democracy: Participatory politics for a new age.* Berkeley: University of California Press.

Bartholet, E. (1999). *Nobodys' children: Abuse and neglect, foster drift, and the adoption alternative.* Boston: Beacon Press.

Bazemore, G., & Schiff, M. (2004). *Juvenile justice reform and restorative justice: Building theory and policy from practice.* Cullompton, Devon, England: Willan.

Bazemore, G., & Umbreit, M. (2001, February). A comparison of four restorative conferencing models. *Juvenile Justice Bulletin.* Retrieved March 3, 2004, from http://www.ncjrs.org/html/ojjdp/2001_2_1/contents.html

Beauchamp, T., & Childress, J. (1983). *Principles of biomedical ethics.* New York: Oxford University Press.

Berg, I. K., & Kelly, S. (2000). *Building solutions in child protective services.* New York: W. W. Norton.

Berzin, S. C. (2004, June). *California's waiver demonstration project: Results from an experimental project.* Paper presented at the From Margin to Mainstream: 2004 Conference on Family Group Decision Making workshop, Harrisburg, PA.

Best, J. (1999). *Random violence: How we talk about new crimes and new victims.* Berkeley: University of California Press.

Best, J. (Ed.). (2001). *How claims spread: Cross-national diffusion of social problems.* New York: Aldine de Gruyter.

Beyer, M. (2003, April). Best practices in juvenile accountability: An overview. *JAIBG Bulletin.* Retrieved February 2, 2004, from http://www.ncjrs.org/pdffiles1/ojjdp/184745.pdf

Bilchik, S. (1995, June). Bridging the child welfare and youth justice systems. *Juvenile Justice Bulletin.*

Bilchek, S. (2003a, April 8). "CWLA testimony." Retrieved May 23, 2005, from www.cwla.org/advocacy/asfatestimony-implementation.htm

Bilcheck, S. (2003b, July 14). "Evolving federal child welfare law and policy: Where do we go from here?" Retrieved May 23, 2005, from www.cwla.org/execdir/edremarkschildlaw.htm

Braithwaite, J. (2000). Democracy, community and problem solving. In G. Burford & J. Hudson (Eds.), *Family group conferencing: New directions in community-centered child and family practice* (pp. 31–39). New York: Aldine de Gruyter.

Braithwaite, J. (2002). *Restorative justice and responsive regulation.* New York: Oxford University Press.

Braithwaite, J., & Strang, H. (2001). Introduction: Restorative justice and civil society. In H. Strang & J. Braithwaite (Eds.), *Restorative justice and civil society* (pp. 1–13). Cambridge, England: Cambridge University Press.

Braithwaite, J., & Strang, H. (2002). Restorative justice and family violence. In H. Strang & J. Braithwaite (Eds.), *Restorative justice and family violence* (pp. 1–22). Cambridge, England: Cambridge University Press.

Briar-Lawson, K., Lawson, H. A., & Hennon, C. B. (2001). *Family-centered policies and practices: International implications.* New York: Columbia University Press.

Brown, E., Limb, G., Munoz, R., & Clifford, C. (2001, December). *Title IV-B Child and Family Services Plans: An evaluation of specific measures taken by states to comply with the Indian Child Welfare Act.* Seattle: Casey Family Programs.

Bureau of Justice Assistance. (2003). *Engaging the family in juvenile drug court.* Retrieved March 3, 2004, from http://www.ncjrs.org/pdffiles1/bja/197449.pdf

Burford, G., & Hudson, J. (Eds.). (2000). *Family group conferencing: New directions in community-centered child and family practice.* New York: Aldine de Gruyter.

Burford, G., & Nixon, P. (2003, June). *And the survey said? The results of the World Wide Web survey on family group conferencing.* Paper presented at the American Humane Association's 2003 Conference on FGDM, Minneapolis.

Burford, G., & Pennell, J. (1995). *Family group decision making: New roles for 'old' partners in resolving family violence. Implementation report summary.* St. John's, Newfoundland, Canada: Memorial University of Newfoundland School of Social Work.

Burford, G., & Pennell, J. (1998). *Family group decision making: After the conference—Progress in resolving violence and promoting well-being: Outcome report* (Vols. 1–2). St. John's, Newfoundland, Canada: Memorial University of Newfoundland, School of Social Work.

Burford, G., Pennell, J., & MacLeod, S. (1995). *Family group decision making: Manual for coordinators and communities.* St. John's, Newfoundland, Canada: Memorial University of Newfoundland, School of Social Work, Family Group Decision Making Project. Retrieved May 3, 2004, from http://social.chass.ncsu.edu/jpennell/fgdm/Manual

Campbell, J., Rose, L., Kub, J., & Nedd, D. (1998). Voices of strength and resistance: A contextual and longitudinal analysis of women's responses to battering. *Journal of Interpersonal Violence, 13,* 743–762.

Campbell, J. C., Webster, D., Koziol-McLain, J., Block, C., Campbell, D., Curry, M. A., et al. (2003). Risk factors for feminicide in abusive relationships: Results from a multisite case control study. *American Journal of Public Health, 93,* 1089–1097.

Carter, J. (2003, October). *Family team conferences in domestic violence cases* (2nd ed.). San Francisco: Family Violence Prevention Fund.

Casey Outcomes and Decision-Making Project/American Humane Association (CODMP/AHA). (1998). *Assessing outcomes in child welfare services: Principles, concepts, and a framework of core outcome indicators.* Englewood, CO: American Humane Association.

Cashmore, J., & Kiely, P. (2000). Implementing and evaluating family group conferences: The New South Wales experience. In G. Burford & J. Hudson (Eds.), *Family group conferencing: New directions in community-centered child and family practice* (pp. 242–252). New York: Aldine de Gruyter.

Center for the Study of Social Policy, Center for Community Partnerships in Child Welfare. (2002, March). *Bringing families to the table: A comparative guide to family meetings in child welfare.* Washington, DC: Author.

Chaskin, R. J., Brown, P., Venkatesh, S., & Vidal, A. (2001). *Building community capacity.* New York: Aldine de Gruyter.

Child Abuse and Prevention, Adoption and Family Services Act of 1988, P.L. 100-294, 102 Stat. 102.

Child Abuse Prevention and Treatment Act (CAPTA) of 1974, P.L. 93-247, 88 Stat. 4.

Child Abuse Prevention and Treatment Act, Amendments of 1996, P.L. 104-235, 110 Stat. 3063.

Child Welfare League of America. (2000). *Relationship between juvenile justice data and child welfare data.* National Data Analysis Systems. Retrieved November 27, 2003, from www.ndas.cwla.org

Child Welfare League of America (CWLA). (2003). *Making children a national priority: A framework for community action.* Washington, DC: CWLA Press.

Child Welfare Practice and Policy Group (CWPPG). (2001). *The origins of family team conferencing.* Unpublished manuscript.

Child Welfare Practice and Policy Group. (2003). *The origins of family team conferencing. Unpublished report.* Montgomery, AL: Author.

Child Welfare Practice and Policy Group. (2002). *Handbook for family team conferences.* Montgomery, AL: Author.

Cohen, J. L. (2001). Civil society. In P. B. Clarke & J. Foweraker (Eds.), *Encyclopedia of democratic thought* (pp. 67–71). London: Routledge.

Cohen, N. A. (2000). *Child welfare: A multi-cultural focus* (2nd ed.). Boston: Allyn & Bacon.

Connolly, M., & McKenzie, M. (1999). *Effective participatory practice: Family group conferencing in child protection.* New York: Aldine de Gruyter.

Corby, B., Millar, M., & Young, L. (1996). Parental participation in child protection work: Rethinking the rhetoric. *British Journal of Social Work, 26,* 475–492.

Cornman, J., Henkin, N. Z., & Kingson, E. R. (1999, Fall). Building communities with intergenerational strategies. *Community, 2*(2), 12–16.

Crampton, D. S. (2001). *Making sense of foster care: An evaluation of family group decision making in Kent County, Michigan.* Unpublished doctoral dissertation, University of Michigan, Ann Arbor.

Crampton, D., & Jackson, W. L. (2000). Evaluating and implementing family group conferences: The family and community compact in Kent County, Michigan. In G. Burford & J. Hudson (Eds.), *Family group conferencing: New directions in community-centered child and family practice* (pp. 324–333). New York: Aldine de Gruyter.

Crawford, A. (1996). Alternatives to prosecution: Access to, or exits from, criminal justice? In R. Young & D. Wall (Eds.), *Access to criminal justice: Lawyers, legal aid and the defense of liberty.* London: Blackstone Press.

Crow, G., & Marsh, P. (1997). *Family group conferences, partnership and child welfare: A research report on four pilot projects in England and Wales.* Sheffield, England: University of Sheffield Partnership Research Programme.

Crozier, L. (2000). The evolution of conferencing within child welfare in Northern Ireland. In G. Burford & J. Hudson (Eds.), *Family group conferencing: New directions in community-centered child and family practice* (pp. 218–223). New York: Aldine de Gruyter.

Daly, K. (1999, October). *What is the future of the youth court? Reflecting on the relationship of informal and formal justice.* Adelaide, AU: Australian and New Zealand Youth Court Judges and Magistrates. Retrieved May 4, 2004, from http://www.gu.edu.au/school/ccj/kdaly_docs/kdpaper8.pdf

Daly, K. (2001). Conferencing in Australia and New Zealand: Variations, research findings and prospects. In A. Morris & G. Maxwell (Eds.), *Restorative justice for juveniles: Conferencing, mediation and circles* (pp. 59–83). Portland, OR: Hart Publishing.

De Jong, P., & Berg, I. K. (1998). *Interviewing for solutions.* Pacific Grove, CA: Brooks/Cole.

DeMuro, P., & Rideout, P. (2002). *Team decisionmaking: Involving the family and community in child welfare decisions* (Rev. ed.). Baltimore: Annie E. Casey Foundation.

DePanfilis, D. (2000). How do I develop a helping alliance with the family? In H. Dubowitz & D. DePanfilis (Eds.), *The handbook on child protection* (pp. 36–40). Thousand Oaks, CA: Sage Publications.

DeStephen, R. S., & Hirokawa, R. Y. (1988). Small group consensus: Stability of group support of the decision, task process, and group relationships. *Small Group Behavior, 19*(2), 227–239.

Dignan, J., & Marsh, P. (2001). Restorative justice and family group conferences in England: Current state and future prospects. In A. Morris & G. Maxwell (Eds.), *Restorative justice for juveniles: Conferencing, mediation and circles* (pp. 85–101). Portland, OR: Hart Publishing.

Dillman, D. (2000). *Mail and Internet surveys.* New York: John Wiley & Sons.

Doolan, M. (2002). *Restorative practices and family empowerment: Both/and or either/or?* London: Family Rights Group.

Doolan, M. (2003). Restorative practices and family empowerment: Both/and or either/or? *Family Rights Group Newsletter.* London: Family Rights Group.

Doolan, M., & Phillips, P. (2000). Conferencing in New Zealand: Child protection. In G. Burford & J. Hudson (Eds.), *Family group conferencing: New directions in community-centered child and family practice* (pp. 193–197). New York: Aldine de Gruyter.

References

Dowden, C., & Andrews, D. A. (1999). What works in young offender treatment: A meta-analysis. *Forum on Corrections Research, 11,* 21–24.

Duquette, D., & Hardin, M. (1999, June). *Guidelines for public policy and state legislation governing permanence for children.* Washington, DC: Children's Bureau.

Edleson, J. L. (1999). The overlap between child maltreatment and woman battering. *Violence Against Women, 5,* 134–154.

Edleson, J. L. (2004). Should childhood exposure to adult domestic violence be defined as child maltreatment under the law? In P. G. Jaffe, L. L. Baker, & A. Cunningham (Eds.), *Protecting children from domestic violence: Strategies for community intervention* (pp. 8–29). New York: Guilford Press.

Edleson, J. L, Mbilinyi, L. F., & Shetty, S. (2003, March). *Parenting in the context of domestic violence.* San Francisco: Judicial Council of California/Administrative Office of the Courts.

Family Preservation and Support Services Program of 1993; Title XIII, Ch. 2 Subch. C, Part I, Section 13711 of the Omnibus Budget Reconciliation Act of 1993, P.L. 103-66, 107 Stat. 650.

Farrow, F. (1997). *Child protection: Building community partnerships, getting from here to there.* Cambridge, MA: Harvard University Press.

Fercello, C., & Umbreit, M. (1998). *Client evaluation of family group conferencing in 12 sites in the First Judicial District of Minnesota.* St. Pau, MNl: Center for Restorative Justice and Mediation.

Fetterman, D. M., Kaftarian, S. J., & Wandersman, A. (Eds.). (1996). *Empowerment evaluation: Knowledge and tools for self-assessment and accountability.* Thousand Oaks, CA: Sage Publications.

Fleury, R. E., Sullivan, C. M., & Bybee, D. I. (2000). When ending the relationship does not end the violence. *Violence Against Women, 6,* 1363–1383.

Francis, S. (2002, Spring). *Results of focus groups with domestic-violence advocates.* Unpublished paper, North Carolina Family Group Conferencing Project, North Carolina State University, Raleigh.

Foster Care Independence Act of 1999, P.L. 106-169, 113 Stat 1822.

Freedman, P. (2003). *What makes a solution? Lessons and findings from solutions for America.* Charlottesville, VA: Pew Partnership for Civic Change.

Fulcher, L. (1998). Acknowledging culture in child and youth care practices. *Social Work Education, 17,* 321–338.

Fullinwider, R. K. (Ed.). (1999). *Civil society, democracy, and civic renewal.* Lanham, MD: Rowman & Littlefield.

Gal, T. (2004, December). *Child victims and restorative justice: The appeal, the risks.* Paper presented at New Frontiers in Restorative Justice, Massey University, Auckland, New Zealand.

Gambrill, E., & Shlonsky, A. (2000). Risk assessment in context. *Child and Youth Services Review, 22,* 813–837.

Garbarino, J. (1976). A preliminary study of some ecological correlates of child abuse: The impact of socioeconomic stresses on mothers. *Child Development, 47,* 178–185.

Garvin, C. D. (1997). *Contemporary group work* (3rd ed.). Boston: Allyn & Bacon.

Gondolf, E. W. (2000). Human subject issues in batterer program evaluation. In S. K. Ward & D. Finkelhor (Eds.), *Program evaluation and family violence research* (pp. 273–297). New York: Haworth Press.

Goodkind, J. R., Gillum, T. L., Bybee, D. I., & Sullivan, C. M. (2003). The impact of family and friends' reactions on the well-being of women with abusive partners. *Violence Against Women, 9,* 347–373.

Goodman, R. M., Wandersman, A., Chinman, M., Imm, P., & Morrissey, E. (1996). An ecological assessment of community-based interventions for prevention and health promotion: Approaches to measuring community coalitions. *American Journal of Community Psychology, 24,* 33–61.

Government Performance and Results Act of 1993, P.L. 103-62, 107 Stat. 285.

References

Graham-Bermann, S. A. (2000). Evaluating interventions for children exposed to family violence. In S. K. Ward & D. Finkelhor (Eds.), *Program evaluation and family violence research* (pp. 191–215). New York: Haworth Press.

Gray, B. (1989). *Collaborating: Finding common ground for multiparty problems*. San Francisco: Jossey-Bass.

Green, J. W. (1999). *Cultural awareness in the human services: A multi-ethnic approach* (3rd ed.). Boston: Allyn & Bacon.

Greenwood, P. W., Model, K. E., Rydell, C. P., & Chiesa, J. R. (1998). *Diverting children from a life of crime: Measuring costs and benefits*. Santa Monica, CA: Rand.

Guetiérrez, L. M., Parsons, R. J., & Cox, E. O. (Eds.). (1998). *Empowerment in social work practice: A sourcebook*. Pacific Grove, CA: Brooks/Cole.

Gunderson, K., Cahn, K., & Wirth, J. (2003). The Washington State long-term outcome study. *Protecting Children, 18* (1/2), 42–47.

Halpern, R. (1999). *Fragile families, fragile solutions: A history of supportive services for families in poverty*. New York: Columbia University Press.

Hassall, I. (1996). Origin and development of family group conferences. In J. Hudson, A. Morris, G. Maxwell, & B. Galaway (Eds.), *Family group conferences: Perspectives on policy and practice* (pp. 17–36). Monsey, NY: Willow Tree Press.

Health Care Advisory Board. (1993). *Outcomes strategy: Measurement of hospital quality under reform*. Washington, DC: Author.

Hegar, R. (1999). The cultural roots of kinship care. In R. Hegar & M. Scannapieco (Eds.), *Kinship foster care: Policy, practice, and research* (pp. 17–27). New York: Oxford University Press.

Henderson, S., Pennell, J., & Family Group Members. (2004, June). *Family perspectives on FGC: Focus groups in a rural county*. Paper presented at the From Margin to Mainstream: 2004 Conference on Family Group Decision Making workshop, Harrisburg, PA.

Henggeler, S. W., Borduin, S. K., Schoenwald, C. M., Rowland, M. D., & Cunningham, P. B. (1998). *Multisystemic treatment of antisocial behavior in children and adolescents*. New York: Guilford Press.

Henggeler, S. W., & Randall, J. (2000). Conducting randomized treatment studies in real-world settings. In D. Drotar (Ed.), *Handbook for research methods in pediatric and clinical child psychology: Practical strategies and methods* (pp. 447–461). New York: Kluwer Academic/Plenum.

Horwitz, M. (2003). *Building permanency with family group decision-making: The kinship connections project. Final report*. Northampton: University of Massachusetts Medical School, Center for Mental Health Services Research.

Hoyle, C., Young, R., & Hill, R. (2002). *Proceed with caution: An evaluation of the Thames Valley police initiative in restorative cautioning*. Layerthorpe, York, England: Joseph Rowntree Foundation.

Hudson, J., Morris, A., Maxwell, G., & Galaway, B. (Eds.). (1996). *Family group conferences: Perspectives on policy and practice*. Monsey, NY: Willow Tree Press.

Hudson, W. W. (1992). *The WALMYR Assessment Scales scoring manual*. Tempe, AZ: WALMYR.

Hughes, M. J., & Jones, L. (2000, January). *Women, domestic violence, and posttraumatic stress disorder (PTSD)*. Retrieved March 3, 2003, from http://www.csus.edu/calst/Government_Affairs/Reports/ffp32.pdf

Indian Child Welfare Act of 1978, P.L. 95-608, 92 Stat 3069.

International Confederation of Midwives. (2000). Protecting the heritage of indigenous people (cultural safety). *In Position statements 2000*. Retrieved December 3, 2003, from http://www.international midwives.org/Statements/Heritage

Kansas Code for the Care of Children, Kan. Stat. Ann. § 39-1559, art. 15 (1994).

Kaplan, M. S., Henkin, N. Z., & Kusano, A. T. (Eds.). (2002). *Linking lifetimes: A global view of intergenerational exchange*. Lanham, MD: University Press of America.

References

Kaplan, R. (2003). *Information packet: Child welfare class action lawsuits.* Retrieved April 3, 2004 from http://www.hunter.cuny.edu/socwork/nrcfcpp/downloads/cw-class-action-lawsuits.pdf

Kelly, K. (2003). *Domestic violence and the politics of privacy.* Ithaca, NY: Cornell University Press.

Kelly, S., & Blythe, B. (2000). Family preservation: A potential not yet realized. *Child Welfare, 79,* 29–42.

Kemp, S., Whittaker, J., & Tracy, E. (1997). *Person-environment practice: The social ecology of interpersonal helping.* New York: Aldine de Gruyter.

Kempe, C. H., & Helfer, R. (1972). *Helping the battered child and his family.* Philadelphia: Lippincott.

Keys, T. (1996). Family decision making in Oregon. *Protecting Children, 12*(3), 11–14.

Knapp, M. (1984). *The economics of social care.* London: Macmillan.

Kretzmann, J. P., & McKnight, J. L. (1993). *Building communities from the inside out: A path toward finding and mobilizing a community's assets.* Evanston, IL: Northwestern University, Institute for Policy Research.

Latimer, J., Dowden, C., & Muise, D. (2001). *The effectiveness of restorative justice practices: A meta-analysis.* Ottawa: Department of Justice, Canada, Research and Statistics Division.

Levin, H. M. (1983). *Cost effectiveness: A primer.* Thousand Oaks, CA: Sage Publications.

Leyton, E., O'Grady, W., & Overton, J. (1992). *Violence and public anxiety.* St. John's, Newfoundland, Canada: ISER Books.

Love, C. (2000). Family group conferencing: Cultural origins, sharing, and appropriation—A Maori reflection. In G. Burford & J. Hudson (Eds.), *Family group conferencing: New directions in community-centered child and family practice* (pp. 15–30). New York: Aldine de Gruyter.

Lupton, C. (1998). Family group conferences: User empowerment or self-reliance? *British Journal of Social Work, 28,* 107–128.

Lupton, C., & Nixon, P. (1999). *Empowering practice? A critical appraisal of the family group conference approach.* Bristol, England: Policy Press.

Lupton, C., & Stevens, M. (1997). *Family outcomes: Following through on family group conferences* [Report No. 34]. Portsmouth, England: University of Portsmouth, Social Services Research and Information Unit.

Lyon, T. D. (1999). Are battered women bad mothers? Rethinking the termination of abused women's parental rights for failure to protect. In H. Dubowitz (Ed.), *Neglected children: Research, practice, and policy* (pp. 237–260). Thousand Oaks, CA: Sage Publications.

Macgowan, M., & Pennell, J. (2002). Building social responsibility through family group conferencing. *Social Work with Groups, 24*(3/4), 67–87.

Maluccio, A. N., & Daly, J. (2000). Family group conferences as "good" child welfare practice. In G. Burford & J. Hudson (Eds.), *Family group conferencing: New directions in community-centered child and family practice* (pp. 65–71). New York: Aldine de Gruyter.

Mannes, M. (2001). Well-being and family-centered services: The value of the developmental assets framework. In E. Walton, P. Sandau-Beckler, & M. Mannes (Eds.), *Balancing family-centered services and child well-being* (pp. 128–154). New York: Columbia University Press.

Marks, D. (2002, Autumn). A brief study and comparison of time spent to undertake allocated pieces of work within the FGC process. *Family Group Conference Network Newsletter,* pp. 6–8.

Marsh, P., & Crow, G. (1998). *Family group conferences in child welfare.* Oxford, England: Blackwells.

Marsh, P., & Crow, G. (2003). Family group conferences and child protection in a multicultural community—1998. *Protecting Children, 18*(1–2), 131–132.

Martin, M. E. (1997). Policy promise: Community policing and domestic violence victim's satisfaction. *Policing: An International*

Journal of Police Strategies & Management, 20, 519–531.

Maxwell, G., Kingi, V., Robertson, J., Morris, A., & Cunningham, C. (2003, December). *Achieving effective outcomes in youth justice: The full report.* Wellington, NZ: Ministry of Social Development.

Maxwell, G., & Morris, A. (1993a). *Family participation, cultural diversity and victim involvement in youth justice: A New Zealand experiment.* Wellington, NZ: Victoria University of Wellington.

Maxwell, G. M., & Morris, A. (1993b). *Family, victims, and culture: Youth justice in New Zealand.* Wellington, NZ: Victoria University of Wellington, Social Policy Agency and Institute of Criminology.

Maxwell, G., & Morris, A. (2001). Family group conferences and reoffending. In A. Morris & G. Maxwell (Eds.), *Restorative justice for juveniles: Conferencing, mediation and circles* (pp. 243–263). Portland, OR: Hart Publishing.

Maxwell, G., Robertson, J., & Anderson, T. (2002). *Police youth diversion: Final report.* Wellington, NZ: Victoria University of Wellington, The Crime and Justice Research Centre.

Mayer, J. P., & Davidson, W. S. (2000). Dissemination of innovation as social change. In J. Rappaport & E. Seidman (Eds.), *Handbook of community psychology* (pp. 421–438). New York: Kluwer Academic/Plenum.

Mbilinyi, L. F., Edleson, J. L., Beeman, S. K., & Hagemiester, A. K. (2002). *How violence against women and children co-occurs: Results from a four-city anonymous telephone survey.* Unpublished manuscript, University of Minnesota, St. Paul.

McCold, P. (2001). Primary restorative justice practices. In A. Morris & G. Maxwell (Eds.), *Restorative justice for juveniles: Conferencing, mediation and circles* (pp. 41–58). Portland, OR: Hart Publishing.

McCold, P., & Wachtel, B. (1998, May). *Restorative policing experiment: The Bethlehem Pennsylvania police family group conferencing project: Summary.* Retrieved May 16, 2005, from the International Institute for Restorative Practices Web site: http://www.iirp.org/library/summary.html

Walter R. McDonald & Associates, Inc. (2000, November). *The Santa Clara County family conference model outcome evaluation.* Sacramento, CA: Author.

McGillivray, A., & Comaskey, B. (1999). *Black eyes all of the time: Intimate violence, aboriginal women, and the justice system.* Toronto: University of Toronto Press.

McLaughlin, J. A., & Jordan, G. B. (1999). Logic models: A tool for telling your program's performance story. *Evaluation and Program Evaluation, 22,* 65–72.

Mears, D. P., & Aron, L. Y. (2003, November). *Assessing the needs of youth with disabilities in the juvenile justice system: The current state of knowledge.* Washington, DC: Urban Institute Justice Policy Center.

Mendel, R. A. (2000). *Less hype, more help: Reducing juvenile crime, what works—And what doesn't.* Washington, DC: American Youth Policy Forum.

Merkel-Holguin, L. (2000a). Diversions and departures in the implementation of family group conferencing in the United States. In G. Burford & J. Hudson (Eds.), *Family group conferencing: New directions in community-centered child and family practice* (pp. 224–231). New York: Aldine de Gruyter.

Merkel-Holguin, L. (2000b). US implementation of family group decision making processes. In H. Walker, G. Allan, T. Featherston, A. Hewitt, G. Keith, & D. Smith, et al. (Eds.), *Family decision making: A conferencing philosophy* (pp. 179–191). Masterton, NZ: Kinpower Associates.

Merkel-Holguin, L. (2001). Family group conferencing: An "extended family" process to safeguard children and strengthen family well-being. In E. Walton, P. Sandau-Beckler, & M. Mannes (Eds.), *Balancing family-centered services and child well-being: Exploring issues in policy, practice, theory, and research* (pp. 197–218). New York: Columbia University Press.

Merkel-Holguin, L. (2002, June). *Follow-up: The missing link*. Paper presented at the 2002 Conference on Family Group Decision Making, Monterey, CA.

Merkel-Holguin, L. (Ed.). (2003). Promising results, potential new directions: International FGDM research and evaluation in child welfare [Special issue]. *Protecting Children, 18*(1–2).

Merkel-Holguin, L. (2004). Sharing power with the people: Family group conferencing as a democratic experiment. *Journal of Sociology and Social Welfare, 31*(1), 155–173.

Merkel-Holguin, L., Nixon, P., & Burford, G. (2003). Learning with families: A synopsis of FGDM research and evaluation in child welfare. *Protecting Children, 18*(1/2), 2–11.

Merkel-Holguin, L., & Wilmot, L. (Eds.). (2000). *2000 National roundtable on family group decision making: Summary of proceedings*. Englewood, CO: American Humane Association.

Mika, H., Achilles, M., Halbert, E., Amstutz, L. S., & Zehr, H. (2003). *Taking victims and their advocates seriously: A listening project*. Harrisonburg, VA: Eastern Mennonite University, Institute for Justice and Peacebuilding.

Milliken, E. (2002). *Margin or center: Building a culturally safe context in which Aboriginal students can develop social work practice competencies*. Unpublished manuscript, Memorial University of Newfoundland, Canada.

Milner, J. (2003, January). *Results of the 2001/ 2002 child and family service reviews*. Washington, DC: U.S. Department of Health and Human Services, Children's Bureau.

Milstein, R. L., & Wetterhall, S. F. (1999). Framework for program evaluation in public health. *Morbidity and Mortality Weekly Report, 48*(RR11), 1–40. Retrieved December 2, 2003, from http://www.cdc.gov/mmwr/preview/mmwrhtml/rr4811a1.htm

Moore, D. B. (1997). Pride, shame and empathy in peer relations: New theory and practice in education and juvenile justice. In K. Rigby & P. Slee (Eds.), *Children's peer relations*. London: Routledge.

Moore, D. B., & McDonald, J. A. (2000). Guiding principles of the conferencing process. In G. Burford & J. Hudson (Eds.), *Family group conferencing: New directions in community-centered child and family practice*. New York: Aldine de Gruyter.

Moore, D. B., & O'Connell, T. (1994). Family conferencing in Wagga Wagga: A communitarian model of justice. In C. Alder & J. Wundersitz (Eds.), *Family conferencing and juvenile justice: The way forward or misplaced optimism?* (pp. 45–86). Canberra, ACT: Australian Institute of Criminology.

Morris, A. (2002). Children and family violence: Restorative messages from New Zealand. In H. Strang & J. Braithwaite (Eds.), *Restorative justice and family violence* (pp. 89–107). Cambridge, England: Cambridge University Press.

Multi-Ethnic Placement Act of 1994, P.L. 103-296, 108 Stat. 1464.

National Association of Social Workers. (2000). *Code of ethics of the National Association of Social Workers*. Washington, DC: Author.

National Association of Social Workers. (2001). *NASW standards for cultural competence in social work practice*. Washington, DC: Author.

National Center for Juvenile Justice. (2003). *National overviews*. Retrieved May 8, 2004, from http://www.ncjj.org/stateprofiles/overviews/faq10t.asp

National Child Abuse and Neglect Data System Web site: www.acf.dhhs.gov/programs/cb/publications/ncands

Nelson, K.E., & Landsman, M. J. (1992). *Alternative models of family preservation: Family-based services in context*. Springfield, IL: Charles C Thomas.

Netten, A. (1996, September). *The experience with cost effectiveness analysis in the United Kingdom*. Paper presented at the Crime Prevention: Money Well Spent? seminar of the National Crime Prevention Council, Ottawa.

New Zealand Department of Child Youth and Family. (1995). *Mihi's Whanau*. Wellington, New Zealand: Author.

References

New Zealand Department of Social Welfare. (1989). *Children, Young Persons, and Their Families Act 1989*. Wellington, New Zealand: Government Printer.

New Zealand Department of Social Welfare. (1999). *Children, Young Persons, and Their Families Act 1989 (Amended 1994): Information pack for NZCYPS staff*. Wellington, New Zealand: Author.

Nixon, P. (1998). Exchanging practice: Some comparisons, contrasts, and lessons learned from the practice of family group conferences in Sweden and the United Kingdom. *Protecting Children, 14*(4), 13–18.

Nixon, P., Merkel-Holguin, L., Sivak, P., & Gunderson, K. (2000). How can family group conferences become family-driven? Some dilemmas and possibilities. *Protecting Children, 16*(3), 22–33.

North Carolina Family Group Conferencing Project. (2002). *Family group conferencing in child welfare: Practice guidance for planning, implementing, training, and evaluation*. Raleigh: North Carolina State University, Social Work Program, Retrieved July 15, 2004, from http://social.chass.ncsu.edu/jpennell/ncfgcp/pracguid

Northen, H., & Kurland, R. (2001). *Social work with groups* (3rd ed.). New York: Columbia University Press.

Oregon Department of Human Resources, State Office for Services to Children and Families. (1998). *Client services manual I*. Salem, OR: Author.

Oregon Department of Human Resources, State Office for Services to Children and Families. (1999, April). *The Oregon family decision meeting guide*. Salem, OR: Author.

Oregon House Bill 2787, 69th Oregon Legislative Assembly, 1997.

Palmer, T. (2002). *Individualized intervention with young multiple offenders*. New York: Routledge.

Parsloe, P. (1996). *Pathways to empowerment*. Birmingham: Venture.

Parsons, R. J. (1998). Evaluation of empowerment practice. In L. M. Gutiérrez, R. J. Parsons, & E. O. Cox (Eds.), *Empowerment in social work practice: A sourcebook* (pp. 204–219). Pacific Grove, CA: Brooks/Cole.

Parton, N. (Ed.). (1997). *Child protection and family support: Tensions, contradictions and possibilities*. London: Routledge.

Paterson, K., & Harvey, M. (1991). *An evaluation of the organisation and operation of care and protection family group conferences*. Wellington, New Zealand: Department of Social Welfare.

Patton, M. (1986). *Utilization-focused evaluation* (2nd ed.). Beverly Hills, CA: Sage Publications.

Pavlich, G. (2001). The force of community. In H. Strang & J. Braithwaite (Eds.), *Restorative justice and civil society* (pp. 56–58). New York: Cambridge University Press.

Pecora, P. J., Reed-Ashcraft, K., & Kirk, R. S. (2001). Family-centered services: A typology, brief history, and overview of current program implementation and evaluation challenges. In E. Walton, P. Sandau-Beckler, & M. Mannes (Eds.), *Balancing family-centered services and child well-being* (pp. 1–33). New York: Columbia University Press.

Pecora, P. J., Whittaker, J. K., Maluccio, A. N., & Barth, R. P. (2000). *The child welfare challenge: Police, practice, and research* (2nd ed.). New York: Aldine de Gruyter.

Pedhazur, E. J. (1982). *Multiple regression in behavioral research: Explanation and prediction* (2nd ed.). New York: CBS College Publishing.

Pennell, J. (with Hardison, J., & Yerkes, E.). (1999). *North Carolina Family Group Conferencing Project: Building partnerships with and around families: Report to the North Carolina Division of Social Services, Fiscal year 1998–1999*. Raleigh: North Carolina State University, Social Work Program, North Carolina Family Group Conferencing Project.

Pennell, J. (with Turner, T., & Hardison, J.). (2001a). *North Carolina Family Group Conferencing Project: Building partnerships with and around families: Report to the North Carolina Division of Social Services, Fiscal year 2000–2001*. Raleigh: North Carolina State

University, Social Work Program, North Carolina Family Group Conferencing Project.

Pennell, J. (2001b). *Research/evaluation instruments for the North Carolina Family Group Conferencing Project*. Raleigh: North Carolina State University, Social Work Program.

Pennell, J. (2002a, March). *Integration of family involvement models*. Paper presented at Children 2002: Making Children a National Priority workshop, Child Welfare League of America National Conference, Washington, DC.

Pennell, J. (with Turner, T., & Hardison, J.). (2002b). *North Carolina Family Group Conferencing Project: Building partnerships with and around families: Final report to the North Carolina Division of Social Services, fiscal year 2001–2002*. Raleigh: North Carolina State University, Social Work Program, North Carolina Family Group Conferencing Project. Online executive summary, retrieved May 15, 2004, from http://social.chass.ncsu.edu/jpennell/ncfgcp/NCFGCPExecSummary

Pennell, J. (2002c). Principles for FGC evaluation. In C. Harper, J. Pennell, & M. Weil (Eds.), *Family group conferencing: Evaluation guidelines* (2nd ed., pp. 13–32). Englewood, CO: American Humane Association.

Pennell, J. (2003a). Are we following key FGC practice? Views of conference participants. *Protecting Children, 18*(1/2), 16–21.

Pennell, J. (2003b, June). FGC key principles—Are we following them in practice? *Pathways to Permanence: 2003 Family Group Decision Making Conference and Skills-Building Institutes* workshop, Minneapolis.

Pennell, J. (2004). Family group conferencing in child welfare: Responsive and regulatory interfaces. *Journal of Sociology and Social Welfare, 31*(1), 117–135.

Pennell, J. (in press-a). Restorative practices and child welfare: Toward an inclusive civil society. *Journal of Social Issues*.

Pennell, J. (in press-b). Stopping domestic violence or protecting children? Contributions from restorative justice. In D. Sullivan & L.

Tifft (Eds.), *Handbook of restorative justice: A global perspective*. London: Routledge.

Pennell, J., & Burford, G. (1994). Widening the circle: The family group decision making project. *Journal of Child & Youth Care, 9*(1), 1–12.

Pennell, J., & Burford, G. (1995). *Family group decision making: New roles for 'old' partners in resolving family violence: Implementation report* (Vols. I–II). St. John's, Newfoundland, Canada: Memorial University of Newfoundland, School of Social Work.

Pennell, J., & Burford, G. (2000a). Family group decision making: Protecting children and women. *Child Welfare, 79*, 131–158.

Pennell, J., & Burford, G. (2000b). Family group decision making and family violence. In G. Burford & J. Hudson (Eds.), *Family group conferencing: New directions in community-centered child and family practice* (pp. 171–185). New York: Aldine de Gruyter.

Pennell, J., & Francis, S. (2005). Safety conferencing: Toward a coordinated and inclusive response to safeguard women and children. *Violence Against Women, 11*, 666–692.

Pennell, J., Noponen, H., & Weil, M. (2004). Empowerment research. In M. Weil (Ed.), *Handbook of community practice* (pp. 620–635). Newbury Park, CA: Sage Publications.

Pennell, J., & Weil, M. (2000). Initiating conferencing: Community practice issues. In G. Burford & J. Hudson (Eds.), *Family group conferencing: New directions in community-centered child and family practice* (pp. 253–261). New York: Aldine de Gruyter.

Polaschek, N. R. (1998). Cultural safety: A new concept in nursing people of different ethnicities. *Journal of Advanced Nursing, 27*, 452–457.

Ptacek, J. (1999). *Battered women in the courtroom: The power of judicial response*. Boston: Northeastern University Press.

Quinnett, E., Harrison, R. S., & Jones, L. (2003). Empirical research on the San Diego model of family unity meetings. *Protecting Children, 18*(1/2), 98–103.

References

Radford, L., & Hester, M. (2001). Overcoming mother blaming? Future directions for research on mothering and domestic violence. In S. A. Graham-Bermann & J. L. Edleson (Eds.), *Domestic violence in the lives of children: The future of research, intervention, and social policy* (pp. 135–155). Washington, DC: American Psychological Association.

Ramsden, I. (1993). Kawa Whakaruruhau: Cultural safety in nursing education in Aotearoa (New Zealand). *Nursing Praxis in New Zealand, 8*(3), 4–10.

Ramsden, I. (1997). Cultural safety: Implementing the concept. The social force of nursing and midwifery. In P. T. Whâiti, M. McCarthy, & A. Durie (Eds.), *Mai I Rangiâtea: Mâori wellbeing and development* (pp. 113–125). Auckland, NZ: Auckland University Press.

Rangihau, J. (1986). *Pau-te-Ata-tu (Daybreak): Report of the Ministerial Advisory Committee on a Maori perspective for the Department of Social Welfare*. Wellington, NZ: Department of Social Welfare, Government Printing Office.

Retzinger, S., & Scheff, T. (1996). Strategy for community conferences: Emotions and social bonds. In B. Galaway & J. Hudson (Eds.), *Restorative justice: International perspectives* (pp. 315–336). Monsey, NY: Willow Tree Press.

Rivard, J. C., Johnsen, M. C., Morrissey, J. P., & Starrett, B. E. (1999). The dynamics of interagency collaboration: How linkages develop for child welfare and juvenile justice sectors in a system of care demonstration. *Journal of Social Service Research, 25*(3), 61–82.

Roberts, D. (2002). *Shattered bonds: The color of child welfare*. New York: Basic Books.

Roberts, D. E. (2003). The child welfare system's racial harm. In S. Macedo & I. M. Young (Eds.), *Child, family, and state* (pp. 98–133). New York: New York University Press.

Roche, D. (2003a). *Accountability in restorative justice*. Oxford, England: Oxford University Press.

Roche, D. (2003b). Gluttons for restorative justice. *Economy and Society, 32*, 630–644.

Rodgers, A. (2000). *Family decision meetings: A profile of average use in Oregon's child welfare agency*. Portland, OR: Child Welfare Partnership Final Report.

Rossi, P. H., Freeman, H. E., & Lipsey, M. W. (1999). *Evaluation: A systematic approach*. Thousand Oaks, CA: Sage Publications.

Rossman, B. B. R. (2001). Longer term effects of children's exposure to domestic violence. In S. A. Graham-Bermann & J. L. Edleson (Eds.), *Domestic violence in the lives of children: The future of research, intervention, and social policy* (pp. 35–65). Washington, DC: American Psychological Association.

Rowe, A. (2003). Evaluation of environmental dispute resolution programs. In R. O'Leary & L. B. Bingham (Eds.), *The promise and performance of environmental dispute resolution* (pp. 175–191). Washington, DC: RFF Press.

Saleeby, D. (1997). (Ed.). *The strengths perspective in social work practice* (2nd ed.). New York: Longman.

Saunders, S. (2002). Team decisionmaking—The past, present and future. *Heart Beat, 15*, No. 5-02.

Scheirer, M. A., & Rezmovic, E. L. (1983). Measuring the degree of program implementation: A methodological review. *Evaluation Review, 7*, 599–633.

Schiff, M., & Bazemore, G. (2002). *Understanding restorative conferencing: A case study in informal decision making in the response to youth crime*. Fort Lauderdale: Florida Atlantic University, Department of Criminology and Criminal Justice.

Schmid, J., & Goranson, S. (2003). An evaluation of family group conferencing in Toronto. *Protecting Children, 18*(1/2), 110–112.

Schorr, L. (1997). *Common purpose: Strengthening families and neighborhoods to rebuild America*. New York: Doubleday.

Seita, J. (2000). In our best interest: Three necessary shifts for child welfare workers and children. *Child Welfare, 79*, 77–92.

Seymour, J. (1997). Children's courts in Australia: Their current role and function. In A. Borowski & I. O'Connor (Eds.), *Juvenile crime, justice, and corrections*. South Melbourne, AU: Addison-Wesley Longman.

References

Shadish, W. R. Jr., Cook, T. D., & Leviton, L. C. (1991). *Foundations of program evaluation: Theories of practice.* Newbury Park, CA: Sage Publications.

Shepard, M. F. (1999). Evaluating a coordinated community response. In M. F. Shepard & E. L. Pence (Eds.), *Coordinating community responses to domestic violence: Lessons from Duluth and beyond* (pp. 169–191). Thousand Oaks, CA: Sage Publications.

Sherman, L., Strang, H., Barnes, G., Braithwaite, J., Inkpen, N., & Teh, M. (1998). *Experiments in restorative policing: A progress report on the Canberra reintegrative shaming experiments.* Retrieved May 8, 2004, from the Australian Institute of Criminology Web site: www.aic.gov.au/rjustice/rise/progress/1998.html

Shook, E. V. (1985). *Ho'oponopono: Contemporary uses of a Hawaiian problem-solving process.* Honolulu: Institute of Culture and Communication, East-West Center.

Shore, N., Wirth, J., Cahn, K., Yancey, B., & Gunderson, K. (2002, September). Long term and immediate outcomes of family group conferencing in Washington state. Retrieved May 4, 2004, from the International Institute for Restorative Practices Web site: www.restorativepractices.org

Shulman, L. (1999). *The skills of helping individuals, families, groups and communities* (4th ed.). Itasca, IL: F. E. Peacock.

Simon, B. L. (1994). *The empowerment tradition in American social work: A history.* New York: Columbia University Press.

Social Services and Research Information Unit [SSRIU], University of Portsmouth. (2003, June). *The Dove Project: The Basingstoke domestic violence family group conference project.* Unpublished manuscript, Hampshire, United Kingdom.

Solomon, B. M. (1976). *Black empowerment: Social work in oppressed communities.* New York: Columbia University Press.

Speck, R. V. (1998). Network therapy. *Marriage & Family Review, 27*(1/2), 51–69.

Speck, R. V., & Attneave, C. L. (1973). *Family networks.* New York: Pantheon Books.

Statutes of New Zealand. (2004). *Public access to Legislation Project.* Retrieved April 2, 2005, from http://www.legislation.govt.nz

Strang, H. (2002). *Repair or revenge: Victims and restorative justice.* Oxford, England: Clarendon Press.

Strang, H., Barnes, G. C., Braithwaite, J., & Sherman, L. W. (1999). *Experiments in restorative policing: A progress report on the Canberra Reintegrative Shaming Experiments (RISE).* Retrieved May 8, 2004, from the Australian Institute of Criminology Web site: http://www.aic.gov.au/rjustice/rise/progress/1999.html

Sullivan, C. M., Juras, J., Bybee, D., Nguyen, H., & Allen, N. (2000). How children's adjustment is affected by their relationships to their mothers' abusers. *Journal of Interpersonal Violence, 15,* 587–602.

Sundell, K., & Vinnerljung, B. (2004). Outcomes of family group conferencing in Sweden: A 3-year follow-up. *Child Abuse & Neglect, 28,* 267–287.

Sundell, K., Vinnerljung, B., & Ryburn, M. (2002). Social workers' attitudes towards family group conferences in Sweden and the United Kingdom. *International Journal of Child & Family Welfare, 5*(1/2), 28–39.

Thoburn, J. (1995). Social work and families: Lessons from research. In F. Kaganas, M. King, & C. Piper (Eds.), *Legislating for harmony: Partnership under the Child Act 1989.* London: Jessica Kingsley.

Thoennes, N. (2003). Family group decision making in Colorado. *Protecting Children, 18*(1/2), 74–80.

Thomas, K. L., Berzin, S. C., & Cohen, E. (2005). Fidelity of family group decision making: A content analysis of family conference and case plans in a randomized treatment study. *Protecting Children, 19*(4), 4–15.

Thomas, K. L., Cohen, E., & Berrick, J. D. (2003). California's waiver evaluation of FGDM: A unique opportunity. *Protecting Children, 18*(1/2), 52–56.

Titcomb, A., & LeCroy, C. (2003). Evaluation of Arizona's Family Group Decision Making Program. In Merkel-Holguin, L. (Ed.), *Promising results, potential new directions: International FGDM research and evaluation in child welfare* (pp. 58–64). Denver: American Humane Association.

Toseland, R. W., & Rivas, R. F. (2001). *An introduction to group work practice* (4th ed.). Boston: Allyn & Bacon.

Tracy, E. M., & Whittaker, J. K. (1990). The social network map: Assessing social support in clinical social work practice. *Families in Society, 71,* 461–470.

Travis, J., Cincotta, E. M., & Solomon, A. L. (2003, October). *Families left behind: The hidden costs of incarceration and reentry.* Retrieved May 7, 2004, from http://www.urban.org/UploadedPDF/310882_families_left_behind.pdf

Trochim, W.M.K. (1985). Pattern matching, validity, and conceptualization in program evaluation. *Evaluation Review, 9,* 575–604.

Trotter, C. (1999). *Working with involuntary clients: A guide to practice.* Thousand Oaks, CA: Sage Publications.

Trotter, C., Sheehan, R., Liddell, M., Strong, D., & Laragy, C. (1999). *Evaluation of the statewide implementation of family group conferencing.* Victoria, AU: Department of Human Services.

Tuell, J. A. (2003). *Understanding child maltreatment and juvenile delinquency: From research to effective program, practice, and systemic solutions.* Washington, DC: Child Welfare League of America.

Turnell, A., & Edwards, S. (1999). *Signs of safety: A solution and safety oriented approach to child protection casework.* New York: W. W. Norton.

Unrau, Y., Sieppert, J., & Hudson, J. (2000). Data collection in a family group conference evaluation project. In G. Burford & J. Hudson (Eds.), *Family group conferencing: New directions in community-centered child and family practice* (pp. 298–311). New York: Aldine de Gruyter.

U.S. Department of Health and Human Services. (2000). *Rethinking child welfare practice under the Adoption and Safe Families Act of 1997.* Washington DC: Children's Bureau.

U.S. Department of Health and Human Services, Administration on Children, Youth and Families. (2002). *Child maltreatment 2000.* Retrieved July 2, 2004, from www.acf.hhs.gov/programs/cb/publications/cm00

U.S. Department of Health and Human Services, Administration for Children and Families, Children's Bureau. (2003). *Results of 2001 & 2002 child and family service reviews,* Retrieved July 2, 2004, from http://www.acf.hhs.gov/programs/cb/cwrp/results/sld001.htm

U.S. Department of Justice, Bureau of Justice Statistics. (2000, May). *Intimate partner violence* [Bulletin NCJ 178247]. Washington, DC: Author.

van Beek, F. (2004, April). *'According to plan?' Research into the plans and follow-up of Eigenkracht conferences* (S. Noorman, Trans.). Voorhout, The Netherlands: WESP Jeugdzorg and Eigen Kracht Centrale.

Vesneski, W., & Kemp, S. (2000). Families as resources: The Washington State Family Group Conference Project. In G. Burford & J. Hudson (Eds.), *Family group conferencing: New directions in community-centered child and family practice* (pp. 312–323). New York: Aldine de Gruyter.

Waites, C., Macgowan, M. J., Pennell, J., Carlton-LaNey, I., & Weil, M. (2004). Increasing the cultural responsiveness of family group conferencing. *Social Work, 49,* 291–300.

Waldfogel, J. (1998). *The future of child protection: How to break the cycle of abuse and neglect.* Cambridge, MA: Harvard University Press.

Waldfogel, J. (2000). Reforming child protective services. *Child Welfare, 79,* 43–57.

Walker, H. (1996). *Whanau Hui,* family decision making, and the family group conference: An indigenous Maori view. *Protecting Children, 12*(3), 8–10.

Walter R. McDonald & Associates, Inc. (1998, May). *The Santa Clara County Family Group Conference Model: Year one process evaluation report.* Sacramento, CA: Author.

Walter R. McDonald & Associates, Inc. (1999, June). *The Santa Clara County family conference model: Strategy for system change.* Sacramento, CA: Author.

References

Walter R. McDonald & Associates, Inc. (2000, November). *The Santa Clara County Family Conference Model outcome evaluation*. Sacramento, CA: Author.

Warner-Roberts, A., & Masters, G. (1999). *Group conferencing: Restorative justice in practice*. St. Paul: University of Minnesota, Center for Restorative Justice and Mediation, School of Social Work.

Weil, M. (2002). Assessing community building in family group conferencing. In C. Harper, J. Pennell, & M. Weil (Eds.), *Family group conferencing: Evaluation guidelines* (2nd ed., pp. 31–53). Englewood, CO: American Humane Association.

Weiss, C. H. (1997). How can theory-based evaluation make greater headway? *Evaluation Review, 21*, 501–524.

Wenston, S. (1987). Applying philosophy to ethical dilemmas. In G. Anderson & V. Glesnes-Anderson (Eds.), *Health care ethics: A guide for decision makers* (pp. 22–33). Rockville, MD: Aspen.

Wiebush, R., Freitag, R., & Baird, C. (2001, July). Preventing delinquency through improved child protection services. *Juvenile Justice Bulletin*. Washington, DC: U.S. Department of Justice, Office of Juvenile Justice and Delinquency Programs.

Wiig, J., & Widom, C. S. (with Tuell, J. A.). (2003). *Child maltreatment & juvenile delinquency: From research to effective program, practice, and effective solutions*. Washington, DC: Child Welfare League of America.

Williams, A. I., & Weisz, V. (2003). Preliminary results from the Nebraska family group conferencing evaluation. *Protecting Children, 18*(1/2), 90–92.

Wollstonecraft, M. (1792/1975). *A vindication of the rights of woman*. New York: W. W. Norton.

Yates, B. T. (1996). *Analyzing costs, procedures, processes, and outcomes in human services*. Thousand Oaks, CA: Sage Publications.

Young, I. M. (2000). *Inclusion and democracy*. Oxford and New York: Oxford University Press.

Zehr, H., & Mika, H. (1998). Fundamental concepts of restorative justice. *Contemporary Justice Review, 1*, 47–55.

Index

About the Editors

Joan Pennell, MSW, PhD, is professor and head of the Department of Social Work, North Carolina State University. She received her PhD in social work at Bryn Mawr College and her MSW from Dalhousie University, Canada. She is the principal investigator of the North Carolina Family-Centered Meetings Project and previously directed the North Carolina Family Group Conferencing Project, both with the goal of fostering inclusive approaches to planning in child welfare. Before her return to the United States, she served with Gale Burford as the principal investigator for a Newfoundland & Labrador (Canada) demonstration of family group conferencing in situations of child maltreatment and domestic violence. Her writings particularly focus on empowerment approaches to practice, program development, and research. She coauthored *Community Research as Empowerment: Feminist Links, Postmodern Interruptions* (Oxford University Press, 1996) and *Family Group Conferencing: Evaluation Guidelines* (American Humane Association, 2002). She has made presentations on family group conferencing in Australia, Canada, England, the Netherlands, New Zealand, and across the United States.

Gary R. Anderson, MSW, PhD, is professor and director of the School of Social Work at Michigan State University. He received his PhD from the University of Chicago, School of Social Service Administration, and his MSW from the University of Michigan. He is the principal investigator for the State of Michigan Department of Human Services Family Group Decision Making evaluation. He was previously the founding director of the National Resource Center for Permanency Planning at Hunter College in New York City. He coedited *The Challenge of Permanency Planning in a Multicultural Society* (Haworth Press, 1997) and edited *Courage to Care: Responding to the Crisis of Children with AIDS* (Child Welfare League of America, 1990). He is the editor of the Child Welfare League of America's journal, *Child Welfare*.

About the Contributors

Gale Burford, MSW, PhD, is professor and director of the University/State Child Welfare Training Partnership at the University of Vermont Department of Social Work. He received his PhD from the University of Stirling, Scotland, and his MSW from the University of Washington. With Joan Pennell, he served as the principal investigator for the Newfoundland & Labrador (Canada) Family Group Decision Making Project. He has carried out research, writing, project design, and management in the use of family group conferencing and, with Joe Hudson, edited *Family Group Conferencing: New Directions in Community-Centered Child & Family Practice* (Aldine de Gruyter, 2000). With Lisa Merkel-Holguin and Paul Nixon, he conducted an international survey of Family Group Decision Making.

Carol J. Harper, MPA, is the director of Systems and Community Program at American Humane. She received her graduate degree from Troy State University, European Division. She oversees the design, implementation, and evaluation of programming for both Children's Services and Animal Protection Services. She began conducting field studies of family group conferencing implementation in the United States during the late 1990s. She has coauthored three guidebooks on the implementation and use of family group conferencing/family group decision making, conducted implementation trainings, and made presentations at numerous conferences regarding the strengths and considerations of family group conferencing, including at the International Congress on Child Abuse and Neglect, New Zealand, where she addressed cultural adaptations.

Lisa Merkel-Holguin, MSW, is the director of the American Humane National Center on Family Group Decision Making. She received her degree from the University of Illinois. Since 1997, she has directed American Humane's family group decision making initiative, providing training and technical assistance to more than 100 communities, developing various publications and other resources, and co-organizing a national network of individuals working to advance family group decision making as a viable approach in child welfare.

Andy Rowe, PhD, is a principal with London-based GHK International and works on assignments in North America, Europe, and Asia. He has a PhD from the London School of Economics, where his thesis topic addressed informational sector and household production. In addition, he has an MPhil in regional economics from Memorial University of Newfoundland and was a research student at the Institute for Soviet and East European Studies at the University of Glasgow. He has worked for provincial/state government in Canada and the United States and the federal government in Canada, held academic appointments in Canada and Scotland, and has been consulting for more than 20 years. He is a former president of the Canadian Evaluation Society and currently chairs the International Committee of the American Evaluation Association. Rowe and his colleague, Jon Waterhouse, estimated the costs of the Newfoundland & Labrador Family Group Decision Making Project.

Peg Whalen, **MSW,** is a project evaluator and advanced doctoral student (Interdisciplinary Doctoral Program in Social Science with Specialization in Social Work) at Michigan State University. She has an MSW from the University of Michigan and a bachelor's degree in psychology from Smith College. She is currently the project director for a federally funded evaluation of the Michigan Adoption Medical Subsidy Program. She has more than 20 years of experience in research methods, statistical analysis, and program evaluation. Her work for the past eight years has focused on evaluation of innovative child welfare programs, including her work as coordinator and research director on the Michigan Department of Human Services, Family Group Decision Making evaluation project.

Leslie Wilmot, **MSSW,** is the manager of American Humane's National Center on Family Group Decision Making. She received her MSSW from the University of Wisconsin–Madison. She first became involved in family group decision making in 1997 as a family group conferencing coordinator for the Dane County Department of Human Services in Madison, Wisconsin. In 2000, she joined American Humane, where her responsibilities include family group decision making curricula development, training and technical assistance, Web site content management, and co-organization of the annual conference on family group decision making. In this capacity, she has been able to work with communities engaged in family group decision-making practices throughout the United States and Canada, and she deeply appreciates their enthusiasm and diligence in advancing this important work.

MORE RESOURCES ON CHILDREN & FAMILIES FROM NASW PRESS

Widening the Circle: *The Practice and Evaluation of Family Group Conferencing with Children, Youths, and Their Families, Joan Pennell and Gary R. Anderson, Editors. Widening the Circle* is about developing family leadership, cultural safety, and community partnerships to safeguard children, young people, and other family members. This volume describes family group conferencing and critically analyzes its contributions to widening the circle. The practices presented are based on the authors' extensive experience with family group conferencing in the United States and Canada as applied primarily in child welfare but also extended into juvenile justice and domestic violence.

ISBN: 0-87101-367-3. 2005. Item #3673. $49.99.

When Their World Falls Apart: *Helping Families and Children Manage the Effects of Disasters,* by *Lawrence B. Rosenfeld, Joanne S. Caye, Ofra Ayalon, and Mooli Lahad.* Born out of necessity and tested in the real world of natural and technological disasters as well as disasters of human design, this timely and critically important new volume is a comprehensive and clear examination of the effects of disasters on children and families from cognitive and behavioral, family systems, and ecological perspectives. Many special activities throughout the book provide a "touch of reality" that bridges the gap between cognitive and affective learning.

ISBN: 0-87101-358-4. 2004. Item #3584. $54.99.

Risk and Resilience in Childhood: *An Ecological Perspective, 2nd Edition,* Mark W. Fraser, Editor. Why are some children so resilient when others are not? Building on the concepts and models presented in the best-selling first edition, *Risk and Resilience in Childhood* takes a major leap forward from other social work texts to probe both risk and resilience and the protective factors that promote positive developmental outcomes. Firmly research based, it bridges the gap between ecological theory and strengths-based practice and provides a foundation for developing case-specific interventions.

ISBN: 0-87101-356-8. 2003. Item #3568. $52.99.

Making Choices: *Social Problem-Solving Skills for Children,* by *Mark W. Fraser, James K. Nash, Maeda J. Galinsky, and Kathleen M. Darwin.* Based on a cognitive problem-solving approach, *Making Choices* addresses the urgent need for children to acquire competence in meeting the demands of childhood within social, school, and family parameters. The book is designed for children from kindergarten through middle school whose behavior is impulsive, oppositional, or aggressive. Recognizing that a great deal of children's behavior is tied to problem solving, the volume focuses on how children solve instrumental and relational issues in different social settings.

ISBN: 0-87101-323-1. 2000. Item #3231. $36.99.

Clinical Intervention with Families, by *Mark A. Mattaini.* (Companion Volume to *Clinical Practice with Individuals.*) Written for social workers in family practice as well as for instructors and advanced-level students, this book is a state-of-the-art and state-of-the-science treatment guide of family practice. An essential volume for those seeking to understand the extrinsic family factors affecting the theory and practice of family social work.

ISBN: 0-87101-308-8. 1999. Item #3088. $42.99.

Children & Schools: *A Journal of Social Work Practice,* Wilma Peebles-Wilkins, Editor-in-Chief. *Children & Schools* (formerly *Social Work in Education*) is a trusted tool for those who provide critical social work services in education for children. Articles present innovations in practice, interdisciplinary efforts, research, program evaluation, policy, and planning. Topics include student-authority relationships, multiculturalism, early intervention, needs assessment, violence, and ADHD. It is a valuable practitioner-to-practitioner resource that assists readers in developing relevant courses and curricula and encourages multidisciplinary collaboration. Available online at www.naswpressonline.org.

ISSN: 1532-8759. Published quarterly in January, April, July, and October. NASW Member (#6001) $54.00; NASW Student Member (#6101) $36.00; Individual Nonmember (#6201) $89.00; Library/ Institution (#6301) $125.00.

(Order form and information on reverse side)

ORDER FORM

Qty.	Title	Item #	Price	Total
__	Widening the Circle	3673	$49.99	_____
__	When Their World Falls Apart	3584	$54.99	_____
__	Risk and Resilience in Childhood	3568	$52.99	_____
__	Making Choices	3231	$36.99	_____
__	Clinical Intervention with Families	3088	$42.99	_____
Children & Schools				
___	NASW Member	6001	$54.00	_____
___	NASW Student Member	6101	$36.00	_____
___	Individual Nonmember	6201	$89.00	_____
___	Library/Institution	6301	$125.00	_____

POSTAGE AND HANDLING
Minimum postage and handling fee is $4.95. Orders that do not include appropriate postage and handling will be returned.

DOMESTIC: Please add 12% to orders under $100 for postage and handling. For orders over $100 add 7% of order.

CANADA: Please add 17% postage and handling.

OTHER INTERNATIONAL: Please add 22% postage and handling.

Subtotal	_____
Postage and Handling	_____
DC residents add 6% sales tax	_____
MD residents add 5% sales tax	_____
NC residents add 4.5% sales tax	_____
NJ residents add 6% sales tax	_____
Total	_____

❐ **Check** or **money order** (payable to NASW Press) for $ _____.

❐ **Credit card**
   ❐ Visa ❐ MasterCard ❐ American Express

_____   _____
Credit Card Number   Expiration Date

Signature _____

Name _____

Address _____

City _____ State/Province _____

Country _____ Zip _____

Phone _____ E-mail _____

NASW Member # (if applicable) _____

(Please make checks payable to NASW Press. Prices are subject to change.)

NASW PRESS
P. O. Box 431
Annapolis JCT, MD 20701
USA

Credit card orders call
1-800-227-3590
(In the Metro Wash., DC, area, call 301-317-8688)
Or fax your order to 301-206-7989
Or order online at www.naswpress.org

CPWC05